In Their Own Image

In Their Own Image

NEW YORK JEWS IN JAZZ AGE POPULAR CULTURE

TED MERWIN

RUTGERS UNIVERSITY PRESS
New Brunswick, New Jersey, and London

LIBRARY OF CONGRESS CATALOGING-IN-PUBLICATION DATA

Merwin, Ted, 1968–
   In their own image : New York Jews in Jazz Age popular culture / Ted Merwin.
     p.   cm.
   Includes bibliographical references and index.
   ISBN-13: 978–0–8135–3808–2 (hardcover : alk. paper)
   ISBN-13: 978–0–8135–3809–9 (pbk. : alk. paper)
   1. Jews in the performing arts—New York (State)—New York—History—20th
century. 2. Jewish entertainers—New York (State)—New York—History—20th
century. 3. Jews—New York (State)—New York—Social life and customs—20th
century. 4. Jews in motion pictures—United States—History—20th century. 5.
Popular culture—United States—History—20th century. 6. United States—Social
conditions—1918–1932. I. Title.
   PN1590.J48M47 2006
   791′.089′924—dc22   2005019945

British Cataloging-in-Publication data for this book is available
from the British Library.

Manufactured in the United States of America

*Dedicated to my grandparents, Jean and Louis Kaplan,
two proud second-generation New York Jews*

Contents

Illustrations

Preface and Acknowledgments

WHILE BROWSING ONE DAY in the early 1990s at a book sale at the Theatre Collection of the New York Public Library at Lincoln Center, I happened upon Edward Coleman's catalog, *The Jew in English Drama*. In the late 1930s, Coleman had taken on the Herculean task of going through everything in the Theatre Collection, listing vaudeville routines and plays with Jewish content, along with references to productions and reviews. I used this invaluable resource to do research for a graduate school paper on the popularity of Anne Nichols's *Abie's Irish Rose*, a legendary comedy that had attracted almost no scholarly attention.

That paper eventually germinated into an article, the article sprouted into a chapter, the chapter flowered into a dissertation, and the dissertation has now become a book. I am deeply grateful to the late Egon Mayer, the professor of that graduate school course who helped and encouraged me at every step along the way of the dissertation. I am extremely saddened that he did not live to see this book in print. He remains very much in my thoughts. His ideas about Jewish identity, history, and culture have shaped every page of this monograph.

I also want to thank my dissertation advisor, Alisa Solomon, who patiently read draft after draft; she always had time to meet in a coffee bar on Tenth Avenue to shmooze in Yiddish, give me encouragement, and help me refine my ideas. Daniel Gerould and David Nasaw were also extremely important mentors in graduate school. I was also fortunate to discuss my work with Hasia Diner and Jenna Weissman Joselit, both of whom are trailblazers in the field of American Jewish popular culture.

Deborah Dash Moore's book on the second generation is a major inspiration for, and foundation of, this study. Deborah was extremely generous with her time, reading extensive sections and giving me very helpful and insightful comments that have tremendously enhanced the final result. Rick Altabef was also a constant source of help and support; his wit, wisdom, and sense of humor sustained me through the difficult process of fleshing out my ideas. I also thank my analyst, Judith Katz, for taking every step with me along the often perilous path to self-knowledge.

I am also deeply indebted to my editor, Melanie Halkias, and to the readers of the manuscript for Rutgers, including Joel Berkowitz, who took a great deal of time and energy to make incisive comments that helped me push the work in new directions.

I also would like to thank my students in my "Jews and Judaism in the United States," "Jews and Hollywood," and "Jewish Masculinities" courses at Dickinson College, whose ideas stimulated and extended my own. I am also extremely grateful to Yale Asbell, whose astounding generosity to the Jewish community at Dickinson has immeasurably enriched my life and work, as well as to senior administrators Bob Massa and Neil Weissman for all their support and good counsel. I also want to thank my colleagues at Dickinson, including Sharon O'Brien, Mara Donaldson, and Ted Pulcini, for all their encouragement. A grant from Dickinson's Research and Development Committee, for which I am extremely grateful, helped to cover the costs of reproducing and getting permission for the illustrations, as well as for some of the costs of indexing the manuscript.

Tina Maresco of the Interlibrary Loan Service at Dickinson never complained about my almost daily torrent of requests for materials; I am very thankful to her for her help. I also thank Rob Goldblum, my editor at *The Jewish Week*, for giving me the opportunity to critique so many contemporary plays of Jewish interest. The experience of being a theater critic has immeasurably enhanced my abilities to understand, appreciate, and write about the performing arts.

My research would not have been possible without the help of librarians and archivists across the country. I am especially indebted to the marvelous staff at the Billy Rose Theatre Collection at Lincoln Center, including Christopher Frith, Christine Karatnytsky, Jeremy Megraw, Brian O'Connell, Dan Patri, and Louis Paul. It was Dr. Roderick Bladel, a senior archivist there, who first told me about *Kosher Kitty Kelly*, a musical that became very important in my research. I would also like to thank Lorin Sklamberg, music archivist at the YIVO Institute, for helping me locate forgotten music recordings for the chapter on vaudeville.

Rosemary Hanes, reference librarian at the Motion Picture Broadcasting and Recorded Sound Division of the Library of Congress, was also extremely helpful in arranging for me to view silent films. I would also like to thank Kristine Krueger of the Academy of Motion Picture Arts and Sciences and the staffs of the Museum of Modern Art Film Archive in New York and the National Center for Jewish Film at Brandeis University. Murray Glass, of Em-Gee Film Library, also screened films for me and rented films to me that were extremely useful in my research.

I owe a special debt of gratitude to my cousins, Peter and Regi Merwin, and their children, Amelia and Linus, for hosting me for a week while I did research in the various film archives in the Los Angeles area, including at the UCLA Film Archive. Although she is no longer alive, my grandmother, Jean C. Kaplan, played a crucial role, in multiple senses, in the creation of this project. It was her volunteer job on Friday afternoons in the Student Activities office at the New York University School of Medicine that made it possible for my family to attend the theater as often as we did when I was growing up. It is only fitting that this book is an attempt to connect to the generational experience that she and my grandfather, Louis Kaplan, had as the children of Jewish immigrants.

In addition to my parents and sister, my greatest overarching debt is to my wife, colleague, and mentor, Andrea, whose love is constant and pure, and who always helps me to understand and challenge myself in new ways. And to Hannah Shira and Sarah Jean, both fifth-generation American Jews, who represent the best evidence there can be that the world is still, as Anne Frank wrote, "a beautiful place." Looking into my daughters' eyes, I cannot help but have confidence in a brighter future, in which, as Jews pray when we announce the coming of the New Month, "all of the yearnings of our heart will be fulfilled for the good."

In Their Own Image

Introduction

AT THE LAST Passover seder she attended before her death, my maternal grandmother, already suffering from senile dementia, took up a different book from the one the rest of us were all reading. Instead of following along in the Haggadah, which tells the story of Moses leading the Israelites out of Egypt, Grandma kept flipping the pages of a catalog from a company called The Source for Everything Jewish, which sells merchandise like Chanukah menorahs, Passover plates, and Jewish-themed jewelry, toys, and clothing. Grandma interrupted the seder from time to time with loud exclamations as she saw things in the catalog that caught her fancy. We laughed, but it was hard not to feel sad that in a sense she was already no longer with us.

I trace my Jewish identity in many ways to my maternal grandparents—they were, in my imagination, truly the source. And yet my grandparents kept few religious customs, almost never went to synagogue, and had no Jewish friends. What was Jewish about them, other than the few Yiddish expressions my grandmother used (always bemoaning the fact that I could not understand them), the traditional Eastern European—although often not kosher, in any strict sense—foods they ate, the summer vacations they took in the Catskill Mountains, and the winter vacations they took in Miami Beach?

Born in America, children of immigrants who spoke only Yiddish, my maternal grandparents were both proud and patriotic Americans. Yet something about them remained Jewish to the core, and it permeated all of their feelings, attitudes, and perceptions of the world. It was their culture, and it mixed somehow with American culture in complicated ways that I could not fully comprehend.

My father's parents, on the other hand, seemed much more ambivalent about being Jewish. According to my father, they always went to synagogue on the High Holidays, celebrated Passover and Chanukah, and had many Jewish friends. But my paternal grandfather, who graduated from Harvard Law School in 1920, at a time when few Jews were admitted to Ivy League schools of any kind, changed his name from Harry Meirowitz to Harry Merwin. In

I

the court documents that he filed, he stated that he "desires that his children be spared the burden and handicap of carrying a foreign sounding, mis-pronounceable and mis-spellable name with its resulting business and social disadvantages." He got his wish; the papers went through on the day that his first child, my Uncle Don, was born.

My father always understood his father's name change to be driven by the fear that a Jewish-sounding name would impede his prospects of attracting legal clients. He clearly felt self-conscious about carrying an obviously Jewish name, as did his wife; my grandmother wrote in her diary that she "always hated the name Meirowitz" and was very happy to be rid of it—she changed her name at the same time her husband did—even though both of them were having trouble getting used to their new surname.

SECOND-GENERATION JEWISHNESS

This book attempts to make sense of the Jewishness of this second generation of American Jews. Deborah Dash Moore, in her book of the same title, has called them "at home in America" in their sense of comfort with both their Jewish and American identities. The reality, however, seems quite a bit more complex. Second-generation Jews needed to reconcile their Jewish identity (based, at least traditionally, on a strict code of behavior and a constant stream of rituals) with the relative openness of American society, with its fundamental principles of freedom and personal choice. My argument is that they did so, in part, through the production and consumption of popular culture.

As Charles Hardy has written of the United States in the early twentieth century:

> America's rise as an urban-industrial society was accompanied by the growth of a new mass culture more concerned with consumption than moral uplift; an urban, popular culture that challenged the values of genteel society and small town America. It was a rebellious, exuberant, and commercial new culture that appealed to city dwellers and immigrants, and which found expression in the movies, radio, amusement parks, jazz, and in the comic strips.[1]

In his seminal book, *The 7 Lively Arts,* the Jewish critic Gilbert Seldes made a persuasive case for the importance of what he deemed these under-appreciated elements of American culture—the "lowbrow" arts such as cartoons, vaudeville, musical comedy, popular songs, and "slapstick" moving pictures. (The number seven, based on the seven arts of classical civilizations, was always flexible in this context in Seldes's mind.) Seldes celebrated silent film actors like Charlie Chaplin, jazz musicians like Paul Whiteman, comic writers like Ring Lardner, clowns like the Fratellini brothers, and vaudeville actors like Frank Tinney and Raymond Hitchcock. He saw these figures as essentially practitioners of modernist art forms, as worthy of appreciation and study as modernist writers like James Joyce, F. Scott Fitzgerald, Ernest Hemingway, and Virginia Woolf—some of whom actually began using vaudeville-type characters in their works or who, like the critic Edmund Wilson, also wrote appreciatively and perspicaciously about popular entertainment.[2]

Unlike many other critics, Seldes exhibited a definite predilection for Jewish performers (especially Eddie Cantor, Fanny Brice, and Al Jolson), and even speculated at times on whether their Jewishness contributed to their success. But while much has been written on the effect that Jews (from Jewish comedians to Jewish writers to Jewish film producers) have had on American culture, there has been few attempts to make a connection between the role that Jews played in the arts and the important changes that occurred in Jewish life as Jews began to join the mainstream of American society.

George Lipsitz, following Ramon Gutierrez, has argued that what we call "popular culture" is a description that we impose upon a work, rather than one that its creator would self-consciously use; creators, in his words, "see themselves merely creating signs and symbols appropriate to their audiences and themselves." He also points out that popular culture "has no fixed forms: the historical circumstances of reception and appropriation determine whether novels or motion pictures or videos belong to a sphere called popular culture." Finally, he says that particular products of popular culture "have no fixed meanings; it is impossible to say whether any one combination of sounds or set of images or grouping of words innately expresses one unified political position."[3]

All of this is true, but I think it understates the role of popular culture in creating the reality of lived experience. Lipsitz is clearly right that the "complicated relationship between historical memory and commercial culture, between the texts of popular culture and their contexts of creation and reception, resist conventional forms of cultural criticism."[4] But this is exactly what we need to get at if we want to understand how popular culture shapes people's perceptions, both of themselves and of each other. One needs only to listen to young people when they talk casually to one another to see the ways in which their lives revolve around popular culture, and in which the cultural icons of music, movies, and television have become their common language, which can bridge vast geographical and class divides.

My sense of my grandparents' generation is that they were much the same, in the universality of their appreciation for Jewish culture. Indeed, popular culture was a kind of lifeline for them; in the 1920s, I will suggest, the "at-home-ness" of the second generation was made possible by the uses that Jews made of popular culture. As Elizabeth Crocker has written of George

Herriman's Krazy Kat (featuring a Jewish mouse named Ignatz), the setting of which was transplanted in 1913 from the streets of New York City to the deserts of Coconino County in New Mexico: "The urbanites of Herriman's Coconino, nearly all children of immigrants if not immigrants themselves, try continually to shake off old ethnic identities that are wrapped up in home-spun culture and the working class, in an attempt to embrace a new, bourgeois, mechanically reproduced culture. Herriman positions Krazy Kat in opposition to the other characters and their aspirations to modernization and assimilation."[5]

But these old ethnic identities were not so easy to "shake off." The new culture that Jews were embracing was in large part a culture of their own making, and one that dramatized and depicted many of their own conflicts in being both Jewish and American. I see the 1920s as a crucial period for American Jewish life, the true entrance of Jews into American society. This was accomplished in an almost ritualistic way, through the adoption of cultural images of Jews and then through the adoption of Jews themselves.

In order for Jews to be accepted as "true" Americans, perceptions of Jews had to shift. Consequently, this was the period in which Jews began to be viewed, by sociologists at least, as a cultural group rather than a race.[6] In 1921, the scholar Thaddeus Sleszynski pointed out that although the second generation was considered "thoroughly American" by many, and their "assimilation . . . taken for granted," the situation was actually much more complex in terms of the attitudes that immigrants' children retained toward their ethnic culture.

Sleszynski divided these children into four categories, based on their relationship to the "foreign colony" or ethnic group: those in the first "conformed to the standards" of the group; those in the second were entirely separated from it; those in the third (composed of musicians, writers, and other artists) were "claimed" by it even though they "belong entirely to the larger community"; and those in the fourth were actually leaders both in their own ethnic group and in American society as a whole.[7] Sleszynski's categories are interesting in that, despite their gross oversimplifications, they argue against the adoption of easy conclusions about the abandonment of ethnic identity by the second generation. But his categories are useful only when they are permitted to overlap; most second-generation Jews often maintained an ambivalent relationship to the ethnic group, and were thus neither wholly attached to, nor wholly detached from, group affiliation.

In line with contemporary scholarly writing on the subject, I will also use the concept of "acculturation" rather than "assimilation" to suggest that Jews in this period did not jettison their ethnic identity in joining the mainstream of American life. While the "melting pot" term was popularized by an Anglo-Jewish playwright, Israel Zangwill, in a play of the same name that premiered in Washington, D.C., in 1908, the melting pot concept fell out of favor among intellectuals by the 1920s, to be revived only in the 1950s with the assertion by Will Herberg, in his *Protestant-Catholic-Jew,* that these three major religious traditions had become a "triple melting pot."[8]

THE JEWISH IMAGE IN POPULAR CULTURE

It has become accepted by scholars that Jewish characters, especially on stage, were virtually invisible in the 1920s. Harley Erdman calls this a "disappearing act," which he says lasted through the middle decades of the twentieth century. "Jewish bodies," he asserts, "seemingly vanished into the air, leaving Jewishness less present to the eye but still floating in the air, audible through aggressive verbal wit or ventriloquized through the bodies of gentile characters, both black and white."[9] Ellen Schiff goes even further, stating that "it is a matter of history that in between the two world wars the Jewish image in popular culture was often disguised or invisible."[10]

The fact is that Jewish characters were extremely common and extremely visible in 1920s popular culture, in hundreds of vaudeville routines, Broadway shows, and films. However, except for a few famous Jewish entertainers like Al Jolson, Eddie Cantor, and Fanny Brice, there has been almost no scholarly attention to this gigantic body of material. And even those studies of famous Jewish entertainers have rarely focused on the Jewish characters (or vaudeville caricatures) that they played.

Yet a simple glance through Edward Coleman's catalog *The Jew in English Drama,* published in 1968, shows that Jewish-themed entertainment was extraordinarily popular in the 1920s; Coleman lists literally hundreds of Jewish-themed entertainments in the United States alone (produced both by professionals and by amateurs) that can be found in the archives of the New York Public Library.[11] Jewish theater in particular was so popular that a Broadway comedy about a Jewish family, Anne Nichols's *Abie's Irish Rose,* was not just the longest-running play of the decade, but one of the most successful Broadway plays of all time; it spawned endless imitators on both stage and screen. I have chosen only a few representative examples from this extremely large body of work. One could easily spend a lifetime reading through only those Jewish-themed works that the New York Public Library's Billy Rose Theatre Collection possesses, which is probably only a fraction of the total.

Why scholars have chosen to ignore such a vital period in the history of Jewish entertainment is mystifying. It may spring to some extent from a distaste, deriving from the post-Holocaust era, for what are considered overly stereotypical depictions of Jews. There is no question that Jews often were represented in highly stereotypical ways in the 1920s, but Jews are represented extremely stereotypically nowadays as well, in plays and films ranging from Mel Brooks's musical *The Producers* to Adam Goldberg's film *The Hebrew Hammer,* and many others too numerous to mention.

Indeed, if one will only consider "nonstereotypical" depictions of an ethnic group, then it becomes difficult to say what one is looking for. When Jewish stereotypes disappear, what marks the character as Jewish at all? Many critics seem to want to have it both ways, complaining both about the preponderance of immigrant stereotypes in the late nineteenth and early twentieth centuries, and then complaining about the "whitewashing" of explicitly "ethnic" characteristics beginning in the 1930s.

Rather than merging into American society, Jewish performers and audiences exteriorized their ethnic identities in important ways, acculturating into American society through a circle (or spiral) of producing and consuming images of themselves in popular culture. There were many divisions in the American Jewish community, then as now, between religious and secular Jews, Zionist and anti-Zionist Jews, socialist and nonsocialist Jews. It was American popular culture that, according to historian Henry Feingold, "increasingly acted as the cultural cement for all segments of American Jewry."[12] And, Feingold might have added, as a way of binding Jews to other Americans.

New York Jewish Life

Although Jews were living in different areas of the country by the 1920s, I will focus on New York because it remained the home for almost half of America's Jewish population. As Deborah Dash Moore has persuasively argued, "the pulse of New York Jewish life decisively influenced all New York Jews. . . . New York Jews devised the grammar of American Jewish life."[13] Jews represented 29 percent of the city's population in 1920, falling only to 26 percent by 1940. As Robert Warshow suggested in his famous essay on the Jewish playwright Clifford Odets, "The elements that make up for most American Jews the image of their group are to be found in the Jewish culture of New York City; more specifically in the culture of the Jewish lower middle class, in the apartment houses and two-family houses of the Bronx and Brooklyn."[14]

Most Jewish immigrants had come to the Lower East Side of Manhattan, which had become identified as the Jewish "ghetto" in America. But Jews actually escaped the overcrowded, crime- and disease-ridden Lower East Side tenements as rapidly as they could. The opening of the Williamsburg and Manhattan Bridges in the first decade of the twentieth century, as well as the inauguration of subway service to Brooklyn during the same period, led to hundreds of thousands of Jews leaving Manhattan for the fresh air and wide-open spaces of the "suburbs" in the Bronx and Brooklyn. Jewish immigrants kept arriving to replace those who had left. Nevertheless, by 1916, according to Moses Rischin, only 23 percent of Jews in New York lived on the Lower East Side, compared to 50 percent in 1903 and 75 percent in 1892.[15]

This exodus continued throughout the 1920s, during which decade, according to Moore, an additional 160,000 Jews left the Lower East Side.[16] By 1930 the population of the Bronx was 49 percent Jewish, and the neighborhoods south of Tremont Avenue boasted a Jewish population of more than 80 percent.[17] From the Grand Concourse to the East Bronx, and from Brownsville to Flatbush in Brooklyn, these newer Jewish neighborhoods thrived with synagogues, Jewish schools, kosher butchers and bakeries, and delicatessens.[18]

As Jews began to fan out through the city, the influence of Jewish life on the surrounding non-Jewish culture increased. As Zalmen Yoffeh wrote in *The Menorah Journal,* "The Ghetto is spreading out, is taking in more territory, and becoming, in the process diluted. . . . It has given the very Gentiles a Jewish tinge."[19] During the 1920s in Bensonhurst (a section of Brooklyn), Jews quickly became 62 percent of the population, while in neighboring Brownsville they became 95 percent of the population. Bernard Postal wrote in the English-language section of the Yiddish daily *Der Tog* that the schools of Bensonhurst might just as well shut down from now on during Jewish holidays, for "even the non-Jewish children become Mosaic on such occasions."[20]

Yet even as they created residential enclaves, Jews also became increasingly more involved in the wider society. The Jazz Age was the age of Art Deco, Prohibition, the flapper, the New Woman. It brought to New York a dizzying set of cultural shifts, and Jews were at the center of many of these transformations as builders, brokers, and Broadway producers.

Even as Jews raised their own profile in society, they helped to create the skyline of Manhattan; many of those who built skyscrapers were Jews and many of the buildings they built were for Jewish-owned companies, like the downtown Singer Building (headquarters of the Singer Sewing Machine Company) and the midtown Chanin Building, an Art Deco masterpiece that housed the offices of prominent developer Irwin S. Chanin's real estate empire. Indeed, the Chanin Brothers built six Broadway theaters in the mid-1920s, in a bid to challenge the Shubert organization for dominance of the legitimate theater in New York. To some extent, the "Art Deco" Jew—the creator of glamor and prestige—was the unlikely progeny of the "ghetto" Jew, who had been ostracized and marginalized by polite society.

Everywhere in the Jazz Age was movement and activity, re-creation and readjustment. Mobility became a feature of Jewish life in multiple senses. The Jewish performers like Eddie Cantor and Fanny Brice who could twist their faces into different shapes or knock about the stage in gleeful slapstick, were showing a talent for physical mobility that might be seen as symbolizing the freedom of movement—both social and economic—that New York Jews in general were experiencing. As Robert Park and Ernest Burgess wrote in 1925, in their seminal study *The City,* "Mobility . . . involves change, new experience, stimulation. . . . Mobility is perhaps the best index of the state of metabolism of the city."[21]

Second-generation New York Jews moved quickly into the lower middle class. For the most part, they eschewed the manual labor of the immigrant generation; they became active and successful in business, politics, and finance.[22] According to Lloyd Ultan and Barbara Unger, "The Bronx was *the* place for people who saw themselves and their children taking a step up the socioeconomic ladder."[23] Part of this mobility was made possible by education; by 1919, according to Sherry Gorelick, 78 percent of students at the City College of New York (CCNY) were Eastern European Jews.[24] Yet the overall percentage of Jews who were enrolled in college was so small, as Gorelick points out, that college attendance was more a result of rising class position than a cause of it.

Jews helped each other to advance professionally and take advantage of expanding economic opportunities. As Moore has put it, "Participation in the myriad aspects of New York culture did not mark the decline of Jewish group life—as some had feared and others had hoped. Rather, as they became middle-class New Yorkers, second-generation Jews created the framework for their persistence as an ethnic group."[25] In other words, since Jews moved into the middle class together, their Jewish identity and class position reinforced one another.

The maintenance of Jewish identity did not, however, necessarily translate into religious observance. Between 1914 and 1924, according to Feingold, consumption of kosher meat, which he calls "usually the last thing to be abandoned by secularizing Jews," dropped by 30 percent.[26] Historians have also emphasized that despite a large number of synagogues in the new Jewish neighborhoods, relatively few Jews attended them except on the High Holidays. Jewish identity began to be defined partly as a simple matter of association with other Jews. As Jeffrey Gurock has noted, "while 1920s–1930s Jews at home on the Bronx's Grand Concourse might never set foot in their local synagogues . . . they could still spend their lives among Jews."[27]

This basic redefinition of Jewishness occurred partly through a transformation of the meaning of leisure. David Nasaw has noted that recreational activities were "not luxuries but necessities in the modern city."[28] As Kate Simon wrote in her memoir, *Bronx Primitive,* about her childhood in the interwar Bronx, Saturday became a day for many Jews to go not to synagogue but to the cinema. The Sabbath thus became associated with "recreation" in a nonreligious sense, but it still retained the aura of a day set apart for a particular kind of pleasure. As we will see, this sanctification of secular forms of leisure had parallels in the ways in which Jews reconstituted their Jewishness through the production and consumption of images of themselves in popular culture.

RECONSTRUCTING THE LOWER EAST SIDE

Despite their confidence in the promises of American society, second-generation Jews remained in many ways haunted by their childhood memories of the ghetto. As the second generation moved away from the Lower East Side both economically and socially, it read back into the ghetto the external qualities of Jewishness that it was attempting to reproduce in the pushcart-filled outer borough neighborhoods. Much more than, as Mark Slobin has called it, "a kind of Old World to be recalled in a rosy haze," the Lower East Side was reconstructed in Jewish popular culture as a place of both conflict with, and accommodation to, American values.[29] As Beth Wenger has written, "The neighborhood helped to frame their collective experiences as American Jews, helped them to make sense of change, and to create a narrative history and a physical context for locating Jewish communal origins."[30]

The Lower East Side became a tourist destination and locale for religious school field trips, a place for dining, shopping, and entertainment where middle-class Jews could go "slumming," and a tangible reminder of their ethnic "roots." The Lower East Side thus functioned as a kind of theater for the temporary reliving of the poor immigrant experience in New York. In Wenger's words, the development of nostalgia for immigrant life fed by the ghetto "was no retreat from the modernization and acculturation of Jews but rather an integral part of the ongoing reconstruction of Jewish consciousness in an American context."[31]

Second-generation American Jews thus made a home for themselves, as Jews had done for millennia, not by discarding immigrant Jewish culture but by adapting it to the culture in which they found themselves. Jenna Weissman Joselit has argued that they "generated an independent sense of what was culturally meaningful and enduring, deriving it as much from American notions of consumerism, gender, privacy and personal happiness as from Jewish notions of tradition, ritual, memory and continuity."[32]

In other words, these "American" and "Jewish" ideas transformed and redefined each other in a dynamic process. The differences between what was "American" and what was "Jewish" began in many ways to be elided. Seeing America through a Jewish lens, but also adopting American values that altered—in both subtle and dramatic ways—the nature of their Jewish beliefs and practices, second-generation Jews changed American culture in their own image. This is seen especially clearly in the performing arts, where Jewish-themed vaudeville routines, plays, and films displayed the tensions that living in an open and capitalist society caused in Jewish families, and the ways in which Jewish families creatively dealt with these tensions while still preserving Jewish traditions and culture.

In addition, because Jewish producers, actors, comics, and composers dominated the field of entertainment, New York Jewish culture had a disproportionate effect on American culture. To continue Moore's analogy, New York Jews structured not just the language of American Jewish life, but the patterns of its visual representation. These representations diverged in important ways from the ways in which Jews were depicted in American popular culture prior to the First World War, as I will discuss in chapter one. However, Jewish-themed entertainment remained extraordinarily popular with non-Jews as well as with Jews. In fact, as Michael G. Corenthal has noted, Jewish comedians whose routines sold millions of records effected a kind of metaphorical intermarriage with Christian America, so that, as he puts it, through the use of the Victrola "a Jewish personage became a permanent fixture in a majority of non-Jewish homes."[33]

I am primarily interested in how Jews rehabilitated their cultural representations and mobilized their newfound cultural capital to accelerate their integration into American life. I will thus focus on the interplay between the ways in which Jews performed their ethnic identities on stage and screen and the changing social and economic position of Jews in New York. As Harley Erdman and others have noted, performances determine economic and cultural reality as much as they reflect it.

How New York Jews lived, how they consolidated their class position, how they expressed their sense of having joined the mainstream—all of these were mirrored on both the stage and screen. In turn, the representations and images of themselves that second-generation Jews viewed in popular culture affected the ways in which they conceived of themselves both as Jews and as Americans. Paul Buhle has called this "reflexiveness," which he defines as "audience cravings for themes and objects that they can recognize as their own."[34] Buhle's study of American Jewish popular culture is comprehensive in scope, but seemingly based almost entirely on secondary sources; one finds few detailed descriptions of specific plays, films, radio broadcasts, songs, or vaudeville routines. (His section on comic strips is interesting, but again he seems not to have gone back to the original newspapers to look at any strips that do not happen to have been reprinted in book form, thus missing crucial developments in the strips he is describing.)

Buhle, Whitfield, and others who have written about American Jewish popular culture also have had little interest in how the saturation of American culture by Jewish- themed entertainments affected the lives of both Jews and non-Jews. While it is not possible to determine how watching a Jewish film, for example, affects an individual's decision on where to live, what to eat, whom to marry—or even how it affects his or her "identity"—the representations of Jewish life in popular culture did help create and sustain ideas and feelings about Jewishness for both Jews and non-Jews. To quote Buhle again, popular culture "invariably contains the particulars (of the creators) cast as the universal (of the audience): the special talent of Jews working in commercial entertainment."[35]

My interest is in the intersection of sociology and performance. As Chandra Mukerji and Michael Schudson have written, "Popular culture studies have undergone a dramatic change during the last generation—from an academic backwater to a swift intellectual river where expansive currents from different disciplines meet."[36] This book is a multidisciplinary contribution to the study of a particular species of popular culture from a particular decade. It is a kind of combination of what has been often termed "folk" culture with what is often called "mass" culture. According to Mukerji and Schudson, it has "become hazardous to make an invidious distinction between popular culture and high culture or a rigid separation of authentic, people-generated 'folk' culture from unauthentic and degraded, commercially borne 'mass' culture."[37] In the case of Jewish culture, what had been the province of a minority group became the entertainment of a nation.

ANTI-SEMITISM IN THE 1920S

It is crucial to recall that anti-Semitism was a pervasive feature of American life in the 1920s. The Ku Klux Klan was at its height in 1922, and Jewish newspapers throughout the country anxiously chronicled its activities. In fact, fear and distaste of immigrants of all nationalities—spurred by eugenicist thinkers like Madison Grant—led to the passage of the Immigration Acts of 1921 and 1924 that practically ended immigration from exactly those European countries from which most American Jewish families had come. John Higham has noted that in 1920, both an economic depression (and the mounting radicalism that accompanied it) and a fresh wave of immigration (with five thousand new immigrants a day passing through Ellis Island) provoked predictions of national economic and social collapse.[38]

Immigrants personified many Americans' fears of the unknown at a time of rapid technological change and economic uncertainty. As Joan Hoff Wilson has written, in the 1920s the "degree of tolerance exhibited toward change and innovation was highly selective. People were usually less inclined to oppose technological developments than they were political and social ones."[39] According to the powerful Henry Ford, who demonized Jews in his newspaper *The Dearborn Independent,* Jews corrupted not just agriculture, journalism, and finance, but popular entertainment as well. His idea was that Jewish involvement in the arts, particularly in theater, would "Judaize" them in an evil way, spreading the influence of "Jewish values" throughout the country.[40]

In fact, quite the opposite took place. Popular culture played a large role in encouraging tolerance among Americans toward different ethnicities. Many of the vaudeville acts, plays, and films I will analyze focused on the relationships between second-generation Jews and Irish. One reason for this may be that both groups lived in close proximity in outerborough neighborhoods (as they had to some extent on the Lower East Side) and both suffered discrimination in American society.

Before the 1920s, performing a Jewish character on stage or screen was a matter of reproducing a catalog of supposed ethnic traits—Yiddish accent, gesticulations, swarthiness, long hair (for women) or long beard (for men), long nose, etc. These visual aspects of Jewishness accompanied a performance of perceived Jewish traits such as greediness, dishonesty, slovenliness, and sexual cupidity. Erdman explores how the repeated performance of these ethnic caricatures served the interests of the majority in reinforcing its hegemony. As long as Jews were associated with bad manners and bad breeding, they could not be accepted into society. But these stereotypes changed, quite slowly and gradually, as Jews began to be viewed as no more objectionable in their behavior as their non-Jewish counterparts. For Jews to "clean up their act" meant to change the ways in which non-Jews perceived them.

Assimilation had performance-like qualities as well. In her study of interwar and postwar musical theater, Andrea Most has argued that while race was presented as immutable, ethnicity was viewed as largely a matter of performance, "a set of transient qualities that were non-threatening because they could easily be performed away. As long as the characters could learn to speak, dress, and sing or dance in the American style, they were fully accepted into the stage community. To be labeled 'ethnic' on the stage was an important step toward becoming a full-fledged member of the white community." But, as Most points out, blacks were excluded from the "ethnic" category; in her words, "ethnicity . . . became a protection from blackness."[41]

BEYOND BLACKFACE

Nevertheless, almost all vaudeville entertainers, including Jewish ones, started their careers by using blackface. The blackface minstrel show was the most popular form of entertainment in mid- and late-nineteenth-century America. Blackface continued to be popular into the twentieth century even as other ethnic caricatures, which grew out of hostility to European immigrants, also became the staples of the vaudeville stage. But by the 1920s, many of the Jewish comics had either abandoned blackface or made it much less central to their work. Al Jolson's use of blackface has attracted an extraordinary amount of critical attention in the last few years, spurred by Michael Rogin's book on Jewish involvement in Hollywood and the politics of blackface. Rogin's controversial thesis was that Jews shed their own racial otherness and "whitened" themselves by performing in blackface.

In contrast to Rogin and other historians who have emphasized these blackface performances in Jewish American culture, I see an equally pervasive phenomenon of Jews performing Jewishness—creating openly Jewish-themed entertainment that reflected the changing nature of Jewish life in New York. From the vaudeville entertainers Fanny Brice and Eddie Cantor, to the playwrights Aaron Hoffman and Montague Glass, to the film actors Jean Hersholt and Rosa Rosanova, Jewish artists helped create a burgeoning Jewish popular culture in the 1920s—a veritable golden age of Jewish enter-tainment—that has gone largely unexamined by serious scholars. By the late 1930s, representations and images of Jews were already much less visible, as Henry Popkin wrote in a famous 1946 article in *Commentary* entitled "The Vanishing Jew of Our Popular Culture."[42]

Of course, many—if not most—American Jewish writers, performers, directors, and producers rarely, if ever, worked with explicitly Jewish themes. Indeed, Stephen Whitfield's book *In Search of American Jewish Culture* restricts itself for the most part to the study of works by American Jews that have little or no explicit Jewish content. He writes that "to expel from consideration [of American Jewish culture] whatever omits Jewish subject matter unnecessarily diminishes the effort to understand the Jews who created such works."[43] But explicitly Jewish material is also important, since it reflects the ways in which Jews were actively reshaping Jewish identity.

After all, many Jewish entertainers did not perform Jewish material exclusively; it was simply a part of their overall repertoire. However, it is not true, as Abel Green and Joe Laurie, Jr., have argued, that "as each immigrant minority prospered during the boom years before World War I, it achieved a new economic and social dignity. It no longer cared to laugh at itself or have other nationalities laugh at it."[44] The ethnic stereotypes may have changed, but they did not disappear; they became a part of American middle-class culture. And they served a unifying purpose for Jewish immigrants and their children.

Many Yiddish vaudeville routines, plays, and films dealt with issues of assimilation and adjustment to American life, from Leon Kobrin's *Sonya of East Broadway, East Side Ghetto,* and *Riverside Drive* to H. Leivick's *Rags* and *Shop.* Furthermore, as Mario Maffi has put it, in discussing the Yiddish dramas that were written in America, "Tenements, sweatshops, roofs, stoops, [and] streets were the usual settings of plots which repeatedly dealt with the rela-tionship of greenhorns and settlement workers, Jews and America, Jews and other ethnic groups, and old and young generations facing the New World."[45] As the non-Jewish observer Hutchins Hapgood wrote in his famous book

The Spirit of the Ghetto, among the Yiddish plays that were presented on the Lower East Side were ones that "portray the customs and problems of the ghetto community, and are of comparatively recent origin."[46]

In his authoritative study of Yiddish film, J. Hoberman has found that many of these themes were also present in early talkies like *Uncle Moses* (1930) and *Mayn Yidishe Mame* (1930), films that were set in America and that likewise showed the challenges of living in a new culture.[47]

It may thus be overstating the case somewhat to argue, as Ellen Schiff has, that the Yiddish stage and the American Jewish stage "are poised on separate axes and serve different constituencies," with the Yiddish stage looking "inward" and the American Jewish stage "outward."[48] In 1920, there were still about a million Yiddish speakers in New York, but only about half of them were foreign born, meaning that there was a large number of Jews (both immigrant and second generation) who undoubtedly spoke both Yiddish and English, and could enjoy entertainment in either language.

In addition to the similarity of many of their themes, both Yiddish and English-language plays served to reinforce ethnic identity for Jewish audiences. But the direction of Jewish culture was moving away from Yiddish. A. Mukdoni, an expert in Yiddish literature, could thus lament in 1940 with a certain amount of truth that "the large mass of Jewish immigrants have learned the English language, developed cosmopolitan attitudes, and acquired a taste for the entertainment offered by the American theaters and movies."[49]

Minority groups undergo constant shifts in their relationship to the dominant culture. As Adina Cimet has argued, ethnic minorities acculturate by "straddling" the divide between their own culture and that of the majority, and they participate in a process of exchange in which they renounce parts of their culture in order to establish themselves. In her thinking, the ethnic culture is in constant negotiation with the majority culture, adapting itself (or pretending to adapt itself) to the priorities and policies of the majority, while retaining as much as it can of its difference and distinctiveness.[50] But the minority culture is always being transformed in the act of undergoing this process, and members of the minority culture are caught in the middle, never fully advancing or retreating.

My analysis of Jewish ethnicity in popular entertainment is inspired by contemporary theoretical understandings of ethnicity as a historically conditioned social construct rather than an essentialized quality. David Hollinger, for example, proposes a new model of ethnic self-identification, which he calls "postethnic," in which voluntary, often temporary affiliations replace hereditary, deeply rooted commitments.[51]

Hollinger and other postmodernists (influenced heavily by Werner Sollors's influential distinction between consent and descent in American history and literature)[52] disagree with Edward Shils's concept of the "primordial affinities" that sustain loyalty to an ethnic group. Instead, they point to the ways in which modern identities are multiple, flexible, and shifting rather than unitary, rigid, and unchanging over time. Semioticians like William Boelhower see ethnic identity as a kind of force field, which emerges only out of the process (or flux) generated by ethnic groups coming into contact and reciprocal relationship with one another—out of, in other words, a process of looking and being looked at.[53]

I will show how this process took place by analyzing and tracing connections between different realms of the performing arts: vaudeville, popular songs, comic strips, Broadway theater, and film. The various forms of popular culture are interconnected in ways that have only recently begun to be appreciated. Comic strip characters and vaudeville routines made the leap onto Broadway and into Hollywood films; plays were turned into films (and vice versa), and popular songs turned up almost anywhere.

VAUDEVILLE, THEATER, AND FILM

However, I have chosen to focus on only three of these interrelated forms of popular entertainment: vaudeville, Broadway theater, and film. These are all obviously visual forms of culture, which allow me to discuss the nature of representation and image. I have chosen not to discuss radio, since it is not a visual medium and since few Jewish performers appeared on it before the 1930s. (Also, most American families did not have radios until the 1930s.) I have also chosen not to discuss literature, since it is not generally viewed as a form of popular culture. By contrast, comic strips and popular songs (which were often performed as part of vaudeville routines) do receive some significant attention in this study. I believe that the influence of comic strips on the Broadway theater has been insufficiently recognized, particularly as they conditioned audience response to Jewish characters.

This book begins with a rehearsal of Jewish stereotypes on stage and then discusses a number of important second-generation Jewish vaudeville stars, with a particular focus on Fanny Brice, Eddie Cantor, George Jessel, and Sophie Tucker. I argue that the Jewish routines performed by these entertainers expressed a highly conflicted attitude toward their Jewish identity. That at least part of the audience was expected to be Jewish as well is indicated by the popularity of routines that incorporated Yiddish expressions, that showed the comedians acting out familiar immigrant Jewish personas in stereotypical Jewish occupations or family roles, and that depended for their humor on a basic knowledge of Jewish religion and culture.

The second chapter analyzes the 1920s Broadway comedies that showed Jewish families coping with peculiarly "American" problems—conflict between the generations, intermarriage (especially with the Irish), and assimilation. Most of these plays were written by Jews, including Aaron Hoffman's

Two Blocks Away (1921), Montague Glass's *Partners Again* (1922), Leon De Costa's *Kosher Kitty Kelly* (1925), Bella and Samuel Spewack's *Poppa* (1928), and David Freedman's *Mendel Inc.* (1928). Many were produced by Jewish producers, from Sam and J. J. Shubert to David Belasco and Sam Harris.

Interestingly, it was the comic strips of the period, particularly Harry Hershfield's *Abie the Agent,* which reviewers most often mentioned in searching for the roots of the new Jewish characters. I trace the way in which Americans' familiarity with ethnic humor in the comic strips increased their receptivity to Jewish characters on Broadway. A transformation of the Broadway audience occurred, as these plays attracted tremendous numbers of Jews to Broadway for the first time, helping to democratize the face of Broadway. As second-generation Jews saw their lives mirrored on the Broadway stage, they celebrated a sense of having arrived in American culture.

The third and final chapter looks at silent films from the period that are almost all set on the Lower East Side. Since Jews had already left the immigrant neighborhood in large numbers, these films are both highly nostalgic and strikingly forward-looking. I argue in this chapter that as images of Jews began to be widely disseminated in American culture, tolerance for Jews gradually increased. The emphasis in this chapter is on the ways in which perceptions of Jews changed in the majority culture.

Despite the mostly negative attitudes toward Jewishness on the part of the highly assimilated Jewish film producers, there was a significant body of films that showed Jews in highly sympathetic ways. These films showed Jews as sharing the same kinds of family relationships, economic struggles, nostalgia for the past, and fantasies of a better life that all Americans did in the turbulent twenties. I will demonstrate this by analyzing not just the films themselves but the marketing campaigns undertaken by the studios, and the reactions to the films in both the mainstream and Jewish press.

During the Golden Age of Jewish culture in the 1920s, it was possible to live, work, and enjoy recreational activities exclusively with other Jews and yet never attend synagogue. Steven Whitfield has argued that there is "no longer a serious way of being Jewish—and of living within Jewish culture—without Judaism."[54] Were my grandparents members of the last generation to be able to ground a transmissible Jewish identity in a nonreligious way?

CHAPTER ONE

Jews on the Vaudeville Stage

HARRY JOLSON, brother of the Jewish superstar entertainer Al Jolson, once recalled an act that the two brothers did together in 1900 called "The Hebrew and the Cadet," in which Harry played a "Hebrew with a big hat and a beard" while Al, who was fifteen at the time, wore a cadet's uniform. At one point in the act Al calls Harry a monkey and Harry responds, "Sure I am a monkey. Vot is more I want to tell you that my brothers and sisters is monkeys, my father and mother is monkeys, and all of my ancestors was monkeys." According to Harry, who told this story in the late 1940s to one of Al's biographers, "This got a huge laugh, and it will today, if you try it on an audience of tender years."[1]

The Jew as monkey? While it was hardly uncommon in the past for immigrants and African Americans to be described as animals, it seems shocking that Jews would take satisfaction in the laughter that such an association suggested. If we imagine how this sketch was performed for maximum comedic effect, the "cadet," sharply attired in his uniform, provides a clear contrast to the disheveled immigrant in his big (probably too big) hat and beard. The Jewish immigrant is proud of his lineage, yet his ancestors have all been sub-human, as he even pronounces himself to be.

Harley Erdman, Paul Distler, and Esther Romeyn have all analyzed late-nineteenth- and early-twentieth-century Jewish vaudeville in terms of the presentation of "types," or characteristics that performers used in order to signify stereotypically Jewish attributes.[2] Variety sketches, like contemporary *Saturday Night Live* skits, are based on obvious, often unrealistic markers of identity—switching hats, sticking on a mustache, adopting an exaggerated accent, and so forth. To impersonate an immigrant Jewish man (Jewish immigrant women were much less often the butt of humor), this meant gluing on a long beard and a big nose, pulling a derby hat over the ears, and speaking with a grotesque Yiddish accent.

Specialists in performing Jewish caricatures were called "Hebrew comics," and most of these were non-Jews. At a time when to make fun of ethnic minorities could help to assuage one's anxieties about immigrants, these performers were second in popularity only to minstrel show performers—

white entertainers who donned blackface to make fun of black people. Jews gradually began to take over their own representations and to work out what it meant to them to be Jewish. When second-generation Jews took over their own representations, transforming the tradition of Jewish "racial" comedy, they reinvented Jewish ethnicity. In creating Jewish self-representations, I will argue, they changed the ways in which non-Jews viewed Jews, and in which Jews viewed themselves.

Not all Jewish American entertainers were known for their Jewish comedy routines. Al Jolson, perhaps the most successful of all second-generation Jewish entertainers, did almost no Jewish comedy after he became famous. (He did, however, record a Yiddish song called "A Chazen oyf Shabbos," or "A Cantor on the Sabbath," which was cut from the 1946 film *The Jolson Story* because it was viewed as "too ethnic.") The Marx Brothers also had no Jewish routines; Groucho Marx told his son that although the Marx Brothers were Jewish, "the world thinks we're Italian."[3] (Nevertheless, as Arthur Berger has pointed out, Groucho Marx played all his ridiculous WASP characters like Hugo Hackenbush and Rufus Firefly with Jewish gestures and inflections—not to mention impudent Jewish verbal humor—thereby poking fun at WASPs.)[4]

Part of this avoidance of Jewish material may have sprung from these entertainers' ambivalence about their own Jewishness. Herbert Goldman, who wrote a major biography of Jolson, tells the story (via George Jessel) of Jolson flying out to California to do radio broadcasts and being met by his two-and-a-half-year-old adopted son, Al Jolson, Jr. "Who am I, Sonny Boy?" asked Jolson. "You're the little Jew," was the response. It was, Jessel told Goldman, the only time he ever saw Jolson completely mortified.[5] However, when Jessel eulogized Jolson, he called him the "happiest portrait that can be painted about an American of the Jewish faith," and noted that Jolson was the first famous entertainer whom everyone knew to be Jewish and who seemed openly proud of being Jewish.[6]

Almost all of the notable Jewish entertainers of the early twentieth century performed explicitly Jewish-themed material only as a part of a larger repertoire that often included blackface performances. Nevertheless, these entertainers' Jewish-themed material is worthy of study for the complex feelings about Jewishness that they encapsulated and the ways in which they signaled greater acceptance of Jews by American society. And often their signature songs or routines were their Jewish-themed material, such as Fanny Brice's "Second Hand Rose" and Sophie Tucker's "My Yiddishe Mama."

The "Hebrew" Comics

Vaudeville grew out of the entertainment format known as the variety show, in which different types of performers (including singers, dancers, jugglers, magicians, animal trainers, etc.) were all presented on the same bill. A producer named John W. Ransome first used the word "vaudeville" to describe the group he formed in the 1880s. The word comes from the French "Val de Vire" (or "Vau de Vire"), meaning the valley of the Vire River in Normandy, a region where lively ballads were sung.[7] Ransome himself played a "Dutch" comic (a caricature of a German-speaking immigrant) with this group, and vaudeville quickly became known for its "racial" comedy, its presentation of stereotypes of immigrants. The Irish were most often the butts of humor, especially in the early days of vaudeville, followed by blacks and then German-speaking immigrants.[8]

But there were many "Hebrew" comics as well, performers whose name came not from their own ethnicity, since most of the actors were not Jewish themselves, but from the Jewish stereotypes they performed on stage. As James Madison, who published compilations of popular vaudeville gags, put it in 1900, "The time is ripe for Hebrew dialect comedians. Good stories illustrative of the traits and peculiarities of the Jewish race always create a laugh."[9] These entertainers created caricatures that exploited the anti-Semitic attitudes of the time; their acts recapitulated negative stereotypes of Jews including their supposed unkempt appearance, unattractive faces, and pervasive dishonesty.

By wearing crepe hair, exaggerated noses made from putty, and long dark clothes, these actors were able, with a few distinguishing features, to give audiences, many of whom did not know any Jews, the pleasure of indulging anti-Semitic feelings. Whether starting a building fire to collect from their insurance company, overcharging their customers, or demonstrating their ignorance of both the English language and of American culture, Jews remained in the Shylock and Fagin tradition, albeit with a comic twist.

Audiences were able to laugh at these stereotypes partly because they were comic rather than threatening. In her study of images of the Jew in nineteenth-century American culture, Louise A. Mayo has found that the most pervasive stereotype was of the greedy, money-hungry Jew. However, she points out that these depictions "did not demonstrate any real rancor or fear."[10] In contrast to European representations of the Jew as the devil incarnate who sucked the lifeblood out of the economic system, Americans saw Jews as more ridiculous than dangerous—a rational being whose pursuit of wealth summed up the ambivalence of Protestant Americans toward their own (more socially acceptable) acquisitiveness.

They also fell into familiar styles. When actors like Frank Bush and Julian Rose performed Jewish roles, they fell into two basic categories, according to Distler: "the fast-talking, aggressive winner and the pathetic, world-weary loser."[11] For example, Ben Welch exemplified the latter type, while his brother, Joe Welch, represented the former. According to Joe Laurie, Jr.,

Joe Welch was a widely imitated comic who entered the stage to almost "funereal music" clad in "misfit coat and pants, hands in his sleeves, derby hat over his ears and beard brushed to a point." Welch then "stood center stage, faced the audience for half a minute, and with the saddest look ever on a human pan, said, 'Maybe you tink I'm heppy?'"[12] He seemed to sum up all the misery that Jews had experienced throughout the ages, in somewhat the same way as did the silent film actor Charlie Chaplin, who was not Jewish, although many people mistakenly believed that he was.

Vaudeville stars who played Jewish characters in the first two decades of the twentieth century continued in many ways to play the "loser." (This changed significantly in the 1920s, as I will demonstrate.) One exception was Jess Dandy, who played a "stout, genial, business Jew," who, according to Gilbert, "never whined or deplored but stressed good humor and pleasantries to win his audience."[13] Gilbert sees him as a forerunner of the Potash and Perlmutter plays of Montague Glass, an enormously popular series featuring two Jewish businessmen that I will examine in greater depth in the next chapter.

1. Frank Bush, an important "Hebrew" comic, clad in stereotypical immigrant Jewish costume. Courtesy of Billy Rose Theatre Collection, New York Public Library for the Performing Arts, Astor, Lenox and Tilden Foundations.

Almost all comics, of whatever ethnic stripe, started by doing blackface comedy, and then branched out into impersonating other ethnic minorities. In fact, vaudeville comics often changed vaudeville "identities" in rapid-fire succession; the most salient feature of ethnic identities on stage was their seeming interchangeability. As Robert Snyder has pointed out, "anyone could play any nationality. All that was needed was a convincing presentation of stock traits (down to skin color: sallow greasepaint for Jews, red for Irishmen, and olive for Sicilians)."[14] Small wonder then that Eddie Cantor, whom everyone knew to be Jewish, recorded a foxtrot song about an Italian grocery store owner, in which the character is described as illiterate but "ruling with a hand like Mussolini's."[15] There were many Jewish grocers as well, but the immigrant groups were somewhat interchangeable when it came to ethnic comedy.

Perhaps because the Jews and Irish lived in close proximity on the Lower East Side of New York, many Americans seemed to view these two immigrant groups as especially similar. As Anne Nichols, who wrote the long-running Broadway comedy *Abie's Irish Rose* (to be discussed in depth in the next chapter), once said, the Jews and Irish "have both known hunger and privation," and both are "intense and mystic in religious matters," with a "strong strain of melancholy." She added that both traditions are "highly imaginative and strongly inclined to superstition," with poetry that is "similarly high-strung with a common lyric strain."[16] While this was a highly romanticized view of both ethnic groups, it does seem to sum up a prevailing sense that Jews and Irish were both outcasts from European society whose cultures were steeped in mysterious-seeming myth and ritual.

In the field of popular entertainment, the Jewish-Irish connection was reflected in the fact that Jewish and Irish caricatures were often performed in tandem. Snyder quotes a theater manager, R. E. Irwin, about a vaudeville team called Morris Allen, who appeared in 1911 at Keith and Proctor's Fifth Avenue Theatre; Irwin trumpets, "Two Jews singing Irish songs with a little talk and some bag pipe singing. This act is a find for any house and is as good an act of the Hebrew brand as has been around in many a day."[17] Only blacks, who were perceived as fundamentally inferior even to immigrant ethnics, were limited in the repertoire of ethnic identities that they were permitted to perform.[18]

While performing other ethnic identities, Jewish performers often slipped back into what they were most familiar with. For example, two prominent Jewish performers from the Lower East Side, Weber and Fields, who never did explicitly Jewish routines, wittily covered their noses with their hands when they sang about being Irish, a gesture that brought down the house.[19] Since Jews stereotypically had large noses, they created humor out of reinforcing their Jewishness at the same time as they masqueraded as Irishmen.

Indeed, according to Harry Jolson, "There were few specialists who played only one type of character. A comedian was expected to do anything. He would be a Dutchman in one act, a Jew in another, and an Irishman in a third, with a perfect rendition of the dialect of each. You were either versatile or out of a job." Harry usually played in a Jewish dialect. In one show, he recounts:

> I was unexpectedly assigned the part of Emperor of Ireland. When the "Wearing of the Green" sounded, I strutted on the stage in a supposed Hibernian costume. Habit was too strong for me. Instead of speaking my lines with an Irish brogue, I made a speech in approved Eastside Yiddish-American gumbo.
>
> When called on the carpet, I defended myself with the skill of a park-bench lawyer.
>
> "There are Jews in Ireland," I said. "Have you ever been in Ireland?"
>
> "No, I haven't," was the reply.
>
> "Well, I have, and I gave a perfect impersonation of an Irish-Jew. What do you expect for what you are paying me? The real Emperor of Ireland?"[20]

Jolson's attempt to excuse his error could itself have been the basis for an extended version of the routine. Vaudeville performers already played with the audience's expectations of what different ethnic groups would look and sound like, as well as with the audience's preconceptions that the member of an ethnic group will be most expert at reproducing the ethnic traits that he or she is most familiar with, or perhaps already possesses to some degree. Conflating the stereotypes was undoubtedly, if unintentionally, very amusing. In addition, although this aspect of vaudeville is rarely commented upon by contemporaneous observers, part of the fun of going to vaudeville performances was undoubtedly seeing performers trip up in various ways.

Over time, many of these extreme forms of ethnic parody began to seem less funny, as immigrant groups became more accepted in American society. Distler refers to the "reformation" of the stage Jew, which he attributes to the work of protest groups like the Anti-Stage Ridicule Committee and the Anti-Defamation League of B'nai Brith. He argues that ethnic stereotypes declined both because immigrants and their children were assimilating and because the Immigration Acts of the early 1920s prevented new immigrants from arriving—providing fewer examples of unassimilated Jews for American culture to parody. Erdman states baldly that the 1910s was the "last decade (until recent times) in which markedly Jewish characters were commonplace in American popular performance."[21]

The evidence suggests otherwise. For while ethnic humor depends on stereotype (or the ethnic group being parodied would not be identifiable by the audience), there is no reason why Jewish comedy would end or Jewish characters would disappear when older stereotypical depictions of Jews began to decline. New stereotypes are always developing. The stereotype of the Jewish doctor or lawyer, for example, is a mid- to late-twentieth-century stereotype, which could only gain currency after Jews began to move into the professions. In the 1980s in New York it was the Japanese (who were buying up American corporations and real estate) who were seen as much more greedy than the Jews.[22] And nowadays Jewish men are much more likely to be portrayed on stage and screen as good providers and sensitive husbands rather than simply money-grubbing fools.

In other words, how ethnic identities are performed has inevitably changed over time as outcast groups have become more accepted in American society. In addition, as groups have become more comfortable in America, they have felt less of a need to internalize the negative feelings that the mainstream culture has projected upon them. It is the intermediate stage—between marginalization and full participation—that is the most interesting, as the group begins to present a new face to the world and negotiates new ways of being ethnic. This was the paradoxical situation of Jews in the 1920s, as they struggled with intense ambivalence about being Jewish.

Stereotypes also take a long time to fade, much longer than the relatively brief period of time in which Distler and Erdman suggest that Jewish stereotypes essentially disappeared from American popular culture. Edward Coleman's compilation, *The Jew in English Drama*, lists hundreds of vaudeville monologues and two-person sketches from the 1920s (many of which were published by T. S. Denison & Company in Chicago) incorporating stereotypical Jewish "characters." From Arthur Leroy Kaser's "Vait a minute" and "Vell! Vell! Vell!" to E. L. Gamble's "Oi, vhat a bargain" and "Oi, vot a business" to William McNally's "Avernsky by the Seasky" and "Irving Lipshits the Salesman," to Frederick Green Johnson's "Abie's Confessions" and "Mrs. Goldblitz on Matrimony," the stage Jew was a durable—and ubiquitous—type throughout the United States during the 1920s.[23]

Many of these routines, which were heavy on physical, slapstick comedy as well as the liberal use of foreign accents, featured a kind of combination approach to ethnic humor, with members of different ethnic groups finding themselves in the same army platoon, restaurant, or schoolroom, as in Kaiser's "Hey! Teacher!"[24] Jews were presented highly stereotypically, as for example in A. F. Byers's "Abie Eats," in which an oyster-eating Jew is dissatisfied with everything on the restaurant menu—especially the prices! His dishonesty is shown by his feigning illness when the bill comes.[25]

Perhaps the most famous Jewish routine was "Cohen on the Telephone," first performed in England in 1912 by Joe Hayman, in which a heavily accented immigrant Jew, unfamiliar with using the telephone, calls his land-lord to complain about a broken window. This recording sold hundreds of thousands of copies and led to a series of further sketches with Cohen in other difficult situations, including being at a real estate office, sailing on a houseboat, attending a prizefight, and having problems with his automobile. (He even gave "lectures" on telephone etiquette and deportment.)[26]

Cohen sketches were also recorded by a number of American comedians; Monroe Silver, the best-known "Cohen" actor in the United States, per-formed them for thirty years, on two dozen different record labels. As we will see in the next chapter, this basic routine was reprised in different ways in a number of the Broadway comedies about Jewish life in New York.

The popularity of these routines across the country spoke to continuing perceptions of Jews as ethnic and racial outsiders. But did stereotypes decline more quickly in New York, since Jews were relatively visible—as compared to more sparsely populated areas of the country—and moving so quickly into the lower middle class? Or did the persistence, at the same time, of large num-bers of Jewish immigrants give the stereotypes greater durability in New York? I do not think that there is a simple answer to this question. (It is sim-ilar to asking how much anti-Semitism existed in New York as opposed to other parts of America. Is there more racism when a group is more numer-ous, or less racism, since the group is less visible?)

I would argue that the growing confidence that Jews showed in mount-ing Jewish-themed entertainment, the sheer number of Jewish-themed per-formances, and the nature of these performances—many of which challenged traditional attitudes toward Jews on the part of the majority culture—bespoke a fairly rapid broadening of ideas of what Jews looked and acted like. Jews began to seem like good neighbors rather than alien beings. And the presence of Jews in vaudeville, the ultimate democratizing art form, meant that Jews had a place in the more open and less hierarchical society that was emerging in the 1920s.

It also meant that Jews were inventing new ways of being Jewish. This was symbolized by the career of the beloved vaudeville star Ed Wynn, who made comedy out of ridiculous contraptions such as a cheese fork with noseguards, a typewriter carriage-style corn-on-the-cob eater, and an overcoat with pro-truding pieces of steel—this last to give the wearer room on the subway![27] Wynn's humor was not as explicitly Jewish as that of Cantor and Jessel, although he claimed that the best joke he ever told on radio was about a "Yiddish tourist," lost in the Alps, who refuses the brandy offered by a St. Bernard who has come from a nearby monastery to rescue him—he tells the dog to go back and get ginger ale![28] Wynn also said in interviews that he had run away from home as a boy to become a Jewish character comedian, and that his comic style remained less of what he called a "joke comedian" than a "method comedian"—one who makes people laugh less through the jokes he tells than through their delivery, expressions, inflections, etc.

As Gilbert Seldes wrote about Wynn, he played a "perpetual immigrant obsessed by hats and shoes and words and small ideas, instead of bothering about skyscrapers. The deepness of his zanylike appreciation of every-day things is the secret of his capacity for making them startling and funny."[29] At a time when technology was spreading rapidly, Wynn spoke to people's sense that life was getting too complex and difficult to comprehend. At the same time, he seemed like a character out of Yiddish theater who marvels at the changes that are coming to the world of the shtetl.

THE JEWISHNESS OF BROADWAY

A Midwestern Jewish newspaper published a front-page article in June of 1926 entitled "Jewishness—and the Box Office" with the subhead "Why Broadway Stars are More Jewish Than Ever." The article, by Henry Montor, talks about a group of "distinguished Paris businessmen" who came to New York seeking a "typical New York evening." Their host, the author of the article, recommended one Jewish entertainer after another, from Fanny Brice to Al Jolson, Eddie Cantor to Ed Wynn, telling them that these entertainers "represent the Broadway age at its best, and the Yankee art in its most original form."[30]

Jewish comedy as authentic *Yankee* art? Montor's article went on to attempt to resolve this apparent contradiction. Despite having changed their names, American Jewish artists openly proclaimed their Jewishness to their audiences. Montor saw their calling attention to their Jewishness primarily as an effort to combat anti-Semitism in American society. But whether or not the prominence of Jewish comedians helped to reduce anti-Semitism, American society was definitely changed by their performances. For it was the Jewish entertainers, Montor concluded, who were beginning to "express, and to a certain extent, mold, American humor, wit, music, and life in general."[31]

Nevertheless, the source of the Jewish entertainers' humor remained a mystery to Montor. Although he said it would "make a very interesting study if one were to analyze and dissect the art of a Jolson or Cantor," he wondered if such an examination would yield a racial trait that accounted for their pre-eminence in entertainment. There seemed no other way to explain the tremendous success of Jewish artists. (If he could have looked into the future, one wonders what he would have said to the French businessmen about Jerry Lewis, who was only a few months old at the time that the article was written but who would go on to become extraordinarily popular, especially in

France, for a manic style that owed much to the Jewish entertainers of the previous generation.)

Although he did not have the words to express it, Montor seemed to echo the idea that Seldes, Wilson, and others had that Jews brought an intense hunger to succeed that was expressed in the tremendous energy and verve that they brought to their work as entertainers—an explosive energy that vibrated in tune with all Americans' sense of anxiety and excitement in the face of enormous social change. Seldes described Jolson and Brice as "daemonic," in the explosiveness of this energy on stage, which he compares to the frenzy of the stock exchange and grandeur of the skyscraper. While Franklin Delano Roosevelt is also "dynamic," Seldes allowed, "the fury and exultation of Jolson is a hundred times higher in voltage than that of Roosevelt; we can produce courageous and adventurous women who shoot lions or manage construction gangs and remain pale beside the extraordinary 'cutting loose' of Fanny Brice."[32] This volcanic energy and insatiable need for attention, Seldes believed, underlay the Jewish entertainers' success.

Seldes was seemingly not at all religious; his biographer, Michael Kammen, has written that "rather than the sacred and the profane, this totally secular assimilated Jew thought in terms of a different dualism: the aesthetically creative versus the culturally mundane." However, even if Seldes wanted to downplay his own ethnicity, there were also those (often as a result of feeling slighted by his book reviews) who found the need to remind him of it; Kammen quotes writers from Ernest Hemingway to F. Scott Fitzgerald, commenting derisively on Seldes's Jewishness.[33]

And Seldes did seem to take some pride in the Jewishness of the Jewish vaudeville stars he wrote about; in any event, he certainly emphasized their Jewishness in one way or another, such as when he mentions Jolson's "absurd black-face which is so little negroid that it goes well with diversions in Yiddish accents" or praises Brice's "Yiddish Squow"—a reference to the routine called "I'm an Indian" in which she masquerades as an American Indian.[34] And, in an intriguing passage, he adds that

> It is noteworthy that these two stars bring something to America which America lacks and loves—they are, I suppose, two of our most popular entertainers—and that both are racially out of the dominant caste. Possibly this accounts for their fine carelessness about our superstitions of politeness and gentility. The medium in which they work requires more decency and less frankness than usually exist in our private lives; but within these bounds Jolson and Brice go farther, go with more contempt for artificial notions of propriety, than anyone else.[35]

As Seldes suggests, Jews did seem to have an aptitude for vaudeville that stemmed from their ability to question and even violate social conventions.

Irving Howe has written eloquently of the ways in which immigrant Jews on the Lower East Side had been "held in check too long by the repressiveness of old-world moralism and the system of 'respect' for learning." Their children, he said, were "full of sap, excited by the sheer volume of street noise, letting loose sexual curiosities beyond the clamp of Jewish shame. . . . It was a vulgarity in both senses: as the urgent, juicy thrust of desire, intent upon seizing life by the throat, and as the cheap, corner-of-the-mouth retailing of Yiddish obscenities."[36] The combination of a tremendous drive to succeed and the pleasure taken in bursting the bounds of civility, both Seldes and Howe suggest, was at the root of the success of Jewish comics.

However, it was easy for Jewish entertainers to stand out because they represented a culture that was very different, in both style and substance, from Protestant American culture. As Mary Cass Canfield wrote in 1922 in *The New Republic,* "Grotesque or not, vaudeville represents a throwing away of self-consciousness, of Plymouth Rock caution, devoutly to be wished for. Here we countenance the extreme, we encourage idiosyncrasy. The dancer or comedian is, sometimes literally, egged on to develop originality; he is adored, never crucified for difference." Canfield goes on to use Fanny Brice as one of her examples of these entertainers who "have been encouraged into self-emphasis by their audiences."[37]

While the reference to being "crucified for difference" is a bit strange (is she comparing Jewish performers to Jesus?), Canfield's point is well taken: vaudeville performers overturn social conventions and liberate audiences from Puritan morality. The "self-emphasis" that she refers to can perhaps be understood, in the case of the Jewish performers, as an underlining of their Jewishness, which is the original source of the "difference" she points out as constitutive of their performance style. What Seldes called the "absurd and vulgar" on the vaudeville stage was, for Jewish performers, a mark of their freedom that the stage afforded them to shock and delight.

Jewish entertainers thus had a profound effect on American culture. True, Montor's article was published in a Jewish newspaper, so his article has more than a little trace of ethnic boosterism—interesting for its own sake in terms of the ways in which these Jewish celebrities made all Jews feel vicariously successful. But there is no question that a select group of Jewish performers became among the most celebrated entertainers in America during this period.

As I will demonstrate, they seemed to be equally successful in performing openly Jewish material as they were when performing non-Jewish material. But I will argue that even their performances of non-Jewish material inescapably had a Jewish *tam* (Yiddish for "taste" or "flavor"). Their choice of material, performance styles, and the overall flavor with which their work was imbued, all signified a Jewish sensibility at work.

Second-generation American Jews also comprised a significant part of the audience for culture in New York. These Jews were, as Deborah Dash Moore has suggested, "at home in America," in terms of their material success and level of comfort in American society.[38] What they needed to work out was the meaning of their Jewish identity, and they did so, I suggest, in large part through the representations of Jewishness that they produced and consumed in American popular culture.

The Stage Jew Rehabilitated?

When this new generation of American Jewish performers began to take over these representations, the old stereotypes still retained influence. Rather than jettisoning them entirely, the new breed of Jewish entertainers transformed the stereotypes in their own image, updating them to reflect their own experience of being Jewish in America. But acting out these modified stereotypes meant parading before the world a highly conflicted sense of self, conscious of the continuing anti-Semitism in American society and yet attempting to carve out a new way of being Jewish.

As one observer, Eli Levi, wrote in an English-language Jewish newspaper in 1922, a new type of Jewish vaudeville comedian had appeared in the last few years. He called them the "English-speaking Jewish comedians . . . working without facial make-up and grotesque costume. They mimic the 'heavy' broken English of their immigrant elders, make cryptic remarks in Jewish, and exemplify the peculiarities of the 'kike.'" Levi concluded that "Vaudeville is not an elevating form of entertainment, and the characterization of the Jew has no place there."[39]

But few members of the audience expected vaudeville to be "elevating." They simply wanted to be entertained. Perhaps the best example of the new breed of Jewish comics is the team of Joe Smith (Joe Sultzer) and Charlie Dale (Charlie Marks), two Jewish boys from the Lower East Side who formed one of the best-loved vaudeville teams. (Their stage names were the result of a theater manager's using leftover cards from another act to advertise their first big-time performance.) In their trademark act, "Dr. Kronkhite" (taken from the Yiddish word for sickness, *krankayt*), a patient with a heavy Yiddish accent is examined by an unsympathetic and impatient physician. (This routine was later incorporated into Neil Simon's play about a retired vaudevillian team, *The Sunshine Boys*.)

The sarcasm-laden humor is based on verbal mix-ups, such as when the patient, played by Smith, says he's "dubious" that the doctor is really a doctor, leading the doctor, played by Dale, to address the patient as "Mr. Dubious." A typical example of the Yiddish word order (in Yiddish, the object often precedes the verb) causing misunderstanding is when the patient says "Veal I eat," and the doctor says "Look, I don't ask you *vill* you eat, I ask you *what* you eat."[40]

Smith and Dale seemed simultaneously to inhabit both the immigrant world of the Lower East Side and the wider world that lay beyond the ghetto. For example, in the 1935 short called "The Gypsy National Savings Bank" (gypsies being a clear substitution for the believed racial otherness of Jews), Smith plays the president of a fancy but bizarre bank who has to deal with a stingy potential depositor, played by Dale. Dale only has seven dollars (all in quarters) to put in the bank, but he wants the royal treatment, including being able to call the bank president at home in the middle of the night if he needs access to his money. But Smith says he does not have a phone; he tells Dale to call the candy store (a familiar type of business on the Lower East Side, often owned by Jews) and they will get the message to him. At another point in the skit, Smith accuses Dale of wanting free pencils from the bank in order to sell them on the street; he also tries to charge Dale money whenever he offers Dale an apple and the depositor takes a bite out of it.

Similarly, in "What Price Pants?" filmed in 1929, Smith plays a highly skilled pantsmaker in a Lower East Side garment shop who is encouraged by his fellow employees to ask his boss, played by Dale, for a raise. But the fast-talking Dale somehow convinces his employee that a raise for him would lead to mass unemployment, and ends up reducing his salary rather than raising it. After a long interlude in which a pants shortage leads to everyone in the city walking around in their boxer shorts and Smith and Dale becoming business rivals for a saloon that illegally sells slacks (in a gibe at Prohibition, which was in force at the time), Smith gets his revenge by tricking Dale into signing over the garment shop by writing a letter in which Smith is supposedly named heir by a fictitious uncle.

These routines recapitulate many stereotypes about Jews, mostly dealing with their supposed obsession with money. In almost all of Smith and Dale's routines, the two are trying to trick, cheat, and defraud one another. Yet despite their lack of education (evidenced by their constant verbal mix-ups, upon which a very large part of all of their comedy depends), Smith and Dale also appear quite upwardly mobile, confident in their Jewishness, and still connected in many ways to the immigrant world of the Lower East Side. They also maintained connections to Jewish religion in their personal lives. When Joe Smith's father passed away in 1923 while the team was touring the West, Smith worked hard to assemble a minyan (quorum of ten men for prayer) both on the train and in each town in which they appeared.[41]

Unlike Tin Pan Alley composers like George Gershwin and Irving Berlin, who incorporated few Jewish themes in their work, these vaudeville performers thus retained close connections to Jewish culture. Mark Slobin, the foremost historian of American Jewish music, has argued that "Jewish popular culture in the 1920s became increasingly defined in terms of its relationship to the mainstream of American life. To rely on the continuity of internal

2. Joe Smith (standing) and Charlie Dale (seated), the comedy team that traded on malapropisms, remade Jewish comedy into a verbal art form. Courtesy of Billy Rose Theatre Collection, New York Public Library for the Performing Arts, Astor, Lenox and Tilden Foundations.

traditions became ever more risky, as the ethnic thread was stretched thinner and thinner."[42] But Slobin's focus on music leads him to underestimate the Jewish content of other forms of popular culture and to make a generalization that is false. Jewishness continued to permeate American popular culture; the "ethnic thread" was not stretched so thin after all.

REPRISING THE GHETTO

One direction in which the "thread" often led, at least in symbolic terms, was back to the immigrant ghetto. A recurrent notion in Jewish-themed vaudeville sketches of the period is the relationship of the second generation to the Lower East Side, the immigrant neighborhood in which they had almost all grown up. (In 1892, 75 percent of Jews in New York City lived on the Lower East Side.) In fact, the Jewish "ghetto" came to symbolize for the second generation their Jewish heritage itself; in moving away from the ghetto they were detaching themselves from Jewish tradition.

This tension informed much of their work. For their careers seemed to take shape, at least metaphorically, in the shadow of the ghetto, to which they and their audiences remained emotionally connected. As Hasia Diner has written, the Lower East Side came, for American Jews, to be "the place about which they told their stories, where they located the narratives that explained who they were, where they had come from, and how they got there. . . . The Lower East Side loomed large as the setting for memories."[43]

It loomed large as well as the setting for vaudeville skits, and later, as we will see, for full-length plays and films. The ghetto became a crucial frame of reference, even for non-Jews; one critic reviewing a vaudeville performance by the entertainer Belle Baker noted that she sang a Jewish comedy song called "Atlas Is It-less" and calling Baker a "raven-haired, big-eyed, Jewish 'Momma,' who used to sell lemonade at a penny a drink in New York's Delancey Street."[44]

By far the most successful dialect comedian was Fanny Brice. Brice, born Fanny Borach in 1891 on the Lower East Side, made a career of Yiddish dialect comedy, despite the fact that she said she never learned Yiddish. At a time when second-generation American Jews viewed the Yiddish accent as a mark of the uneducated and unacculturated, Brice's use of it enabled her to mock her origins in ways that pleased both Jewish and non-Jewish audiences. Her gleeful performances of "characters" from the ghetto were particularly popular, especially among Jews for whom they stirred nostalgia for the Lower East Side.

One of Brice's three biographers, Barbara Grossman, quotes an interview Brice gave in the 1930s in which she exclaimed, "The Ghetto! It is so old and strong; it is still carrying on all over the earth. It gave us a spirit I can tell you."[45] Although Brice did not explain this remark, the idea that the ghetto would be "carrying on all over the earth" is an interesting one; Brice herself, through her performances, brought the ghetto all across America and to London. The ghetto traveled with her.

Her first big success came in 1909 when she performed a song about a Bronx girl who became a hula dancer. It was written by Irving Berlin and was called "Sadie Salome, Go Home!" Her singing it in a Yiddish accent came

3. Belle Baker, Jewish actress and singer who often performed Jewish material. Courtesy of Photofest.

about, she later recalled, because Berlin sang it for her with what she later called his "little naive inflection."[46] Brice said she "never had any idea of doing a song with a Yiddish accent. I didn't even understand Jewish, couldn't talk a word of it. But, I thought, if that's the way Irving sings it, that's the way I'll sing it."[47]

Berlin's Salome song parodied the late-nineteenth- and early-twentieth-century craze for Salome dancing (sparked, according to Grossman, both by Oscar Wilde's 1893 one-act play and by Florenz Ziegfeld's 1907 spoof of the Richard Straus opera in the first edition of his celebrated *Follies*)[48] by portraying a Jewish girl who leaves home and leaves her disapproving fiancé, Mose, in order to seek stardom as a Salome dancer (a kind of glorified stripper). Singing this song, Brice recalled, brought back, for her, the sights and smells of the immigrant neighborhood: "I saw Loscha of the Coney Island popcorn counter and Marta of the cheeses at Brodsky's Delicatessen, and the Sadie's and the Rachels and the Birdies with the turnover heels at the Second Avenue dance halls. They all welded together and came out staggeringly true to type in one big authentic outline."[49]

In Brice's mind, the personalities of the ghetto merged; "they all welded together," as if they were the various parts of a single entity. Singing her Salome song, Brice recovered the sensory experience of the ghetto for herself—and, presumably, for her audience. The poor working women of the ghetto shared certain common characteristics that Brice saw herself as embodying in her performance. Similarly, in an interview with a Detroit newspaper two years later, the vaudeville star Belle Baker (known as the "Bernhardt of Ragtime" in her day for having introduced Irving Berlin's "Alexander's Rag-Time Band" in 1917) seemed almost to repeat Fanny Brice's words in claiming that she took her Jewish characters from people she had known on the Lower East Side:

> A comic song to be truly comic ought to have a true-to-nature touch. If you don't understand the people you are characterizing, your impersonation is just a burlesque and not real at all. Well, I don't have to make a sightseeing tour to get my types. I was born in New York right among them. . . . All my impersonations are real. When I sing an Italian or Irish or Yiddish song, I have a definite character in mind that I've known for years. I present the character from that point of view—not the outsiders.[50]

In defending her characterizations of Jews, Baker never mentions her own Jewishness. Her claim to be able to represent Jews is based on knowing them—not on being one herself. This enables her to claim that she can represent different ethnic characters with equal skill. However, another article from the same newspaper, while calling Baker a "neat and capable Jewish girl who can give the audience the distilled quintessence of any ballad, or can wring the uttermost drop of pep out of any rag," also pointed out that she "isn't above commercializing some of the characteristics of her own kin."[51] The idea of profiting from one's ethnicity is more familiar in the contemporary world that it was a hundred years ago. What is rap music (promoted, most of the time, by white record producers) but, in part, a commercialization of African American identity?

Brice's use of the Yiddish accent was equally calculating. A newspaper article about her in 1912 says she "lives in daily terror that some day she will speak the way everyone else does, and that she will forget her accent." In order to avoid this, she returns to the ghetto for two or three weeks every summer "listening, imitating, bargaining, quarrelling—using every opportunity for a new trick." Still, Brice continued to distance herself from those she supposedly studied. As she told a Cincinnati newspaper, "I go to their dances and outings, and eat in their restaurants. I do not bother with the Jewish types who have been in this country long enough to be Americanized."[52]

She did not "bother," in other words, with people like herself, who had shed many of the immigrant mannerisms and gestures. The irony is that her second-generation audience was also more "Americanized," and thus she was conspiring in a sense with her audience to present a picture of Jewishness that both she and they knew was outdated, and yet which they could both take pleasure in having grown out of.

Yet Brice, even as she became very successful, continued to demonstrate, at least in her work, an obsession with Jewish immigrants and the neighborhood in which they had settled. One profile of Brice in 1932, in a Jewish journal, is worth quoting at length:

> From the Ghetto to Park Avenue—that is the triumphal march of Fannie Brice, America's most famous and most popular Jewish comedienne. Her journey was begun almost forty years ago on New York's crowded East Side, that colorful habitat of 'Jews Without Money,' and a far cry from the refinement, spaciousness, quiet elegance, and glamorous doormen of the world's wealthiest street. . . .
>
> But Fannie Brice (that's how she signs her checks) did not leave the Ghetto behind. She has not entirely escaped it. A bank account, a hand-wrought, grilled door, a mosaic lobby, a soft-spoken, well-bred elevator man, a French governess for her two children stand between her and the sordidness and ugliness of her early environment; but the vibrant tragedy of all the Ghettoes of the world cries out in her voice. Her eyes broadcast the haunting pathos of Clinton Streets, Suffolk Streets, and Delancey Streets the world over. And right under the noses of the ritzy attendants of 1111 Park Avenue, this colorful character, Fannie Brice, lugged up to her quarters a large parcel of the Ghetto including the courage, the wit, the stamina, the honesty and the real values of the Jewish slums.[53]

The article describes Brice as bringing the ghetto with her in an almost surreptitious way, "right under the noses" of the servants of the rich. The reader is cast in cahoots with Brice, who is preserving the "real values" of the ghetto. Ironically, given the conspiratorial tone, it is the ghetto's "honesty" that Brice is especially lauded for preserving. The honesty seems presented less in moral terms than in fidelity to one's roots. The "parcel" that Brice "lugs," almost as if she still had to carry home her own shopping from the Lower East Side markets, is identified with the ghetto itself. It is characterized as a burden, but also as a source of both physical strength and strength of character. Her success has come from her ability to "broadcast the haunting pathos" of the ghetto streets to the world; the paradox of her career is that she has made a great deal of money by reproducing for the world the experience of poverty.

The ghetto also remained important as both setting and theme in the work of another groundbreaking Jewish performer, Eddie Cantor. Cantor, one of Brice's costars in the Ziegfeld *Follies,* was born Isidore Iskowitz, on Rosh Hashanah, the Jewish New Year, in September 1892. According to Cantor's biographer, Herbert Goldman, Cantor's immigrant mother died of a lung disease when he was an infant and his father abandoned him.

Cantor was raised on the Lower East Side by his maternal grandmother, Esther Kantrowitz; when she registered him for public school, she mistakenly gave her name rather than his, and the school shortened it to "Kanter." Cantor's memories of his stern but self-sacrificing grandmother and his impoverished upbringing on the Lower East Side remained vivid and important to him throughout his life. In both his autobiographies, *My Life Is in Your Hands* and *Take My Life,* Cantor fondly remembered his early job as a delivery boy for the Isaac Gellis Wurst Works (a kosher meat factory). The job gave Cantor his first taste of abundance; he later said he ate so many sandwiches he turned into a "sausage with eyes"[54]—an interesting choice of words given the importance of Cantor's eye movements to his comedy work.

Cantor broke into vaudeville in 1908, when he won first prize at an amateur night contest at Miner's Bowery. Cantor stuck on a beard and told jokes he remembered from vaudeville routines of stage Hebrews like Joe and Ben Welch. As the comedian recalled in his autobiography, "Joe Welsh's [*sic*] line always served as a handy opening. It appeared funny for a young boy with a beard to shake his head gravely and say, 'If I had my life to live over again I wouldn't be born.' It was extremely ironic, Cantor recalled, that he and his partner, Dan Lipsky, once appeared in a Yiddish theater without knowing it; they found themselves speaking in English to an audience that only knew Yiddish. In George Jessel's autobiography, *So Help Me,* he recalls Cantor doing a Yiddish monologue as well at the Imperial Theatre in Manhattan, but Cantor never mentions this in his books.[55]

Nevertheless, Cantor's Jewish vaudeville material is on display in a short film from 1924 called "A Few Moments with Eddie Cantor," which was one of the first experiments with synchronized sound in the history of film. In a brief program of comic songs and other material, Cantor tells two jokes about Jews who are overwhelmed by the circumstances in which they find themselves.

In one, he witnesses a man in New York's Pennsylvania Station who is beating his son. The father is warned by another man to stop or "I'll make trouble for you." The father's response is that his wife left him, his business failed, his baby has mumps, and his son has swallowed the train tickets—there's not much more trouble that he can experience. In the second, Cantor is on a train from Chicago to San Francisco when he observes a fellow passenger moaning "Oy vey" once every day for three days straight; when he asks if he can help, the man says that it is the third day that he is on the wrong train!

Jokes about train travel are a staple of Yiddish humor, as in Sholom Aleichem's comic, often surrealistic "Railroad Stories." Many Yiddish jokes set on trains are about Jews finding out that other passengers are also Jewish, as in the joke about the Jew who only relaxes and puts his feet up on the seat when he realizes that the man across the aisle from him is also a Jew. But these jokes of Cantor seem to ask the audience not just to take pity on the characters he discusses but also to dismiss them as impotent and infantile.

Cantor's first starring vehicle on Broadway was called *The Midnight Rounders,* which opened on November 29, 1920. Although Cantor had acquired a reputation as a blackface comedian (albeit one who wore glasses as part of his costume, which was a departure from stereotype), he performed in whiteface, and played a number of characters. One of his best was that of a tailor's assistant in a second-hand clothing store on the Lower East Side.

The sketch was called "Joe's Blue Front," or "Belt in the Back." The tailor and his apprentice give a squeaky, very timid customer the hard-sell, trying to get him to purchase a succession of ill-fitting, ridiculous-looking outfits. (Each time, he balks, demanding a suit "with a belt in the back." Cantor lifts his arm as if to slug him in the rear.) Cantor leads the customer onto the tailors' platform and around the store, pretending that they are going up the stairs to the next floor. But nothing satisfies the poor man. More merriment ensues when the two tailors lay the customer on the ground, as if measuring him for a coffin, or when they chant the numbers off the tape in the same melody as that used to explicate the Talmud. (The customer mistakenly chimes in with "Sweet Adeline," a song whose tune is completely different from the one they are warbling.)

As they keep forcing him to try on different clothes, adjusting each one in ridiculous fashion (for example, when he complains that a suit is too tight, Cantor rips it down the back seam; when he demands pinstripes, Cantor draws the pinstripes in chalk), the customer gets more and more frustrated and tries to flee. But they keep dragging him back in, trying alternately to flatter or humiliate him in order to get him to make a purchase.

4. Eddie Cantor, Lew Hearn, and Joe Opp in the famous sketch, "A Belt in the Back" or "Joe's Blue Front." Courtesy of Billy Rose Theatre Collection, New York Public Library for the Performing Arts, Astor, Lenox and Tilden Foundations.

After performing this routine again in his next Broadway show, *Make it Snappy*, Cantor also performed versions of it in two films: the silent *Kid Boots* (1926) and the musical *Glorifying the American Girl* (1929). He generally worked with the same two actors, Lew Hearn and Joe Opp. He brought the skit back yet again in his television show in the early 1950s. Writing of the original version, Gilbert Seldes said that the comedian's "terrific rushes from the wings, his appeals to God to strike him dead 'on the spot' if the suit now being tried on wasn't the best suit in the world, his helplessness and his 'Well, kill me, so kill me,' as apology when his partner revealed the damning fact that that happened to be the man's own suit—all of this was worth the whole of the Potash-Perlmutter cycle."[56]

The popularity of this routine was likely due to the many Jewish stereotypes that it referenced, from the history of the Jews in retail (particularly in the clothing industry, as in the Smith and Dale sketch "What Price Pants?" mentioned earlier), to the idea of the Jew doing anything for a buck, to the ways in which the Jewish tailors convince their customer (and, perhaps, themselves) that their run-down little shop is actually an impressive clothing emporium. But the idea of trying on clothes can also be read metaphorically; American Jews are trying on different ways of being Jewish, none of which fit quite right. And what holds them back is the persistence of pernicious stereotypes that they appear both to celebrate and resist at the same time.

Although Brice and Cantor were perhaps the most successful Jewish entertainers of their day, with the possible exception of Al Jolson, other well-known Jewish vaudeville performers also performed Jewish routines that reminded their audiences of their own childhoods in the ghetto. George Jessel, who starred in *The Jazz Singer* both on Broadway and on its national tour, became famous for his vaudeville monologues in which he talked on the telephone with "mama," reassuring her that he did not take money from her dresser, or steal a cake from her cupboard. (Three decades later, Mike Nichols became famous with a similar routine, in which he placed a telephone call to his guilt-inducing mother, played by Elaine May.)

In his show *Troubles of 1919,* Jessel also did imitations of comedians who sang like Harry Cooper, an actor who appeared on stage as an old Jewish man, wearing a long beard and a derby hat (a là Frank Bush). But instead of talking in pseudo-Yiddish dialect, when he opened his mouth he would sing in a beautiful tenor. According to one of Jessel's autobiographies, a typical song of Cooper's would begin: "In the green fields of Virginia, in the vale of Shenandoah."[57] By imitating Cooper imitating a Jew, Jessel was expressing a common fantasy for Jews: Jews were really true blue Americans, no matter how foreign they seemed to other Americans.

In the summer of 1920, Jessel produced his own revue; he hired chorus girls and a vaudeville team called Holmes and Wells. With a partner, Andy Lewis, he wrote the script; he also included songs that he had written himself, such as "Oh How I Laugh When I Think How I Cried about You" and "I'm Satisfied to Be My Mother's Baby." Jessel then appeared in the Shuberts'

Passing Show of 1923 with an expanded version of the "conversation with mama" routine called "Mama in the Box."

In this famous sketch, he enters an upper box in the theater with his stage mother, who wears a shawl and ridiculous hat. He tells her that they are going to see a famous French play. When she expresses anxiety about understanding the language, he tells her that no one in the audience will understand it, either; it is his job to translate it into English for them. "But," she reminds him, "English I don't understand much either." When the play begins, Jessel mistranslates the French into English and also gives a funny translation in Yiddish for his mother.

To make matters worse, "Mama" does not know how to behave in the theater; she crunches on fruit, argues with the other people sitting in the box, and talks back to the actors on stage, with Jessel translating furiously back and forth. (At one point the leading actress, forgetting her role, returns her insult in Yiddish.) Ultimately, the play is totally disrupted, with the actors all taking part in a general melee. The curtain falls.

This sketch works on a number of different levels. The second-generation son is caught in the middle, between his immigrant parent and the "high" culture of American society. The sketch makes fun of both, but it is mostly Jessel's Yiddish-speaking mother who does not know the rules of etiquette in a Broadway theater; she behaves as if she is in a Yiddish theater, where there

5. George Jessel, preeminent American Jewish comedian, later Toastmaster General of the United States. Courtesy of Billy Rose Theatre Collection, New York Public Library for the Performing Arts, Astor, Lenox and Tilden Foundations.

are fewer rules of decorum and audience members are expected to participate more freely in the action.

In her book on Yiddish theater, *Vagabond Stars*, Nahma Sandrow reprints a wonderful cartoon from *The Big Stick,* a humorous Yiddish newspaper from the turn of the century that shows the same people as they behave at a Broadway theatre and at their own neighborhood Yiddish theater. At the uptown theater, they sit quietly and attentively; at the Lower East Side theater, they argue with one another, eat, hiss the actors, and generally act as if they are in their own living rooms.[58] Jessel's stage mother "forgets" that she is not in her usual milieu; she acts as if there is no other theater than the Yiddish theater. When the leading actor returns her insult in Yiddish, this fantasy seems to be borne out; perhaps everyone (both in the cast and in the audience) *does* really speak Yiddish.

Jessel's character has one foot in both worlds: he can translate into Yiddish for his mother, but he also understands both English and French; his primary "responsibility" is to make sure that the English-speaking audience understands the play. But his mother humiliates him by forcing him both to expose himself as a Yiddish speaker and to choose sides, so he has to defend her against the actor she has picked a fight with. Jessel is trying to please his mother by taking her to the theater; he is ultimately overwhelmed and dominated by her. The irresistible tide of Jewish culture has pulled him back in. Nothing could express better the ambivalence that second-generation Jews felt toward the culture of their parents.

Second-Generation Jewish Masculinity

In "Mama in the Box," the son is also ultimately dominated by his demanding and overbearing mother. (He probably would like to trap her "in a box," but she bursts the bounds of all limits and propriety.) Indeed, even as Jews were becoming more accepted in American society, the masculinity of male Jews remained questionable, at least in popular culture. The New York critics agreed that one of the hits of the 1918 edition of the Ziegfeld *Follies* was Cantor's routine as an aspiring aviator, Percival Johnson, undergoing a physical examination by an air force doctor. Cantor was set upon by the doctor, played by Frank Carter, who slapped his face, pummeled his body, and twisted his limbs.

As the entertainer described it, "He whacked and banged me, clapped me together and pulled me apart like an accordion, and did everything but twine me around a spool." Hebrew comedians had not been known for their use of slapstick; such an approach was identified more with "Dutch" routines, such as those of Joe Weber and Lew Fields, who chased each other around the stage, hitting one another with canes, pool cues, and other implements. In fact, one newspaper reviewer called Cantor's routine "Good, rollicking, belly-shaking slapstick this, that recalled the palmy days of Weber & Fields."[59]

In many of his routines, Cantor's Jewishness became explicit. He played what the *New York Telegraph* called a "meek and timid" character who is hilariously ill-suited for the bravery and heroism required of military service. (In a Paramount short from 1929, entitled "Insurance," Cantor undergoes a similar medical examination; he plays a Jewish-Irish man named "Sidney B. Sweeback." When asked on what side he is Jewish, Cantor replies, "The East Side.") Just as Jews were continually reminded that they did not belong in America, Cantor's masochistic character learned that his personality and disposition disqualified him from battle, especially from the glamor of the air force. The irony was that Cantor, whom the *New York Sun* called the "favorite of the Midnight Frolic and the Bronx," was beginning his rise to stardom.[60] He did so by allowing himself to be shamed and humiliated on stage, but in a way in which he seemed always to be in control, or at any rate to be complicit in his own victimization.

Cantor's character possessed a kind of serene self-confidence coupled with a physical invulnerability that permitted him, like a cartoon character, to undergo endless abuse. According to Cantor, "audiences love to see somebody knocked and battered about to the point of insensibility so long as they feel he isn't really getting hurt. But if they suspect the punishment has passed the point of fun, they suddenly stop laughing and even show resentment."[61]

One critic who did seem unsettled by the routine was Gilbert Seldes; he complained that the osteopath scene was an "exploitation of meaningless brutality," although he allowed that other sketches starring Cantor were "excellent pieces of construction, holding sympathy all the way through and keeping on the safe side of nausea." Rather than attempt to copy Jolson's success at blackface, Seldes believed, Cantor should stick with his stock character, the "timid, Ghetto-bred, pale-faced Jewish lad, seduced by glory or the prospects of pay into competing with athletes and bruisers."[62]

Cantor reprised a version of the osteopath routine in the silent film *Kid Boots* (1926); it takes place in the infirmary of a golf club where he is working as a caddy, and it follows an attempt by his enemy (who is trying to prevent Cantor's testimony in a divorce case) to kill him by turning up the voltage in some kind of medical "electric chair." Cantor turns the tables not by tying his opponent into knots, but by getting him to sit in the chair.

Cantor's character did not really get hurt, but I would argue that his "punishment" was, in an important sense, directed toward his being Jewish. The self-abasing performance of Jewishness suggested that Jews felt that they deserved to get hurt; they were asking for it. In other words, their (largely unconscious) masochistic behavior provoked society's deepest sadistic urges.

Cantor's stage and screen persona remained childlike in many ways; along with a total confidence in his ability to entertain, it embodied a level of insecurity demonstrated by the persona of a needy, precocious child, dependent on the laughter and applause of others to maintain a stable sense of self. Cantor's portrayals of wise-cracking Jewish tailors, cab drivers, and aviators were fraught both with anxiety and an almost infantile inability to take themselves seriously.

In addition, Cantor's performances played on old stereotypes of Jewish men as undersized, weak, and unable to defend themselves from Gentile aggression—stereotypes that fed into the eugenicist thinking that was at its height of popular acceptance in the late 1910s and early 1920s. His "characters" were oddly effeminate and suggestive of homosexuality—a projection of what Sander Gilman calls the stereotypically demasculinized Jewish body.[63]

Harley Erdman has found a similar strain of effeminacy in the characteristic portrayal of the "sheeny" (a slang word for Jew) in nineteenth-century drama; he writes about the "feminized sheeny villain" who is easily frightened, weak, and sexually deviant.[64] Although he never played an evil or hostile character, Cantor's performance of Jewishness still suggested that Jewish men were lacking in essential components of masculinity.

However, unlike the "Hebrew" comics whom Cantor copied in his early career, Jewishness was no longer principally a matter of wearing certain clothes, speaking with a certain accent and inflection, and using definably "racial" mannerisms that suggested overt anti-Semitism. However, he seemed both supremely self-confident and strangely naive, pugnacious but puny, highly energetic yet unable to accomplish anything.

Interestingly, Cantor referred more and more frequently to his wife and children as his career progressed. One of his most famous songs was about his wife: "Ida, Sweet as Apple Cider." Herbert Goldman argues that Cantor's references to his family helped transform the acting profession in America by humanizing stars, making them not just entertainers but *celebrities*—in both their private and public lives.

But Goldman misses the fact that Cantor's repeated references to his family served generally to deprecate himself and to emphasize his purported shortcomings in the masculinity department. The father of four daughters, he joked throughout his career about his inability to have a son. When asked after the birth of his second daughter, Natalie, if he was disappointed that she wasn't a boy, he replied, "With a fellow like me, I'm lucky it wasn't a rabbit." And on one of Cantor's radio shows on which Al Jolson appeared as a guest, Jolson gave the story of Cantor's life. According to Jolson, rather than Eddie carrying Ida across the threshold in their Bronx apartment, she carried *him*.[65]

Part of what made Cantor's act endearing was the naiveté, the vulnerability, which Cantor so assiduously cultivated. (His trademark little hand-clap suggested a child's excitement and pleasure.) Goldman describes this as an element of what he calls a "presexual youth's sexual awakening—a young man uncertain of his sexual orientation but with a definite susceptibility to the charms of beautiful women."[66] Goldman suggests that Cantor played a powerless character with such a knowing and self-conscious air that it should be seen merely as a way of pleasing audiences. But Cantor stuck with this persona as he became more popular with Jewish audiences, and no longer needed to portray an infantile persona.

The film version of *Kid Boots,* based on the Ziegfeld musical of the same name, begins with a drawing of Cantor, a caricature with gigantic ears. The titles give a few lines of doggerel about his character: "You look a sight. You've got no class. Don't look in a mirror. You'll break the glass" and a title "signed" by Cantor himself calling his character, Samuel, "an example of Nature's wasteful ways" and asking "Why put house detective ears on a tailor?" Of course, one of the first things Cantor does is look in a mirror, shattering it instantly. The anti-Semitic stereotype of the Jew's oversized nose has been changed to outsized ears. The Jew's ugliness is a mark of his exclusion from society.

Cantor's stage persona was thus a mass of contradictions. Goldman calls it "unmistakably Jewish—pushy, slightly nebbishy, but without the intellectual neuroses that would distinguish Woody Allen in the 1960s."[67] But the idea of the "pushy" Jew and of the "nebbish" also seem a reflection of later stereotypes of the Jew in American culture, after Jews had achieved unprecedented postwar economic success and full-fledged entry into the academy. Goldman is closer to the truth when he says that Cantor played the "weakling" and points out that he often did so as an "extremely effeminate character" who could almost be read as homosexual. It was Cantor's lack of virility that, as much an anything, made him the object of ridicule. As both Michael Rogin and Andrea Most have shown, Cantor's feminized characters suggested that the idea of a "Jewish man" was an oxymoron; it was not possible to be Jewish and manly at the same time.

Yet Cantor's characters could still aspire to a kind of heroism. In one of the comic's most popular routines, he played a Jewish aviator from Newark named Gregory Ginsburg being interviewed by an army major for his mental fitness—a twist on the physical examination that was such a standby of his earlier work. (His plane was dubbed "Mosquito—The Spirit of New Jersey.") Without any physical comedy, but with lots of verbal humor, this routine satirizes the very idea of a Jew becoming a pilot. Unlike the hero Charles Lindberg, Cantor doesn't "look like" a pilot, he has never been up in the air, he was sick during the war when other men were fighting, and he still sleeps at home with his brother. Finally, his dietary requirements preclude his eating what soldiers are supposed to eat; he calls off the flight when he realizes that the sandwiches he has been given are all made with ham!

6. Eddie Cantor preparing for the kitchen scene in the 1930 film *Whoopee*. Courtesy of
Billy Rose Theatre Collection, New York Public Library for the Performing Arts, Astor,
Lenox and Tilden Foundations.

Furthermore, Ginsburg (which, Cantor explains, was changed from Levy
when he heard that they were blowing up the levees in the South) keeps
repeating the name of Charles A. Levine, the navigator who accompanied the
pilot Charles Chamberlin on a trans-Atlantic flight in 1927 that broke Lindberg's long-range flying record. (President Calvin Coolidge honored Chamberlin at the White House, but did not invite Levine, leading a Jewish
vaudeville star, Charles Cohen, to try to set the record straight by recording a
heroic song about Levine called "Levine and His Flying Machine.")[68]
Cantor's humor thus both celebrated the visibility of Jews in American society and satirized the ways in which their accomplishments were regarded.

In "Getting a Ticket," a Paramount short from 1929, Cantor is stopped on
Long Island for speeding in his sports car. The witless Irish cop confiscates a
bottle of Cantor's liquor by drinking it, gets misled by Cantor's long irrelevant stories, and gets taken in by Cantor's ridiculous excuses about why he
cannot give out his address. The battle of wits is clearly won by Cantor,
despite the fact that it is the cop who is clearly playing the more masculine
role. The sketch ends with Cantor playing a song on a phonograph (which he

just happens to have in the car) and singing along with it to prove his identity. The song, "My Wife Is on a Diet," compares his wife to an automobile; it sums up Cantor's character's ambivalence toward his wife's being overweight. Not only is she herself seemingly starving herself to lose weight, but she serves him the same food she eats; they have only grapefruit for every meal! The routine is so larded with Freudian implications that it belies the fact that, according to Cantor, "on the Lower East Side, we didn't know from Freud."[69]

SECOND-GENERATION JEWISH FEMININITY

In their performances, Jewish female comedians acted out the ways in which Jewish women were doubly disempowered—both by Jewish men and by American society. As Riv-Ellen Prell has found, one of the most prevalent stereotypes was that of the "Ghetto Girl," the loud, vulgar, garishly dressed, and uncultivated Jewish woman. As Prell puts it, "the Ghetto Girl's taste was far too conspicuous; she was betrayed by the cheapness of what she had and wore."[70] The Ghetto Girl's excessive desires, according to Prell, threatened the precarious masculinity of Jewish men within American culture.

One of Fanny Brice's most famous songs, James Hanley and Grant Clarke's "Second Hand Rose" (first presented in the Ziegfeld *Follies* of 1921), expresses the frustrations of a young woman from Second Avenue (the heart of the Jewish quarter) who is too poor to own anything that is new. As the lyrics go:

Father has a business,
Strictly second-hand,
Everything from tooth-picks to a baby grand.
Stuff in our apartment,
Came from Father's store,
Even things I'm wearing, someone wore before.
It's no wonder that I feel abused;
I never get a thing that ain't been used!

I'm wearing second-hand hats,
Second-hand clothes,
That's why they call me Second Hand Rose.
Even our piano in the parlor,
Father bought for ten cents on the dollar.
Second-hand pearls,
I'm wearing second-hand curls,
I never get a single thing that's new!
Even Jakie Cohen, he's the man I adore,
Had the nerve to tell me he'd been married before!
Everyone knows that I'm just Second Hand Rose,
From Second Avenue.

I'm wearing second-hand shoes,
Second-hand hose,
All the girls hand me their second-hand beaus!
Even my pajamas, when I don them,
Have somebody else's 'nitials on them.
Second-hand rings, I'm sick of second-hand things,
I never get what other goilies do.
Once while strolling through the Ritz, a woman got my goat,
She nudged her friend and said, "Oh, look, there goes my last year's
    coat!"
Everyone knows that I'm just Second Hand Rose,
From Second Avenue.[71]

All her possessions are used, from her hats and clothing to her boyfriend
(Jakie Cohen, who's been previously married) to her pajamas with their previous owner's initials sewed on them. To the extent that such things help one
build and reinforce an identity, she is dominated by other people's identities
and seemingly forestalled from having one of her own. She is the sum total of
other people's cast-offs.

This is quite humiliating, especially when others notice her wearing their
old clothes, such as the fur coat that the former owner recognizes. In trying
to look like a rich person, Brice has been exposed for what she really is, a
poor girl from the Lower East Side. Brice's character's pain is evident: "It's no
wonder that I feel abused. I never have a thing that ain't been used." She is
herself "used" or taken advantage of in the sense that she has become a butt
of jokes. As her name suggests, it is Rose herself who is "second hand." (Is this
a suggestion that she is no longer a virgin?) She suffers from a kind of exis-
tential belatedness. She is defined only in relationship to the past, a past she
can neither escape nor claim as her own.

"Second Hand Rose" is, at root, about the shame of being Jewish in a
Gentile world, a shame that the second generation of American Jews inher-
ited from their parents. As Alfred Kazin wrote in his memoir *A Walker in the
City,* "I was the first American child, their offering to the strange new God; I
was to be the monument of their liberation from the shame of being—what
they were."[72] This pervasive sense of shame shadowed the second generation
throughout their lives. Donald Weber writes perceptively that American Jews
had to cope with "deformations wrought by shame and self-hatred, the
dialectic of nostalgia and memory, and the psychological 'costs' of achieving
the host culture's seemingly 'civilized' manners." Brice was dramatizing these
conflicts in her work.[73]

As sung by Brice in a heavy Yiddish accent, "Second Hand Rose" is likewise about the second generation's feelings about Jewishness. After all, Jewish

tradition is handed down from generation to generation; the more acculturated offspring of Jewish immigrants inherit something that is already "used,"
and that they are expected to cherish partly *because* it belonged to their parents. It is significant that all of Rose's possessions come from her father's store.

But why was this song so popular among second-generation Jews? (It
became popular among third-generation Jews as well, as one of Barbra
Streisand's biggest hits of the 1960s after she sang it in both the Broadway and
Hollywood versions of *Funny Girl,* her tribute to Brice.) The popularity of
"Second Hand Rose" testified to the romanticization of the ghetto that most
New York Jews no longer lived in, having begun to enter the middle class.
Second Hand Rose is very much a ghetto dweller, although she differs in
important respects from the Ghetto Girl stereotype in that she does not seem
excessive in her desires.

In real life, Brice dressed in the most expensive clothes, either new or
used, that she could find. As her daughter, Fran Stark, recalled in an interview
with a fashion magazine in 1968, "Mother was the epitome of elegance.
Among my fondest childhood memories are the many afternoons I spent
with her at couturier fittings. . . . As a child, she made dresses for her neighborhood friends. And as soon as she could afford to buy something she spent
her first money at a place where chic women sold their beautiful used French
clothes." But by the 1920s she could afford to buy new clothes. As Stark
added, "By 1920 she was wearing new Worth, Poiret and Piguet; by 1930,
Chanel, Hattie Carnegie and Adrian. . . . The simple white evening gowns that
she often wore in the Follies' finales became the season's fashion highlight."[74]

While I have not found any pictures of how Brice dressed as she sang this
song in the *Follies,* the cover of the sheet music for her performances in the
Follies (which included a few other songs in addition to "Second Hand
Rose") shows an extremely svelte, curvaceous woman in a fashionable flapper-
style dress with a long flowing sash; she gazes at herself in a mirror she is holding. She is as far from a Jewish stereotype as one could find. She could be one
of the other performers, including one of the chorus girls in the revue. But
she looks nothing like Brice. It is very difficult to see how the cover relates
to the song, even as the song's title is emblazoned in large letters at the top of
the page. Whoever was marketing the song plainly thought that it would sell
more copies if the cover showed a vain, non-Jewish-looking woman rather
than an insecure, Jewish-looking one. Sheet music was sold so that people
could play and sing the songs themselves, not necessarily so they could imitate
the way the stars performed them.

Thus, as much as the song itself gestures toward the history of Jews in the
garment business and even the junk business, the conditions of its reception
are more complex. And in some ways the song itself does gesture toward a
new beginning, both for Rose and for second-generation Jews in general. For

7. Cover of Grant Clarke and James F. Hanley's 1921 song "Second Hand
Rose." Courtesy of Billy Rose Theatre Collection, New York Public Library
for the Performing Arts, Astor, Lenox and Tilden Foundations.

Rose to complain about her possessions being used suggests that she, or perhaps her children someday, will do things differently. Her unhappiness with
her lowly status gives her the desire to change it. The humor from the song
comes from the sense that she is waking up to a situation that presumably
does not need to stay the same. This spoke to the sense second-generation
Jews had that as American society was slowly beginning to open up more to
Jews, they were starting to find themselves in a new world, throwing off some
of the encumbrances of history.

Before World War I, among Brice's most popular acts were her parodies of opera singers and ballet dancers. Whether crashing all over the stage as a Jewish Nijinsky, or losing her voice as a Jewish opera singer, Brice satirized high culture at the same time as she expressed a sense of Jewish exclusion from that high culture. In "Becky is Back in the Ballet," which centers on a Jewish girl who is singularly untalented in dancing, Becky's mother asks her to do an imitation of Pavlova's dying swan. However, Becky slips and falls all over the stage, demonstrating an awkwardness and lack of sophistication that, as Brice's Yiddish accent reminds the audience, are stereotypically Jewish attributes. In satirizing high culture, Brice helped Jews indulge their fantasies of participation in high culture while reassuring them that they did not need it anyway, that it was not worth having.[75]

Rather than directly express her generation's pain at being rejected in so many ways by society, by the 1920s Brice's "characters" complained instead about the ill treatment they received from men. A song like "Oy, How I Hate That Fellow Nathan" (re-recorded by Kaye Ballard early in her own career as "Oh, How I Hate That Fellow Nathan," but with the "oys" restored to the lyrics) is a comic lament about a man who refuses to return her affections but with whom she seems unable to end her involvement. Nathan has agreed to marry her, but when he named the month for their nuptials, he refused to say the year! Although he is content to smoke her father's cigars and eat her mother's cooking, he seems to have little desire to support Brice—"he said he'll lay down and die for me, but he won't get up and work for me!"

Brice has four reasons she "hates" Nathan; she could have married Meyer the Butcher, Jake the Plumber, Hymie the Tailor, or Louie the Lawyer. But for some reason she has stuck by Nathan, despite his unreliability. Nathan also has the stereotypically Jewish trait of stinginess; he refuses to put a quarter in the gas meter in her family's living room. (He says that if her father finds them sitting there in the dark, the father will put a quarter in the meter!) And, Brice says, when all of "my people" brought her something made of gold to celebrate her engagement, Nathan brought goldfish! Many entertainers recorded this song; Irving Howe quotes a line in Carrie Balaban's memoir that the song was a "sure-fire hit in Jewish neighborhoods."[76]

Not all of her material was Jewish. Perhaps her best-known number was "My Man," a torch song that expressed the singer's resolution to remain in an extremely unhealthy and self-destructive relationship. Parallels have often been drawn between Brice's marriage to a gangster, Nicky Arnstein, who took enormous advantage of her both financially and emotionally, and the lyrics of the song.

"My Man" was sung without accent, leading Gilbert Seldes to write that it was "amusing to learn that without a Yiddish accent and without those immense rushes of drollery, without the enormous gawkiness of her other impersonations, Miss Brice could put a song over." But he said he preferred her as her immigrant Jewish character, her "Fanny" character, rather than her "Miss Brice" character.[77] Indeed, a song like "Nathan" expressed the same sentiments, although, by placing the relationship in a Jewish milieu, the situation becomes inevitably comic. Also, Brice's character's freedom to sing about how much she "hates" her beau seems to testify to the very real difficulties Jewish men and women had in relating to one another in an anti-Semitic culture. As Prell has noted, "New World marriage produced anxiety and uncertainty about whether it could deliver its promises of class mobility and Americanization."[78]

Songs about Jewish women unable to get their boyfriends to commit to marriage were extremely popular; the Yiddish dialect singer Rhoda Bernard also recorded one, "Roll Your Yiddishe Eyes for Me," in which a woman frankly asks for her beau to "make me heavy pleasure" and "for me make a little *mazel tov*; I've got such an appetite for making love." She tells him that "love ain't business," and that "even though we aren't married," he can "take a piece on credit" anyway, and that she "doesn't want any security." June Sochen has written that Brice "dealt with subject matter that women often hid from public view."[79] But Bernard did so even more explicitly; such an emphasis on women's sexual needs was unusual in Jewish songs. It was more prevalent in the repertoire of black female performers, and in the "red-hot mama" songs of Sophie Tucker, which I will explore later in this chapter.

Sochen calls Brice, Tucker, and later female entertainers like Bette Midler and Barbra Streisand "reformers" in the sense that they "question forbidden subjects in public spaces previously reserved for men. They reverse traditional sex roles, challenge convention, raise doubts and offer new possibilities for women, new ways to live, new issues and new values."[80] But Brice was hardly overturning patriarchy by singing about cooking breakfast for her husband, about overprotecting her children on a seaside holiday, or about the trials and tribulations of getting someone to marry her.

Although Sochen correctly emphasizes that Jewish women were outsiders in a dual sense in American culture, she does not analyze the Jewishness of Brice's material. The Jewishness of these characters complicated the picture of femininity portrayed in these songs. Riv-Ellen Prell has argued that marriages between Jews in early-twentieth-century America were undermined by the gender stereotypes that Jewish males projected onto Jewish females—stereotypes that reflected Jewish male anxieties about assimilating into an anti-Semitic and materialistic culture.[81]

But a song like "Nathan" seems to be about the stereotypes that Jewish women projected onto Jewish men, in which Jewish men were viewed as indecisive, unmanly, and unable to provide for their women. If Jewish men were not "100 percent American" according to the mainstream culture, then to Jewish women they were often less than 100 percent men. As Prell has realized, anti-Semitism ate away at the heart of Jewish self-confidence and self-esteem, and poisoned relationships between Jewish men and women.

A similar picture of a Jewish man appears in one of Brice's most popular comic monologues, "Mrs. Cohen at the Beach," first performed in 1927, in which the character's Jewishness becomes more complex. Most of the song focuses on Mrs. Cohen's ordeal watching over her three squabbling children on a seaside holiday, with little help from her husband, Abe. In fact, when Mrs. Cohen runs into an acquaintance, a Mrs. Levine, she tells her about Abe's humiliation at the hands of a man who robbed his delicatessen; while the robber held up a pistol, Abe was impotently holding a limp herring. Barbara Grossman writes about this character as a combination of two stereotypes, the *yente* (a pushy, vulgar woman who loves to gossip) and the Jewish Mother (an overbearing woman who dominates her husband and manipulates her children's affections).

The routine reminds Grossman of the "oppressively close Jewish family with its often ineffectual father and domineering, overprotective mother." Mrs. Cohen's "constant carping and complaining, her endless comparisons and criticism, her irrational fears about health and safety, her emphasis on eating, her stinginess and pettiness [and] her skill at creating guilt and playing martyr" are all qualities that Grossman associates with the Jewish Mother.[82]

But the Jewish Mother's excessive nurturing was still nurturing. And sometimes the Jewish Mother did not even act particularly Jewish. When it is time to serve lunch, Mrs. Cohen pulls out the pastrami, salami, and liverwurst and then announces, in a teasing lilt, "And we've got haa-aam." For Brice, the Jewish Mother did not just feed her children; she helped to acculturate them. Like the happy wife singing about "Cooking Breakfast for the One I Love" (a song whose lyrics were written for Brice by her third husband, the Broadway producer Billy Rose), who announces that, "He loves bacon, so that's what I'm makin'," the character seems to straddle the immigrant and American worlds.

Brice did not always conform to the expectations of her Jewish fans, however. When a newspaper published an advertisement for a week-long engagement at the Palace that included the night of Yom Kippur, Jewish organizations protested. The solicitor who placed the ad said it was a mistake, and that she did not intend to perform on Yom Kippur, but a writer for *Variety*, amused at the controversy, opined that Brice was trying to save face. Brice skipped the performance on the night in question.[83]

Sophie Tucker, born Sophie Abuza in Hartford, Connecticut, in 1887, came from a Yiddish-speaking family who ran a delicatessen. But she ran away from home shortly after an abortive marriage to a boy named Louis Tucker (abandoning her infant son to her parents' care, without their permission) to pursue a career on the stage.[84] She began by singing in restaurants in New

York, as she had done in her family's delicatessen, and then graduated to the vaudeville stage. Her first vaudeville performances were in blackface; then, when her trunk supposedly failed to arrive in time for a performance, she was obliged to go on stage without her costume and make-up. Doing the same "coon" songs without the blackface, Tucker found that the routines went over just as well. She did not need the blackface to perform a black caricature; she could enact it with mannerism, gesture, and vocal style.

Pamela Brown Lavitt has written that Tucker's "novel infractions of the blackface form did more than confirm Tucker's 'bona-fide' whiteness; they laid bare her *white* Jewishness" (emphasis in original). Lavitt seems less interested in the Jewish content of Tucker's routines than in the ways in which she performed a racial identity. Still, she writes of both Tucker and Brice that "[t]heir distinctive, exuberant and unapologetic Yiddish breaches of established and transfigured minstrel forms impressed critics and won the affections of an expanding Jewish audience, who probably felt hailed and validated by popular theatre at last."[85] By placing the emphasis on the audience, Lavitt rightly examines the cultural work that these two performers' routines accomplished in the Jewish community in New York, the ways in which they spurred ethnic pride.

Tucker once told her fellow Jewish performers at a benefit that "We all sprang from the same source, the same origin. We were all swept to the shores of this country on the same tidal wave of immigration, the same flight from prejudice and persecution. Our life stories are pretty much the same."[86] But of course almost all of the Jewish performers, including Tucker herself, were born in America. By referring to her parents' experience rather than to her own, Tucker was implicitly grounding her sense of Jewishness in the first-generation experience.

Tucker's repertoire was versatile; she sang ragtime, romantic ballads, comic songs, and novelty numbers with equal ease. But Tucker, who was significantly overweight, was best known for her "red-hot mama" songs, in which she played a sexy maternal figure starved for affection.

Like the major black singers of her day such as Bessie Smith, Ma Rainey, and Billie Holiday, Tucker (who never remarried) connected with her audiences by expressing an aching need for love and sexual fulfillment. But it was this in combination with her Jewishness that created a potent mix. As Nora Ephron has pointed out, after her childhood, Tucker "hit upon the combination of schmaltz ('My Yiddishe Mama'), self-derision ('Nobody Loves a Fat Girl, but Oh, How a Fat Girl Can Love'), and broad sex ('When They Start to Ration My Passion It's Gonna be Tough on Me') which made her the darling of the Borscht circuit, English royalty, Ed Sullivan and the general public."[87]

She always sang the Yiddish songs and ragtime numbers first, before doing the "red-hot mama" songs. The Jewish mother was endlessly self-sacrificing, while the black mother cried out for nurturing. But by singing them so closely together, I would argue, the two stereotypes merged; the Jewish/black mother needed love but also needed to dominate through her smothering nature. If the Jewish mother was, in Beverly Gray Bienstock's words, "gossipy, plump, overprotective of her children, obsessed with the healing powers of chicken soup," then she was—and became in later Jewish American drama, film, and fiction—an object of ridicule and revulsion.[88]

My *Yiddishe Mama* (or Mammy)

To Jewish audiences, what Ephron calls Tucker's "schmaltz" (literally, "chicken fat") song, "My Yiddishe Mama," was her most popular. Although she sang it mostly in English for non-Jewish audiences, she also had a Yiddish version (with different lyrics) that she sang for heavily Jewish audiences. One of the first cities she sang it in was London, where her performances attracted large Jewish audiences. One reviewer (who, like many other London review- ers, misquoted the title of the song; this one used the masculine form of the adjective and called it "Yiddisher Mama") noted that the "Jewish portion of the audience was very much moved" by her rendition of the song.[89] And J. T. Grein, the famous founder of London's Independent Theatre Society (where George Bernard Shaw's plays were first produced), was ecstatic about Tucker. When she appeared again in London in 1930, in *Follow a Star*, her first appear- ance in musical comedy, he wrote: "What a woman! What a dynamic force! What infinite humour, broad, subtle, drastic, insinuating! What understanding of humanity in all its phases. One song about 'If your kisses can't hold the man you love' embraces all the Freudian theories—it literally knocked the natives to a frazzle. But how true it was—as good as a play! And yet she has a round dozen of them, full of the joy of life and knowledge of character. She alone would fill the house for months to come."[90]

It is thus simply inaccurate, as Lewis Erenberg claims, that Tucker "repre- sented the possibility of ethnic success and acceptance if one abandoned much of the ethnic content of one's culture and adapted to the larger world and market of American entertainment and social patterns." His evidence for her supposedly altered approach includes the fact that she changed her name, wore "luxurious" clothes, and "dramatically interpreted songs rather than belting them out"—none of which prevented her from doing Jewish-themed material.[91]

In fact, although Tucker noted in her autobiography that she "was always careful to use ["My Yiddishe Mama"] only when the majority of the house would understand the Yiddish," she also said that throughout the United

8. Sophie Tucker, "last of the red-hot mamas." Courtesy of Billy Rose Theatre Collection, New York Public Library for the Performing Arts, Astor, Lenox and Tilden Foundations.

States and Europe, "Gentiles have loved the song and have called for it."[92] Like the popularity of John McCormack's performance of "Mother Machree," she pointed out, people of every ethnic background seem to have been moved by the song.

Non-Jewish critics, it seemed, could not help commenting on the reaction of the Jewish audience to the song. Tucker connected to these audiences so viscerally that it was astounding. One London critic, reviewing a 1925 performance at the Holborn Empire, did not particularly care for the song, but was amazed by the fact that Tucker "seemed to have things fairly her own way with the audience there—which, be it said, was almost entirely Jewish. She has an enormous fund of personality, and an extraordinarily expressive face and voice, and her 'Yiddishes [sic] Momma' song seemed to arouse in her hearers a whole gamut of emotion, from hilarity to tears—particularly that half which she sang in Yiddish. As far as we were concerned, we liked her 'Ukele Lady' song best, but this was no doubt a question of race."[93]

Tucker recorded both versions of the song; they were released by Decca on different sides of the same 78 rpm record. Mark Slobin has reprinted the lyrics to the English version, and translated (a little oddly) the Yiddish version. He writes that the two texts are "poles apart expressively, and nearly seem to be for different songs."[94] He sees these differences principally in the greater number of ethnic markers that the Yiddish version contains, and thus in the more specific ethnic milieu conjured up by the Yiddish version.

Although Slobin notes that both versions expressed the second generation's ambivalence about assimilation, he analyzes the two versions only superficially, and is content mostly to suggest that Tucker's guilt over abandoning her parents (he does not mention her son; wasn't she supposed to be a Yiddishe mama too?) could have given her a strong unconscious motivation to sing it.

While the English version of the song begins with the singer sitting in the "comfort of a cozy chair," the Yiddish version begins with the singer standing. (A later stanza, not sung in the extant recordings, begins with the singer sitting.) It then goes on to talk about a mother who was not "made-up" or "well-dressed"—who was not, because of her poverty, pleasant to look at. (The English version just says she "never cared for fashion's styles," as if she could have afforded them if she had wanted to.)[95]

The Yiddish version then presents a picture of an old woman who has seemingly spent her entire old age in a single "little room" where now she "sits and cries and dreams of days long ago" when children's voices filled the house and the kitchen "smelled of kugel and tzimmes (pudding and carrot stew—traditional Eastern European Sabbath dishes)." The English version simply says it "wasn't much like Paradise" but that "'mid the dirt and all" sat the angelic mother. The Yiddish version thus emphasizes the description of the mother's feelings. Through tastes and sights and smells, it also gives a much more powerful evocation of the tenement milieu, including summoning up the presence of the voices of the very audience of second-generation Jews who are the target audience for the song. The *yiddishe mama*'s self-sacrificing nature is then detailed; "she used to give us bread out of her own mouth and she would have given up her life for us as well." She was the only thing, the Yiddish version continues, of which God provides only one.[96]

Second-generation Jews constructed their Jewish identity through songs like "My Yiddishe Mama," through which, as an audience, they could share the experience of nostalgia, of returning to their roots. The paradox of second-generation American Jewish culture is that Jews could celebrate their origins by listening to a song about losing them. The song is almost an apologia for Judaism itself: "You don't know how you'll grieve when she passes away." But what Joyce Antler calls the "world of the past that was vanishing even when Tucker herself was growing up" was kept from dying partly through the very songs like "My Yiddishe Mama" that evoked the "lost" world of the immigrant generation.

But perhaps even more important than any of the content of "My Yiddishe Mama" was the very fact that Tucker generally sang it in Yiddish for Jewish audiences. While most second-generation children were native English speakers who recoiled from their parents' embarrassing Yiddish accents, the sound of Yiddish must have also had positive connotations of childhood and nurturing. The Yiddish version of "My Yiddishe Mama" is about much more than the mother who has been left behind, causing acute guilt for her children. In her book *The Journey Home,* Antler has written that the song "mourned the family closeness that immigrants' children lost as they set off on their own paths." But the song is also about the homesickness the immigrants' children had for a childhood saturated with Jewishness; their ambivalence reflects what Antler has termed (referring to the Yiddish version of the song), the "bittersweet experience of assimilation."[97]

The children of immigrants had to an extent abandoned their Jewishness in that Lower East Side tenement; their nostalgia gives them *less* guilt—it gets them off the hook in a sense. By celebrating the immigrant Jewish mother in the song, the second generation is finding a way to leave her behind—to pay tribute as a part of the process of moving on.

The line in the Yiddish version of the song, "You don't know how you'll grieve when she passes away," thus suggests that the children do not appreciate the depth of their own feelings. But the song has already buried the mother; the mother is a kind of Jewish unconscious that her children are struggling to keep from rising to the surface of their own awareness. As much as the song testifies to the second generation's desire to reconnect to their childhood in the ghetto, it also represents their having, at least in their own eyes, to a large extent transcended those origins.

The song was so popular that it spawned the parodic "My Yiddisha Mammy," performed by Eddie Cantor in *Make It Snappy.* The song, reconfigured as a fox trot, was a kind of commentary on Jewish blackface, as if the blackface performer is coming clean about actually being Jewish. While "All the mammies they call divine / Come from below the Mason Dixon line," the performer's "mammy" comes not from "Alabammy" but from New York: "Her cabin door is in a Bronx tenement." She "never heard about dear old Black Joe / She's never been where the sweet Magnolias grow. / She don't play a banjo or ukelele, / But her lullaby is Eli, Eli."[98] The black and Jewish mothers have been melded into a single image. The performer is nurtured not by Southern Black culture but by New York Jewish culture, even while he metaphorically keeps a foot in both worlds.

Recent feminist scholarship on the *yiddishe mama* has revealed the mythic aspects of this stereotype. Rather than giving exaggerated credit to the mother as the transmitter of Jewish culture, feminists have attempted to

9. Cover of Eddie Cantor's "My Yiddisha Mammy," trading on Al Jolson's signature blackface song, "Mammy." Courtesy of Billy Rose Theatre Collection, New York Public Library for the Performing Arts, Astor, Lenox and Tilden Foundations.

understand the complexities of the mother's role in the traditional Jewish home, both before and after emigration from Europe. As Paula Hyman has argued, the Jewish mother was almost always responsible for contributing to the economic upkeep of the family. In the Old World, she writes, women stood in the marketplace, selling roots or home-baked bagels, or clothes they had sewn. (The more prosperous owned stores where they sold food, linen, cooking pots, and glassware.) In America, women continued to work, either in the home or outside it—sewing piecework, taking in lodgers, selling from pushcarts, and so forth. The *yiddishe mama* did not necessarily spend her entire life in the kitchen, eternally available to nurture her children. She wasn't even always home.[99]

Furthermore, some feminists have argued that the stereotype of the *yiddishe mama* is actually a negative one. Male writers, according to Erika Duncan, have portrayed the Jewish mother as the "all-engulfing nurturer who devours the very soul with every spoonful of hot chicken soup she gives, whose every shakerful of salt contains a curse."[100] Duncan reads Jewish women writers, from Anzia Yezierska to Tillie Olsen, as setting the record straight by writing about the self-imposed starvation of the Jewish mother. Duncan sees the stereotypical *yiddishe mama* as so self-sacrificing that she deprives herself of the love and nurturance she provides so unquestioningly to her children. Duncan does not mention Tucker's "Yiddishe Mama" song, which was written by men. However, the fact that it was sung by a woman makes it hard to argue that it was simply a creation of male ambivalence. And the song is more eulogistic than vengeful; its very participation in the process of myth-making is what makes it interesting.

What did second-generation Jewish men and women have at stake in the myth of the *yiddishe mama*? By portraying her as the ideal maternal object, they could mourn her passing. By the 1920s, it was no longer fashionable or even appropriate for American women to sacrifice their own needs to those of their children. Women were emancipated from such servitude; the age of the flapper and of women's suffrage brought a new conception of women's roles. The song both constructed a link to the past and helped to provide a sense of closure on that past. It helped women to remember and even honor their past in the act of letting go of it.

Robert Snyder has argued that when Tucker sang it, "Homesick Jews found . . . a new American ethnic identity." But I think this is too simplistic. I think the song functioned in a broader context of American Jewish popular culture of the 1920s (recall that *The Jazz Singer* also opened on Broadway in the same year, 1925) that helped simultaneously to reinforce and erode the connections Jews had toward their Jewish past. Vaudeville may have been what Snyder calls a "secular faith for its fans," but Jewish vaudeville also incorporated a creative tension with Jewish tradition that gave it much of its power.[101]

Tucker seemed to be comfortable with her own Jewishness. Still, although she observed the High Holy Days and Passover with her family, and refused to work on those days, she makes it clear in her autobiography that she did not follow her own mother's Orthodox religious practices. (This makes for interesting juxtapositions, as when she describes eating a memorable oyster dinner immediately before talking about going back to Hartford to attend synagogue for the High Holidays.)[102] As many of her Jewish colleagues in vaudeville and theater did, she played many benefits for Jewish organizations, such as the Jewish Theatrical Guild in New York.

There were many synagogues in the new neighborhoods to which Jews were moving in the 1920s. But, as Deborah Dash Moore has written, second-generation Jews also established "synagogue centers," which sponsored social and recreational activities in addition to religious services and classes. (They tended to include gyms and swimming pools in addition to classrooms and sanctuaries.) The pioneering rabbi Mordechai Kaplan, founder of Reconstructionist Judaism, developed the idea of Judaism as a "civilization" rather than merely a religion, in which the totality of Jewish spiritual, intellectual, moral, and cultural life maintained a vibrant existence within the larger fabric of American society.[103]

The "American" component of second-generation Jews' identity was thus taken for granted. Seeing the synagogue center as a "physical monument to the completion of the Americanization of the New York Jew," its creators envisioned it as preserving Jewish religion and Jewish culture in a manner consonant with American democratic values.[104] Entertainers like Sophie Tucker and Belle Baker, who sang often at synagogue center benefits, paradoxically contributed to this process of "Americanization" by performing a mixed repertoire of religious and secular songs, English-language and Yiddish-language songs.

Such concerts, whether presented on Broadway or in the auditorium of the synagogue center, blurred the boundaries between the world of Broadway and the world of the synagogue. Like the Jewish vaudeville stars, second-generation Jewish audience members did not just move easily between the two realms; they occupied both simultaneously. While beginning a trend of Broadway attendance which, along with the large proportion of Jewish creators, would have a significant effect on the offerings of the New York theater, they also "patronized" the entertainment sponsored by Jewish centers. Bringing their Jewishness into the public sphere, in a way that sometimes made the whole world seem Jewish, they also imported American popular culture into the world of the synagogue. The two identities were not just compatible with one another; they became impossible to separate.

It is important to emphasize that these entertainers had a choice of what kind of material to perform. Lewis Erenberg's conclusion that the second-generation Jewish entertainers were successful because they were "rootless in a society loosening its traditional boundaries" misrepresents the fact that much of their success derived from their relationship (conflicted as it was) with those self-same Jewish roots.[105] But why would one's Jewishness necessarily enable one to "transcend" or "abandon" Jewishness itself? How is "ethnic success" derived from renouncing "ethnic content"? Successful Jewish-American entertainers were popular with both Jews and Gentiles, but if their very popularity were based on the projection of a Jewish persona, then how could they transcend it without undermining their own success?

Second-generation Jews were still in the process of creating their own distinctively Jewish forms of popular culture. Irving Howe has argued that the "distinctiveness" of these entertainers "seldom appeared in their opinions, and not even in their use of Jewish materials; it came through most vividly in the rhythm and tone of their work, the pulsation of their nerves, the unfolding of what we call 'personality.'" He characterizes their trademark style as a "hysterical frenzy" that derived somehow from immigrant experience and was intensified by a desperate need to prove themselves equal to non-Jews. But non-Jewish entertainers also had "personality" and the quality of "frenzy" that Howe has identified is common to many types of comedy. What set these second-generation Jewish artists apart was their need to work out the meaning of their Jewish identity and their relationship to the world of their parents. As Howe puts it, "Jolson's large-gestured sentimentalism, Jessel's gritty wisecracking, Brice's yente grandeur, Cantor's frantic shakiness; all these were spin-offs from immigrant experience."[106]

This did not mean they had a unitary point of view. June Sochen has written that both Fanny Brice and Sophie Tucker had a peculiarly Jewish "perspective on life" and "angle of vision" that "enabled them to transcend their particularity and become one with large, diverse audiences."[107] But far from transcending a Jewish outlook, both Brice and Tucker built much of their careers on their ability to connect to Jewish audiences through a shared experience of the world.

True, as Sochen puts it, "their public personas spoke to all peoples, while their message often had a particular poignancy for their Jewish audiences."[108] But for Jewish entertainers, to some extent their public persona *was* their message. In becoming prominent both as comedians and as Jews, and in doing so much explicitly Jewish material—much of which was especially geared to Jewish audiences—they were both expressing and fomenting ethnic pride. The next chapter, which examines Broadway comedies about Jewish life in New York during the same period, takes this multivalent, ambivalent process to the next level.

CHAPTER TWO

Jews on Broadway

WHAT HUMORIST H. L. MENCKEN in the 1920s called "America's third-largest industry" was a Broadway play by Anne Nichols about Jewish-Irish intermarriage called *Abie's Irish Rose,* which ran for 2,327 performances, opening on May 23, 1922, at the Fulton Theatre on West 46th Street and closing on October 22, 1927, at the Republic Theatre on West 42nd Street.[1] The comedy opened to mostly negative—if not downright damning—reviews and struggled for the first two months of its run.[2] But by the time it closed, productions of *Abie's Irish Rose* had been seen throughout the world; the play had attracted audiences totaling an estimated eleven million people, and it had grossed close to five million dollars. The play's success was a watershed in the evolution of regional theater in America as well; it ran for months in cities across the country that had never supported a single production for more than a few weeks at a time.[3]

Abie's Irish Rose was perfectly fitted both to its cultural moment and to its era in American Jewish social history. The play that leading theater critic Heywood Broun had called a "synthetic farce" and the "worst play of the season" and that another critic had called a "cheap farce dependent upon stock lines and forced situations" had, according to a Boston newspaper, "not only pleased its public" but "created its public."[4]

I will argue that *Abie's Irish Rose,* which I will discuss in depth later in this chapter, as well as other popular comedies of the period such as Montague Glass's *Partners Again,* Osip Dymov's *Bronx Express,* and Leon da Costa's *Kosher Kitty Kelly,* indeed "created" a public, primarily an ethnic Jewish one. They did so by reflecting images that both reinforced second-generation Jews' perceptions of themselves as "Americanized" and flattered their continuing attachment to their ethnic roots. Deborah Dash Moore has written of the success of second-generation Jews in creating an American Jewish identity that was "not simply a prelude to assimilation." I will contend that these comedies about Jewish families (three of which—*Abie's Irish Rose, The Bronx Express,* and *Partners Again*—opened in the same month, May of 1922) were an integral part of the construction of this proudly, self-consciously Jewish identity.

The emergence of Jewish characters out of vaudeville, comic strips, and comedy recordings (radio and film were just becoming popular) onto the Broadway stage was problematic for Broadway theater critics, who saw them as polluting the genre. Even Gilbert Seldes, surveying plays of Jewish interest in the *Menorah Journal,* a Jewish publication, wrote that he found Jewish stereotypes on stage "excessively banal and distasteful" to the extent that he refused to attend a performance of *Abie's Irish Rose.* His extreme discomfort with Jewish stereotypes is understandable given the anti-Semitic comments that he so often faced from other writers. But his utter dismissal of the comedy is perplexing given his prediction that "no Jewish theme will be completely treated until it has been done by non-Jewish hands as well as Jewish."[5]

Despite not seeing the play, Seldes remained fascinated with *Abie's Irish Rose* and what it represented, both in terms of the depiction of Jews on stage and what the play's popularity suggested about the place of Jews in American society. He later published an outline in *The New Republic* for a proposed preface for a novelized version of the script. Among the points he suggested were: "Creation of a new audience in the theater," "The triumph of the Jews in their 'inferiority complex' submission," "The Jew in Abie, a Slavic immigrant," and "Breakdown of religious observances and tribal customs, especially on the part of the alien." Among the questions Seldes posed were: "Can the value of a critic be judged by the number of times he predicts correctly the popularity of a play?" and "Can a play find its audience in spite of the critics?"[6]

While *Abie's Irish Rose* may have pointed up the ambivalent feelings that some, including many Jews themselves, felt about the increasing visibility of Jews in America, it certainly weathered the negativity of many of the critics. The most vitriolic was Patterson James, who wrote in the *New York Billboard* that "One platter full of *Abie's Irish Rose* filled me with an almost irresistible impulse to start a pogrom of playwrights, managers, actors and critics. And as a side issue set fire to every show house in Manhattan." In addition to his anti-Semitic invocation of the pogroms, the state-sponsored massacres of Jews in Eastern Europe, James thumped his Bible vigorously in complaining that the play "outrages truth, plausibility and good taste at every turn, and it makes either a viciously deliberate attack on or exhibits an incredibly abysmal ignorance of the ordinary practices of the great branches of the Christian religion."[7]

Or as the more gentle but still acerbic Heywood Broun wrote, objecting strenuously to both the Jewish and Irish stereotypes in the play, "No author has ever expressed her contempt for the audience in such flagrant fashion as Miss Anne Nichols. . . . [The play] seems designed to attract the attention of Irish and Jewish theatergoers but is likely to offend such patrons even a little more than any others." (Broun was later was to eat his words, saying in 1931 that "Now that *Abie* is not longer a present menace, I am willing to admit that it was an excellent and tonic thing that the general public succeeded in reversing a critical opinion which was almost unanimous.")[8]

While many still associated Jewish theater in New York primarily with Yiddish theater—one journalist opined in 1922 that "to write a paper about Jewish actors without saying something about the Yiddish Theatre is like talking about modern America without mentioning the flapper and Prohibition"—Jewish-themed plays in English were also beginning to come into their own. Critic Elias Ginsburg opined that the "neglect of bringing to American Jewish audiences the past and present of American Jewish life in the tongue of the country is certainly to be deplored" and called for plays "portraying contemporary Jewish types with their griefs, their joys and their problems."[9] Thus, while the growing black middle class in Harlem sought entertainment mostly in their own neighborhood—racism continued to bar them from Broadway theater seats—Jews hardly restricted their entertainment options to the few Yiddish theaters that sprang up in Brooklyn and the Bronx.

Nichols told Allison Smith of the *American* in 1923 that the idea for her play came from a newspaper story she read about a Bronx boy, Irving Berg, who fell in love with an Irish girl and introduced her to his parents as a Jewess. These "strange people," as Smith puts it, were not so much curiosities to each other, as new to Broadway. The "subway public" that attended the play was largely Jewish. Smith writes that one couple in the audience "laughed about the ham" served to the characters at the end of the play, and "went home to Bushwick Avenue," one of the newer Jewish neighborhoods in Brooklyn.[10]

The "Decline" of the Yiddish Theater

With the progressive loss of their audience, the Second Avenue Yiddish theaters inevitably began to decline and even lose talent to Broadway, as well as to the growing Hollywood film industry. As an article in the *New York Evening Post* put it in 1928, "With the slowing up of immigration, the younger generation is drifting away from the language of its parents and prefers to go uptown to American shows for entertainment." But when the Yiddish theater disappeared, the writer pointed out, the city would lose "some very remarkable plays and productions" that have "trained an extremely talented corps of actors, some of which sooner or later make their way to Broadway."[11] The writer singled out the actor Muni Wisenfrend, the Yiddish stage actor who was appearing at the time on Broadway in Milton Gropper and Max Siegels's comedy about European immigrants called *We Americans* (1926) and who was later to become famous on stage and screen as Paul Muni.

The rise of English-language plays about American Jewish life may even have indirectly benefited the Yiddish stage. One observer, David Barzel, joked

10. Muni Wisenfrend (later renamed Paul Muni), Yiddish stage actor turned Broadway and Hollywood star, in Dana Burnet and George Abbott's 1927 gangster drama, *Four Walls*. Courtesy of Billy Rose Theatre Collection, New York Public Library for the Performing Arts, Astor, Lenox and Tilden Foundations.

at the time that the federal immigration restrictions were a blessing in disguise in that the Yiddish theaters realized that "some means must be devised to keep the Americanized Jewish immigrants from going over to Broadway, and that this could only be done by making their productions as good as those on Broadway."[12] Indeed, the Yiddish theater blossomed artistically in the interwar period, as it incorporated modernist trends of the European avant-garde. In the 1920s, there were more than a dozen Yiddish theaters in Manhattan, Brooklyn, and the Bronx alone.

As Nahma Sandrow has written, "Yiddish actors and writers went back and forth across the Atlantic like bees cross-pollinating. . . . American Yiddish artists and audiences were in closer touch with European currents than were most of their counterparts uptown."[13] In the same era as European companies such as the Moscow Art Theater and the Comédie Française first began making visits to New York, Maurice Schwartz's Yiddish Art Theater was widely acclaimed, by both Jews and non-Jews, for the creativity of its productions. Some of these, like S. Anski's *The Dybbuk* and David Pinski's *Der Oytser* (*The Treasure*), were even translated into English and performed on Broadway.

Performers also began to cross over to Broadway from the Yiddish stage. Celia Adler (daughter of preeminent Yiddish stage actor Jacob P. Adler), Paul Muni, Bertha Kalish, Clara Langsner, and others were well known to patrons of the Second Avenue Yiddish theaters before they achieved fame on Broadway. This was frowned upon by many Yiddish speakers; the expression that was commonly used in the Yiddish press was that an actor was *avek tsu di goyim*— gone off to the non-Jews. Not that every actor needed to leave the Yiddish stage in order to be successful. Mike Burstyn, himself a well-known performer, says that his father, Pesach, was so successful on the Yiddish stage that he repeatedly turned down offers to act on Broadway.[14]

Muni was especially rankled by the implication that he had betrayed his mother culture by acting on the Broadway stage. He defended his decision in an article in *Der Tog* in which he said that the invitation to perform on Broadway offered him an "opportunity to portray a kind of Jew that has never been seen on the English-speaking stage, a Jew who only 'one of us' can play, not an old-fashioned, vulgar type of Jew and also not a creeping sentimental fool, as is portrayed by certain actors in the Jewish-American plays on Broadway." He added that he had taken the "first step on the way to providing a different tone in the portrayal of the Jew on Broadway, correcting the ludicrous and totally false image of the Jew on the English-speaking stage."[15]

The conflict between immigrant parents and Americanizing children remained an especially common theme in Yiddish drama. In the adaptations of Shakespeare on the Yiddish stage, as Leonard Prager, Joel Berkowitz, and others have shown, parents were often recast as representatives of religious Orthodoxy, while children represented either secular or mystical (generally Hasidic) approaches to Jewish tradition. Prager has speculated that in Jacob Gordin's famous *Jewish King Lear,* the parents' insistence that the children follow in their ways spoke to many immigrant Jews' guilt about abandoning their own parents in the Old Country.

"Guilt feelings," Prager writes, "intensified traditionalist loyalties and placed added strain on parent-child relations." The emotional context for this guilt, he theorizes, was that the parents "had difficulty in understanding the alien world outside their Jewish streets, fearing and even despising that alienness. Would their children, free of such fears, learn to despise *them*?"[16]

Yet in some ways the Jewish theater itself may have helped promote understanding between children and parents by presenting familiar conflicts in fictional form. As one critic, Walter Ginsburg, suggested, second-generation Jews could gain a "psychological insight into the character of the immigrant generation" by attending Jewish-themed plays. But it worked both ways, he thought, as reflected in the story he told of the "naïve Jewish lawyer who began to understand his Americanized clients after he became a frequenter of the Yiddish theatre." Ginsburg concluded that, "Just as the gap between children and parents is popularly pictured on the stage so it is often bridged in the audience where the playgoers, old and young, see new light thrown upon their relation to each other."[17]

Even in drama, however, the distinction between the supposedly unacculturated immigrant and his or her Americanized children was never absolute. Reflecting the fact that many immigrant Jews were learning English, Yiddish plays often incorporated large amounts of English words and phrases in their dialogue. Plays like Osip Dymov's *Bronks Ekspres,* which I will discuss in depth later in this chapter, and H. Leivick's sweatshop drama, *Shop,* even had English-language titles.

Even as English words were heard on the Yiddish stage, Yiddish words almost always issued from actors' mouths in the new Jewish comedies on Broadway. All of the new Jewish comedies on Broadway incorporated immigrant Jewish characters, representing the older generation against which the children were invariably rebelling in order to escape their parents' religious and/or ethnocentric values.

Some audience members on Broadway, then as now, seem to have taken pleasure simply in hearing Yiddish expressions flung about on stage. Remarked a writer for the Yiddish daily *Der Tog* about *Abie's Irish Rose:* "The play is very Jewish; the Jewish characters don't just speak English with a Yiddish accent, but they speak Yiddish as well. Many Jews can find a good substitute [on Broadway] for the Yiddish theater on Second Avenue or in Brownsville, where they also speak both English and Yiddish."[18] Even immigrant Jews could potentially feel that they had not been left behind by the beginning of the transformation of a Yiddish-speaking culture into an English-speaking one.

A song by Jewish vaudevillian Rhoda Bernard, "My Yiddish Matinee Girl," poked fun at the way Jewish audiences were beginning to transfer their allegiance from the Yiddish theater to Broadway. Bernard was never as famous or successful as Fanny Brice, although she clearly tried to imitate her style, including the heavy Yiddish accent and gentle tone of ironic self-mockery. Bernard's song was written by Addison Burkhardt, who had worked on four Broadway musicals in different capacities—contributing the book, music, or lyrics in each case. He also wrote dozens of Tin Pan Alley songs. "My Yiddish Matinee Girl," recorded in 1916, satirized the tastes of the growing (heavily female) matinee audience on Broadway during the period—at the same time making fun of Jewish girls in particular. Bernard sang in a high, quavering pitch about the American actors (both Jewish and Gentile) who were beginning to appeal to English-speaking Jews:

> When Rosie lived in Essex Street, she liked the *Yiddishe* plays
> She was so sweet and gentile, all the actors she would praise
> But since she moved up to the Bron-nex, she has got high tone
> She gave up Thomashevsky and she took to Georgie Cohen [*sic*].
> She's now got lots of whims, since father's business pays
> From moving picture flims [*sic*], she changed to Broadway plays.[19]

Rosie, like so many second-generation Jews in New York, has moved out of the Lower East Side to a newer Jewish neighborhood in the Bronx. The cover of the song sheet shows a very slender and stylish girl in a hoop dress and high-heeled shoes, her hat sporting extravagantly long ribbons that rakishly cover her right eye. Her fashion-plate appearance suggests that she no longer lives in the ghetto—she is far from a "second hand Rose." In addition to cultivating a more fashionable appearance, Rosie has gone from enjoying the rough and tumble of the Yiddish theater (symbolized by the great Yiddish matinee idol Boris Thomashevsky) to patronizing the plays of the equally dapper George M. Cohan (a son of Irish immigrants, although the song seems to be suggesting he was Jewish), a producer and composer known for his patriotic shows that included songs like "Yankee Doodle Dandy."

The song goes on to say that Rosie "loves the plays with 'tso-russ'" (meaning *tsuris,* the Yiddish word for trouble). But she also "loves to see 'Abe and Mawruss'"—the first names of the characters in Montague Glass's long-running series of *Potash and Perlmutter* plays, in which the Jewish actors Barney Bernard and Alexander Carr carried on an intense vaudeville-style rivalry, as mismatched partners in the garment trade and later in the automobile industry.

The song's gently satirical lyrics also mention Rosie's admiration for non-Jewish stars from Otis Skinner to Corse Payton to Gaby de Lys. Rosie even attempts to imitate her favorite actors—"She thinks she looks like Billie Burke, and talks like Borr-ow-more" (Lionel Barrymore), while "She tries to dance and skip, like 'Eva I Don't Care'"—the latter being a reference to the highest-paid vaudeville performer of the time, Eva Tanguay.

Rosie fantasizes that some of the Gentile objects of her admiration are Jewish. "To Carus' [the opera singer Enrico Caruso] she'd like to scribble, because he looks like Abe Kabibble," refers to "Abie the Agent," Harry Hershfield's well-known cartoon character who appeared daily in the *New York Journal* throughout most of the teens, twenties, and thirties. Jewish and non-Jewish, fictional and real: the characters become mixed up in her mind. And Rosie herself manages to be both clearly Jewish and fully Americanized at the same time. She seems to prefer Jewish and non-Jewish entertainers equally. She sounds Jewish but her looks (on the cover of the sheet music) are ethnically nonspecific. Rosie occupies an intermediate position, somewhere between the immigrant world and the world of mainstream American society.

It was in this period that Jews became extremely active in all phases of Broadway. In a sense, the Yiddish theater simply moved uptown, bringing its audience with it. Jewish producers were especially prominent. An article in *The American Hebrew,* the most widely read American Jewish magazine, praised David Belasco, Lee Shubert, and Sam Harris in arguing that Jews have "enacted an increasingly important role both in fostering the arts and in . . . creating art."[20] The preeminence of immigrant Jews in Hollywood film production, as described by Neil Gabler in his influential book *An Empire of Their Own,* was matched by an almost equal predominance of Jews in theatrical production.

Indeed, it became a common comic device in various forms of entertainment to have a pair of crass, uncultured Jewish theatrical producers. From the caustic, wise-cracking Kibbitzer and Eppus in J. P. McEvoy's satiric 1928 novel *Show Girl* to vaudeville pros Smith and Dale in the 1932 film *Manhattan Parade* to the bumbling, lovable Max Bialystock and Leo Bloom in Mel Brooks's 1967 film *The Producers* (later, of course, a much ballyhooed Broadway musical), to the strutting, avaricious Gold and Goldberg in Michael John LaChiusa's 2000 musical (set in 1928) *The Wild Party,* Jewish characters often provided the funding and the know-how to get fictional plays up on the stage.[21]

The success of Jewish theatrical producers seemed to confirm stereotypes about the supposedly "natural" talent that Jews had for making money. (Like the idea that African Americans were somehow born with a sense of rhythm—which is nothing if not racist—this stereotype, aside from its pernicious elements, can be seen as actually quite disparaging to the large numbers of Jews who had to work hard to earn a living.) As the eminent theater critic (and Yale University professor) Walter Prichard Eaton wrote in the pages of the *American Hebrew,* theatrical production was "monopolized" by Jews. These Jews were, he opined,

> ludicrously unfitted to control the destiny of a fine art, and have brought into the theatre, into theatre management, a rudeness of manners, a lack

of courtesy and consideration, a general vulgarity and lack of all cultural background, which rightly or wrongly has been attributed to their racial blood, and has greatly intensified racial prejudice among the rank and file of the theatre artists and the more discriminating public. . . . [The Jew] brings with him little or no cultural background, unpleasantly aggressive manners, and, in general, an atmosphere disturbingly at variance with the spirit of the place he enters.[22]

Eaton concluded by remarking that the American theater "has always been a rather easy prey to the shrewd commercialist. That commercialist, in our generation, is a Jew."[23] That such an anti-Semitic raving would be printed in a Jewish publication (indeed, Prichard begins the article by saying that he was solicited by the editor to weigh in on the question of whether or not the primacy of Jews in theatrical production "has tended to increase or decrease prejudice") shows how eager most Jews felt to distance themselves from Jewish stereotypes. It also shows the continuing view of the theater as a high culture preserve, rather than also a place for popular culture to flourish. To say that Jews lacked any kind of "cultural background" is patently ridiculous, unless one believes that the only kind of cultural background to have is a white Anglo-Saxon Protestant one.

However, while the Jewish Hollywood producers had to work themselves up from owning small storefront nickelodeons to running entire film studios, the Jewish producers on Broadway had to invest a significant amount of capital right from the beginning. Thus, their supposed talent for making money could also be seen in complimentary terms, if they were viewed simply as gamblers who had an intuitive sense of what shows to back. As Thomas H. Dickinson opined in *The Nation*, the Jew demonstrated "just that combination of artistic discrimination and initiative in organization—that skill in fusing the diverse elements of an intimate and sensitive art with the touch-and-go, devil-may-care adventure of the curb market that is necessary in creating the modern dramatic production."[24]

Indeed, part of the mystique surrounding the success of *Abie's Irish Rose* was the fact that the gangster Arnold Rothstein, who was known as the "Moses of New York's Underworld," reportedly helped bankroll the original Broadway production. But it was not just Jewish producers who helped get shows on their feet; Jerry Eisenhour has discovered that the managers of *Abie's Irish Rose* kept the show going only by transferring large blocks of tickets to a Jewish cigar store owner named Joseph Leblang who resold them to the public at a discount.[25] Leblang was the forerunner of today's Theatre Development Fund, which sells half-price tickets in Times Square (at the TKTS booth) to Broadway and off-Broadway shows.

THE TURN TO BROADWAY

As "cosmopolitan" as the immigrants and their children might have become, they remained powerfully attracted by Jewish-themed entertainments. Perhaps the consumers of Broadway plays about Jewish life were less discriminating than their counterparts in the Yiddish theaters (some of these, however, were the same people; they attended both). As Ludwig Satz, who took over the role of Abe Potash on Broadway after the death of the popular comic Barney Bernard, once wrote in the *New York Times,* "Your American audience has not definitely made up its mind as to what it likes and what it doesn't like, but is willing to be shown what you have and to enjoy it if it is enjoyable." By contrast, the Yiddish audience "knows exactly what it goes to the theater to buy. . . . It is a homogeneous audience and it knows the life that its theater portrays. You cannot fool its members with false types and with false interpretations."[26]

Some of the most popular Jewish-themed stage productions were really variety shows such as the ones mentioned in the previous chapter that featured well-known Jewish vaudeville performers like Baker, Brice, Jessel, and Cantor reprising versions of their routines. Others, like Fanny Brice's *Fanny,* were attempts to use stars as romantic and/or comic leads in story formats. Almost all were comedies; as Dickinson wrote, "there still exists something of a prejudice against the Jewish actor unless he is a comedian, holding up the traits of his tribe to laughter."[27] But while in many ways Jews remained the butts of humor on the Broadway stage, they also, paradoxically, began to be portrayed in more sympathetic and realistic ways.

Not all the Jewish-themed plays that appeared on Broadway during the 1920s were plays about American Jewish life. There were, for example, a number of productions of Shakespeare's *Merchant of Venice,* one of which, directed by David Belasco, starred the famous Jewish actor David Warfield. Harley Erdman has described Warfield as the actor who "first popularized the turn-of-the-century Hebrew comic type and either directly influenced or strongly overshadowed all the other Jewish performances of the period."[28]

But Warfield's Shylock disappointed the critics, who panned him for delivering a performance devoid of psychological complexity and emotional power. The production was also derided for its excessive sets and absurdly melodramatic acting styles. John Corbin, the critic for the *New York Times,* bitingly called Warfield's Shylock "an appealingly human voice pathetically crying in a producer's weird wilderness of misunderstanding."[29]

Nevertheless, the announcement of Warfield's appearance in the role had caused great excitement in the Jewish community. As one writer in the *American Hebrew* put it, it was hoped that the actor, as "the most representative Jewish actor on the English-speaking stage," would "strengthen the humanity and the Jewishness of the character as it has never been done before." This was in the context of a lively debate that raged in the American Jewish press in the 1920s as to whether or not Shylock was even a Jew![30]

Also well-received by American Jewish audiences was the English playwright John Galsworthy's *Loyalties* (1922). *Loyalties* is about a wealthy young Jew, Ferdinand De Levis, who has a large sum of money stolen by one of his fellow guests while he is staying in the country home of a prominent man of society. When he insists that his money be returned, De Levis is excluded from participation in elite social circles.

As one of the other characters complains, "I don't like . . . 'Ebrews. They work harder; they're more sober; they're honest; and they're everywhere. I've nothing against them, but the fact is—they get *on* so." However, De Levis is ultimately vindicated when an anti-Semitic captain is unmasked as the culprit; as Louis Harap has pointed out, even plays by non-Jewish authors in the 1920s that included Jewish characters did not tend to portray them in entirely unflattering ways.[31]

Indeed, Jewish characters "getting on" became a perennial theme of the Jewish fare on Broadway during the Jazz Age. A plethora of Jewish-themed Broadway plays reflected the second generation's need to stake out its own territory within American society and, more particularly, within the polyglot culture of New York City. Rather than assimilating to a single "Yankee" standard, Jews transformed New York culture in their own image. Not until *Fiddler on the Roof* in the 1960s would the Broadway theater again be such an important source of Jewish ethnic pride.

Some of these plays were set on the Lower East Side; others were set in the outerborough neighborhoods to which the majority of second-generation Jews had relocated. Those set on the Lower East Side, like the vaudeville routines that were set in the ghetto, capitalized on the nostalgia of second-generation Jews for the immigrant neighborhood and its atmosphere of Jewish saturation. By reprising the ghetto on stage, Jews both memorialized the Lower East Side and marked the distance—in physical, social, cultural, and emotional terms—they had traveled to escape it.

THE JEWISH AUDIENCE

In his theater column in the *American* in 1922, Alan Dale said he found *Abie's Irish Rose* "clever, ingenious and possible" but that he "regretted the dialect." According to Dale, "the public absolutely believes that no one can be Hebrew unless he speak a horrible patois in assorted tones." The vaudeville caricature of the Jew, he believed, survived on Broadway not because Gentiles indulged their own prejudices, but because more assimilated Jews were amused by the immigrant stereotypes. Dale wrote: "The Hebrews themselves are largely to blame for the prevalence of the [Jewish] stage type. They laugh at it and enjoy the knowledge of their own superiority. They are greatly amused at jargon, because they have thrown it into the discard. They have been educated out of it, but they like to see stage characters that haven't been thus educated. . . . You seldom see a non-dialected Hebrew on the stage. He wouldn't be 'funny' if he didn't talk with his hands in dialect."[32]

In other words, second-generation Jews needed these stereotypes as much as (if not more than) non-Jews did; they marked the distance the children had traveled from the world of their fathers. As an index of their own acculturation, second-generation Jews could celebrate having shed themselves of the baggage of ethnic stereotypes, even as they sought in many ways to continue to develop a more positive Jewish self-image. It might seem that by laughing at Jewish characters on stage, Jewish audience members were adopting the anti-Semitic attitudes held by the majority of Americans. But, at least in the context of the Broadway audience, where Jews were attending in groups (often theater groups organized by synagogues and other Jewish organizations), there was, I would suggest, almost a ritualistic element to the ways in which Jews both collectively purged themselves of stereotypes and, paradoxically, continued to enjoy the stereotypes and in-jokes on the level of rollicking Jewish entertainment.

Paul Distler has argued that ethnic humor declined on the vaudeville stage when the audience became more middle-class, musical comedies with strong storylines became popular, and fewer immigrants arrived for comedians to parody—or for audience members to feel threatened by, or even to recognize. But for Jews, the popularity of the new Jewish comedies indicates that the immigrant stereotypes were still very much needed as part of the acculturation process. For non-Jews, these ethnic comedies retained enough of the older stereotypes for them to be humorous—Jews were sufficiently maintaining their distinctiveness in order to be identifiable targets of humor. Non-Jews could also take pleasure in seeing Jews and other immigrants "Americanize" themselves by, to various degrees, downplaying or even renouncing the customs of their ancestors.

Another reason that Distler suggests for the so-called reformation of the Jewish stage type was the growing influence of groups like the Chicago Anti-Stage Ridicule Committee that, in 1913, boycotted Jewish performances in Chicago that it viewed as anti-Semitic. Distler concludes that these efforts, which he says were supported by the Anti-Defamation League of B'nai Brith, were extremely successful in curtailing the openly Jewish characterizations that appeared on American stages.

This seems highly improbable. The few sporadic protests that these groups organized did not stem the tide of a whole brand of popular entertainment based on Jewish stereotypes. Edgar Rosenberg's catalog of the New York Public Library's holdings of Jewish-themed plays, published in 1968, has hundreds of listings of such plays, including plot summaries and descriptions of the Jewish characters. A large percentage of these plays were originally published in the years just before and after the First World War, in the same period in which Distler argues that Jewish stereotypes were disappearing from American stages.

Even in New York, where productions of Jewish plays could arguably make a profit even if they just appealed to a Jewish audience, the audiences for these plays was unlikely only to have been Jewish. But critics from mainstream newspapers tended to view the audience as almost exclusively composed of Jews. As the critic for the *New York Herald Tribune* wrote in his review of *The Jazz Singer* in 1925: "It is a well-known fact that plays in which the principal characters are Jews, even in the broadest comedies, appeal particularly to Jewish audiences, and we believe that such will be the case with *The Jazz Singer*. We know of no play that requires so thorough an understanding of and sympathy with the Jew and his faith as does this one. Indeed, many of the lines of the play which were spoken in dialect, while wholly unintelligible to us, were received by an audience almost entirely composed of those of the Jewish race."[33]

The Broadway audience for *The Jazz Singer* could hardly have been entirely Jewish. Nor does the play, despite its grounding in a Jewish milieu, require a deep knowledge of Jewish tradition in order to follow its basic outlines and understand its characters and themes. What comes through in the review is an underlying feeling of resentment; the critic seems to feel excluded and to count himself as one of those who lacks a certain amount of "sympathy" with Jews and Judaism. It is especially interesting that he refers to himself in the plural, which is unusual in reviews from the period, as if to set up an opposition between the Jewish audience that understands and appreciates the play and the rest of society that he claims will be mystified and even irritated by it.

It was partly true that second-generation Jews were creating a kind of entertainment world of their own, one that mirrored their own experience. In the song quoted above, Rosie is still a "Yiddish" matinee girl even though she has stopped going to Yiddish plays. Her identity is in flux; there remains a sense about her "Yiddish" theater-going that she is either the right person in the wrong place, or the wrong person in the right place. But what is most important is that her identity *is* to some extent defined or determined by her theater-going. As in the old adage, "You are what you eat," Rosie (herself a fictional creation) takes her own identity from what she sees on stage. This was the second generation's experience of Broadway. Jews attended Jewish-themed Broadway plays with more than a shock of recognition; they experienced a genuine sense of homecoming that celebrated and reinforced their Jewishness.

THE INFLUENCE OF THE COMIC STRIPS

Many of these Jewish types seemed familiar to critics from the comic strips, which had arisen in the 1890s as part of a circulation war between William Randolph Hearst's *New York Journal* and Joseph Pulitzer's *New York World*. By the 1920s, comic strips were beginning to be taken seriously as an important indigenous art form. Writing about George Herriman's *Krazy Kat,* Gilbert Seldes called it "the most amusing and fantastic and satisfactory work of art produced in America today." While the cat and mouse were of indefinite ethnicity and gender, Seldes was perhaps the first to note that Krazy's accent seemed heavily influenced by Yiddish speech rhythms, calling it "partly Dickens and partly Yiddish." (It also often combined with a Tex-Mex Spanish accent, but Seldes fails to mention this.)[34]

Other comic strip characters, however, were quite explicitly Jewish, such as Harry Hershfield's *Abie the Agent,* which ran in the *New York Journal,* first as a daily strip and later as both a daily and Sunday (color) strip. Hershfield was born in Cedar Rapids, Iowa, of Russian Jewish parents. His first successful comic strip was *Desperate Desmond,* the tales of an adventurer in foreign lands inspired by C. W. Kahles's melodramatic strip called *Hairbreadth Harry: Boy Hero.* When Desmond encountered a cannibal named Gomgatz, Hershfield, needing a strange-sounding speech pattern, employed a Yiddish accent for Gomgatz's utterances. Hershfield's editor, Arthur Brisbane, then prodded Hershfield to create an entire strip featuring Yiddishisms. Abe Kabibble became, according to cartoon historian Donald Markstein, the first Jewish protagonist of an American comic strip. In addition to the strips, Abie also "reviewed" Broadway shows; the reviews were bylined "'Abie the Agent' per Harry Hershfield." One of his reviews is quoted at the end of this chapter, in connection with the Fanny Brice vehicle *Fanny.*

In appearance, Abie was strikingly similar to Barney Bernard, the original Potash of the *Potash and Perlmutter* series. In fact, it seems in retrospect that Bernard was the model for a whole generation of Jewish male stage characters—short and fat, lovable but slightly harebrained, unable to really "make it" in society despite his get-rich-quick schemes.

Speaking English, but with a Yiddish accent, Abie's whole "personality" was a kind of new Jewish stereotype. Lacking "manly" qualities and lacerated by self-doubt, Abie is still an affectionate partner to his girlfriend (later wife) Reba and a good friend to another Jewish guy named Minsk. And he eagerly wants to succeed in the fiercely competitive American society, which, at least in the early years of the strip, meant beating out his competitor Benny Sparkbaum of the "Collapsible" Automobile Company.

Abie marked a clear departure from the type of Jewish character drawing done by Samuel Cahan, who did studies of immigrant Jews for the *New York Sunday World.* As an article in the *Jewish Forum* described his work, they were "psychological masterpieces," depictions of "[o]ld, shrivelled, frozen Jewish peddlers; loquacious and stout Jewish women; a tender and pale *yeshivah bachur* [Talmud student]; [and] the shrewd, keen-eyed businessman."[35] These character studies showed the decline of a highly romanticized Lower East Side (much like the *shtetl* in Eastern Europe) as the immigrant generation battled poverty and disease and the younger generation (other than the *yeshivah* student) moved away.

And there were also comic strips in the Yiddish press, such as the work of Samuel Zagat for the newspaper *Die Wahrheit*: these featured stereotypical immigrant characters such as Gimpl Beynish, the matchmaker; Berl Bedroom, the boarder; Moshe, the Real Estatenik; and Mrs. Pisl from Uptown. (Unfortunately, these have never been reprinted.) When Zagat left *Die Wahrheit* in 1919, he began a four-decades-long career as art director for the *Forvertz* (*Jewish Daily Forward*), a newspaper that survives to this day. John Appel describes Gimpl as a "bearded, top-hatted, beady eyed, frock-coated busybody in striped pants" who had a "frantic desire to make a living from uniting the most unpromising single men with unattached females"—an occupation that took him from the Lower East Side to the Catskills and everywhere in between.[36]

As Appel has written, these Yiddish comic strip characters "inhabited a more self-consciously Jewish milieu than the syndicated types in the Anglo-American press, less circumscribed by the cartoonists' or the syndicates' taboos concerning immigrant speech and characteristics." Appel notes that these Yiddish characters "seem more robustly ethnic, more Jewish even when they do not transcend the broad slapstick farce that was the mainstay of the comics."[37] Just as in the Yiddish theaters, Jews were expected to be the exclusive consumers of this form of entertainment, produced in the immigrants' native language.

Hershfield's strip, which ran from 1914 to 1940, was directed much more to the second generation. As he reminded the readers of the *American Hebrew*, in his strip "you never see the stereotyped derby hat over the ears, with a big beard, and the movement of the arms, as depicted by so-called Hebrew caricatures on the stage." Instead, noted Hershfield, he depicted what he called "American humor, as seen through certain types of Jews and to be read by all Americans without regard for religious belief." Or as he told the members of a Chicago women's club in 1916, he was determined to make Abie a "clean-cut, well-dressed specimen of Jewish humor" to combat prevailing, invidious Jewish stereotypes. In the same year, Bert Levy, creator of the popular *Samuel and Sylenz* strip, told the trade publication *Cartoons Magazine* that he had given up the profitable strip "rather than continue a series which he found offensive to his fellow Jews."[38]

As Gilbert Seldes described him, Abie was "the Jew of commerce and the man of common sense; you have seen him quarrel with the waiter because of an overcharge of ten cents, and, encouraged by his companion, replying, "'Yes, and it ain't the principle either; it's the ten cents.'" In sum, Seldes wrote, Abie was the "epitome of one side of his race, and his attractiveness is as remarkable as his jargon."[39] In other words, he exemplified Jewish stereotypes in such a way that, for the first time, they seemed appealing rather than atrocious. The comedy had a good-natured aspect to it rather than simply an anti-Semitic tinge.

Nevertheless, Peter Marzio points out that Hershfield "put into his comic strips the brand of Yiddish humor that had spiked the vaudeville stage with humor for at least twenty years before."[40] Indeed, Milt Gross, a phenomenally prolific author and comic strip artist, was to use the Yiddish accent for many of the first-generation, urban Jewish characters who populated his strips, from *Nize Baby* and *Gross Exaggerations* (both based on the misadventures of the hapless Feitlebaum Family) in the 1920s to *Dave's Delicatessen* in the early 1930s. Perhaps his greatest achievement is his 1926 version of Longfellow's Hiawatha, done entirely in a Yiddish dialect.[41]

The Yiddish words in the strips of both Hershfield and Gross are spelled phonetically, as in "Oy Vay," "Teeayter," "Eppetite," and "Mozeltoff" (in Hershfield) and "Fiftin meenits from de station" (in Gross). Especially in the earlier strips, Hershfield uses frequent Yiddish words and idioms that obviously were directed at a readership that understood (even if they could not speak) Yiddish. (However, sometimes he translates the Yiddish into awkward English, such as when he calls an unfortunate situation "a shame for the neighbors" rather than the familiar Yiddish expression *a shande far di goyim* [an embarrassment in front of the non-Jews].)

Marzio's comparison between comics and vaudeville is illuminating. Comic strips depended for their humor on the same kind of timing employed by the vaudeville performers, with a punchline at the end of each strip as at the end of each routine. However, in their overall impression they were perhaps more similar to plays; the main character of each strip was embedded in a larger narrative that readers followed from week to week. (The musical version of Garry Trudeau's *Doonesbury,* which opened on Broadway in 1983, showed how adaptable the comic strip format was to the stage.) Like modern-day television, there was also a gallery of recurring characters that the reader needed to keep track of as they drifted in and out of the main character's "life."

It is interesting that Hershfield mentioned that he presents "certain types" of Jews even as he insisted on moving away from stereotypical depictions. What were the new types of Jews that the comic strips portrayed?

As Marzio has written, "There's something funny about a Jewish salesman like Abie trying to analyze mass taste: he, himself, seems so out of touch with the world. . . . Yet, in one episode after another he pursues the task single-mindedly, relentlessly—an urban stumble-bum who'll somehow make his way."[42] It is Abie's very determination to succeed that is both comical and impressive and that likely resonated not just with immigrants looking to fit into American society but with all Americans who were preoccupied with financial success and social mobility.

By the 1920s, Abie's class position had seemingly improved tremendously, much more than most American Jews of the time. Instead of selling cars, he owned a wholesale company and managed what he called a "high class" restaurant ("One more aggravation and I'll turn this into a delicatessen," he threatened in a strip in 1922). In addition to speaking at lodge dinners and making visits to the racetrack, Abie joined a fancy club, began going to benefit performances at the theater (often in support of Jewish charities such as the Israel Orphan Asylum), and even at one point hired a chauffeur. In one strip, he is very nervous about attending a black tie affair, since he is afraid that he will not know any of the other guests; as it turns out, the guests are all introduced to each other by the man who rented tuxedoes to all of them!

11. Al Hershfield's "Abie the Agent," the first comic strip based on a Jewish character. Courtesy of King Features Syndicate.

He may still have the impulses of a salesman (in one strip he goes around the restaurant announcing over and over that the management is not responsible for hats, coats, and umbrellas; he explains that it would not look good to have signs on the wall in such an upscale establishment), but he has already shed many stereotypical Jewish characteristics. Indeed, it is his friend Minsk who is now the cheapskate; when someone rescues Minsk from drowning in the ocean, Minsk asks his savior for change of a half dollar in order to give only a twenty-five-cent reward!

Yet when Abie orders a corned beef sandwich at Max Rosebudd's Delicatessen or attends the Broadway theater (of a 1915 revue by George Cohan, he quipped, "Goulash is mixed up, but it's great, isn't it?"), he seems just like any other second-generation New York Jew who is participating in the cultural and gastronomic pursuits of the era.[43]

The same was true of the comic strip characters invented by Rube Goldberg; as a profile of Goldberg in the *American Hebrew* put it, "The men with bulbous noses and spinach whiskers who romp joyously through his strips might, with a few sobering touches, be transformed into our fellow citizens from the Bronx, Canarsie or Central Park West."[44] While most of the characters created by the San Francisco–born Goldberg were not explicitly Jewish, Goldberg always demonstrated what Rick Marschall has called a "playful approach to human nature. His talent was to see the sham behind the pretention, the absurd in the pompous. He might have written about Society's traditions, 'I'm the guy who put the con in convention.'"[45] (The reference is to Goldberg's signature saying, from a strip called *I'm the Guy*: "I'm the Guy that put the Con in Congress.") Goldberg became most famous, of course, for the elaborate contraptions invented by his inspired creation, Professor Lucifer Gorgonzola Butts, and that seem, like Ed Wynn's "inventions" for his vaudeville routines, a demonstration of intelligence and creativity triumphing over—or perhaps even overcompensating for—almost any challenge.

As John Appel has written of *Abie the Agent,* it "kidded rather than satirized aspects of American Jewish middle class life" since it sympathetically showed Abie trying to make his way in the capitalist economy. Nevertheless, Appel argues that the strip had "only a faint Jewish coloration," because Jews were keeping a low profile in American society and because non-Jewish readers would not understand the Jewish references.[46]

One wonders, however, if Jews really were keeping such a low profile when representations and images of them were appearing with such frequency in so many arenas of popular culture. Indeed, even *Abie the Agent* was nationally syndicated by the Hearst organization, although Don Markstein has written that the strip "tended to be more popular in the large ethnically diverse cities of the Northeast than in small Midwest towns" (www.toonopedia.com/abie.htm.) But it did well enough that as early as 1917 the Hearst organization adapted the strip into two animated cartoons, *Iska Worreh* and *Abie Kabibble Outwitting His Rival.*

Interestingly, given the frequency with which Jews and Irish were paired in popular culture, it was an Irish comic strip, George McManus's *Bringing Up Father,* that was most similar to *Abie the Agent* in its ethnic humor. In McManus's strip, which became one of the all-time most popular strips, an Irish bricklayer named Jiggs wins a million dollars in a sweepstakes, but, over the loud protestations of his wife Maggie (a washerwoman), he wants only to repair to Dinty Moore's saloon to play poker, drink beer, and dine on corned beef and cabbage. The working man could not be kept from his pleasures for very long.

THE NEW JEW ON STAGE

Ironically, second-generation Jews could embrace their own representations on Broadway precisely because those representations were changing. As we saw in the first chapter, the stereotypes of Jews familiar from early-twentieth-century vaudeville were giving way to more acculturated portrayals—Jewish characters who looked and sounded more like real human beings (which, in a Gentile culture, meant more like Gentiles). The "stage Jew" was no longer the exclusive property of "Hebrew" comics, but could accommodate himself or herself to a wide range of portrayals. Jews were still outsiders but they created a world of their own that appealed more and more to non-Jews as well as Jews. As economic opportunities expanded for many Americans, Jews capitalized on the improving national mood, creating entertainment that induced audiences to begin to laugh with them instead of simply at them. The First World War was over, and so was much of the unity forged during wartime. As hellish as the war had been, one could still be nostalgic about how it brought people of different religions and ethnicities together.

Abie's Irish Rose demonstrates the breadth of the range of portrayals. The play begins with a conversation among three visitors—a couple from next door named the Cohens and a rabbi, Rabbi Samuels—in the home of businessman Solomon Levy. Cohen is reading a popular comic strip, *Maggie and Jiggs,* out loud; Mrs. Cohen is complaining about a recent operation; and the rabbi is pleading for quiet. The Cohens, clearly immigrants, both speak with heavy Yiddish accents; the goateed rabbi, better educated and significantly younger, speaks unaccented English. (The Cohens and Solomon Levy were, according to a critic for *The New Republic,* Robert Littell, "thoroughly unmistakably, ridiculously Jewish, with an accent a foot thick, and bits of Yiddish thrown in.")[47]

When the owner of the apartment, Solomon Levy, finally makes his appearance, the phone rings and he launches into a monologue that audiences would have immediately recognized as lifted from the recorded comedy routines of the British comic Joe Hayman, such as his immensely popular "Cohen on the Telephone," in which fractured English, a ridiculous Yiddish accent, and multiple misunderstandings are the sources of humor.[48]

SOLOMON: Hello! Who iss it? Yes vot? Me! Yes, it's me! Who am me? Say who am you? What number? I don't know the number! I didn't get the phone to call myself![49]

Solomon's son, Abraham Levy, then enters with his new bride, Rose Mary Murphy, an actress he met in France during his service in the First World War. Abraham, or Abie, is afraid to incur his father's displeasure, and thus introduces his wife as a friend named Rose Mary Murpheski, a change of name that he knows will cause his father to think her to be Jewish. Although the first thing Solomon wants to know, when he and his son are alone, is how much money Rose Mary has, his next impulse is to exult over his son's choice of a Jewish bride, after a succession of romances with Gentile women. "We'll have no 'Schickies' in this family," insists Solomon. When Rose Mary compliments Solomon on his "blarney," Solomon is angered: "I once had dealings with a fellow named Murphy, and what he didn't do to me," he explains. "Every time I hear dot void blarney it reminds me of dot Irisher."[50]

In the second act, Abie and Rose Mary are married by a rabbi, Dr. Jacob Samuels, as Rose Mary's father, Patrick, and his priest, Father Whalen, arrive by train from California. Patrick's first shock, upon entering the Levy's home, is the sight of the living room decorated with orange trees rather than flowers, the result of an economizing move by Solomon, who prefers edible fruit to perishable blossoms. But Patrick associates oranges with Protestants, and immediately assumes that his daughter is marrying a Protestant. He is quickly disabused of this notion by Solomon, and both men lament their children's deception. However, the rabbi and priest seem to recognize each other from their mutual wartime service, during which both ministered to the dying without regard to the faith of the wounded. Not only that, but, according to Father Whalen, the American soldiers shared an epiphany of religious tolerance: "Shure they all had the same God above them. And what with the shells bursting, and the shrapnel flying, with no one knowing just what moment death would come, Catholics, Hebrews and Protestants alike forgot their prejudice and came to realize that all faiths and creeds have about the same destination after all."[51]

As Patrick threatens legal action, Father Whalen appeases him by suggesting that he himself marry the couple, to legitimate the marriage in the eyes of the Church. Without telling either the rabbi or Solomon, he performs the ceremony. The already married couple is thus ultimately married twice more (all three nuptials, interestingly, occurring offstage, as if showing the intermarriage onstage would be too transgressive for the audience to witness).[52] After a period in which the young couple is estranged from both families, they are finally reconciled over Christmas dinner—the meal consisting of kosher food for Abie's side of the family and ham for Rose's. The couple presents their fathers with twins; the boy to be named for the Irish father, the girl for Abie's deceased mother.[53]

The play parades a series of progressively more acculturated Jewish stereotypes before the audience. Solomon Levy is a prosperous businessman, but he speaks as if he has just stepped off a vaudeville stage. In the first Broadway production of *Abie's Irish Rose*, Levy (created by vaudeville and Yiddish stage veteran Alfred Weisman), appears in cast photographs as wearing an ill-fitting suit, striped vest, baggy pants, a shirt with its collar up around his ears, and a battered beret. By contrast, Abie (played, in the original Broadway cast, by the Gentile actor Robert B. Williams) wears a tuxedo. The goatee-sporting rabbi is clad in a stylish dark suit with starched white-collar shirt.

Characters like Abie were what the social worker Konrad Bercovici, writing in 1923 of the "generation of Bronx Jews quite distinct from the East Side," called "the second-generation Jew with all the outward characteristics minus beard and mustache, playing baseball, great fight fans, commercial travelers, clean-shirted, white-collared, derby-hatted, creased-trousers."[54] Since

12. Various characters in Anne Nichols's 1922 play, *Abie's Irish Rose*, representing the father, son, rabbi, and next-door neighbors. From left, Ida Kramer (Mrs. Isaac Cohen), Alfred Wiseman (Solomon Levy), Harold Shubert (Abraham Levy), Jack Bertin (Rabbi Jacob Samuels), and Milton Wallace (Isaac Cohen). Courtesy of Billy Rose Theatre Collection, New York Public Library for the Performing Arts, Astor, Lenox and Tilden Foundations.

religious Jews were not supposed to shave, the trimming of the beard and mustache was itself significant; it symbolized a more secular lifestyle. Interestingly, however, the derby hat had also been de rigueur for the "Hebrew" comics; the derby could seemingly intensify either an unkempt appearance or a fashionable one. For example, the Levys' neighbor Cohen wears a top hat, which makes him look like a comedian or magician. Played in the original cast by the diminutive Milton Wallace, Cohen's top hat accentuates his short stature, making him look utterly ridiculous.

The change in stereotype, at least for males, is highly significant. The old immigrant costume was viewed as feminizing its wearer, rendering him truly unsuited for the life of American commerce. By contrast, the more fashionable apparel worn by the second-generation Jew marked him as eligible to participate in the new economy. But it was not just his dress that handicapped the immigrant Jew. Even if he did not remain attached to religious rituals, the stereotypical immigrant father still often seemed to lack masculinity; he had to make up in brains what he lacked in brawn.

Even older immigrant Jews could be "Americanized," according to the Broadway theater of the day. A case in point is the heavy-handed but patriotic *We Americans,* the play starring Paul Muni that was later made into a (now lost) silent film. Muni played Morris Levine, an immigrant Jewish presser with a heavy Yiddish accent, who is persuaded by his daughter's boyfriend, Samuel Korn (a second-generation Jew), to attend Korn's night school classes in English.

The comic centerpiece of the play is the second act, in which Levine and his wife, along with representatives of other immigrant groups, struggle to master the English language. (The schoolroom scene with the various immigrants is reminiscent of many vaudeville acts of the time that poked fun at immigrants' accents and malapropisms.) In doing so, they acquire a newfound self-respect and an appreciation for American values. The stage directions to Act 2 instruct the director to make clear that the immigrants have lost their "eye-sore" qualities when they begin to attend school, but that their "improved appearance is attributable to an altered viewpoint and not to the acquisition of money.... [T]here is apparent in them a consciousness of themselves not, as heretofore, merely as members of a race, but a consciousness of themselves as individuals."[55]

Even more complex second-generation Jewish characters are found in the work of Aaron Hoffman, a St. Louis–born playwright who studied at the University of Chicago and then moved to New York, where he wrote vaudeville sketches before penning larger works like his playlet *The Son of Solomon* (1912), which depicted the conflict between Orthodox Jewish parents and their children, who stray from religious observance. According to Ellen Schiff, the playlet "turned its back on the prevailing burlesque and caricatured stage Jews."[56] By the end of his life (he died in 1924, at the age of forty-four), Hoffman was writing full-length plays. His ironically titled *Welcome Stranger* (1920) focuses on the character of Isidor Solomon, a Jewish visitor to a small New England town, who faces prejudice at every turn as he seeks to win acceptance from the anti-Semitic mayor and townspeople. Ironically, it is only when he exposes the mayor's own concealed Jewishness that Solomon replaces him as the leader of the community.

Solomon was played by George Sidney, a short and pudgy actor who was known for his work in vaudeville; he was later to star in the film series *The Cohens and the Kellys.* As Carol Bird wrote in *Theater Magazine* about Sidney's performance in *Welcome Stranger:* "No one ever dreamed that a day would come when a stage comedian would be cast as anything but a comedian—a grotesque, a burlesque of his race, a magnifier of racial characteristics. . . . But the miracle happened. Today theater-goers are given the opportunity to see on the stage a Jew as he really is—say at home—kindly, lovable, childish, affectionate, droll, humorous, extraordinarily fond of his family and all the things connected with his home."[57]

Perhaps the most interesting aspect of this encomium is the rush to replace one set of stereotypes with another, to overcompensate for the negative stereotypes by inventing positive ones. But even Bird seems to presuppose some of these stereotypes herself; she adds that "rarely nowadays is [the Jew] shown as he most assuredly is not, nine cases out of ten—a vulgarian, crudely unfamiliar with the English language, raving constantly about money." She seems to need to concede that there *are* some Jews who do fit the stereotype, which undermines her own argument. Still, Sidney, "without realizing it, or striving for it, has become a sort of propagandist for his race." As Sidney himself said, as quoted by Bird, "I never could go back to the beard and dialect plays. I enjoy too much depicting the average Jew as he actually is," meaning the Jew as "kindly, loveable, sympathetic, eager to help the underdog, and, generally, an all-round regular human being."[58]

Reinventing Jewish Ethnicity

The most popular "stage Jews" of the period were, without doubt, the fictional characters of Abe Potash and "Mawruss" Perlmutter. The first play, *Potash and Perlmutter,* grew out of a series of short stories written by Montague Glass, an Anglo-Jewish author, about two Jewish immigrants who run a clothing business; by 1926 a total of seven Potash and Perlmutter plays had appeared on Broadway, with the two partners entering occupations as diverse as running a film studio (in the 1917 comedy *Business Before Pleasure*), and operating a detective agency (in the 1926 *Potash and Perlmutter, Detectives*).

The concept was so successful that it also migrated to film and to a daily comic strip in Hearst newspapers.

Played originally by Barney Bernard and Alexander Carr (Bernard died in 1924 and was replaced by Ludwig Satz for the last play in the series), the Jews in these stage comedies were portrayed very differently from the ways in which they had been played by the early-twentieth-century "Hebrew" comics. Although an article about the play in the *Sioux Falls Press* noted that Bernard and Carr were "two of the best Hebrew low comedians on the stage," the Potash and Perlmutter series moved Jewish character comedy beyond the early immigrant stereotypes.[59] Clean-shaven, dressed in suits and vests, and speaking with only slight Yiddish accents, the comic duo clashed incessantly but good-naturedly with one another.

After the first Potash and Perlmutter play, Glass transferred the idea to a comedy called *Why Worry?* that opened on Broadway in 1918 and that, rather than featuring two men, focused on two women—this time operating a Jewish restaurant on Second Avenue that somehow became a favored meeting place for German spies. One of the wise-cracking waitresses (who also happens to be a daughter of the chef) was played by none other than Fanny Brice. The Avon Comedy Four (a group of comedians that included both Joe Smith and Charlie Dale) were also on hand to add to the merriment. In the second act, the proprietors exchange the immigrant hangout for an inn in Larchmont (a northern suburb of New York), which is where the Jewish owners ultimately show their loyalty to America by confounding the German spies. One reviewer scoffed that the "text and acting are just as vulgar as the people represented," and called the dialogue a "Yiddish–American version of the mind and speech of Mrs. Malaprop."[60]

Harley Erdman views the work of Montague Glass as a kind of bridge between the slapstick, rollicking humor of Weber and Fields on the one hand, and the essentially verbal humor of Groucho Marx. According to Erdman, Glass's plays marked the end of an era of explicitly "ethnic" Jewish characters on stage. In his words, Jewish characters became "less visibly present in mass culture."[61]

It is difficult, however, to see Glass's work as ethnically denatured. For even as Jewish characters shed some of their recognizably ethnic mannerisms, they still continued to perform a Jewish identity and to reflect a Jewish sensibility. Jewish New Yorkers did not "lose" their Jewishness as they began to move into the lower middle class and live in parts of the city and country other than the Lower East Side. Similarly, Jewish characters on Broadway did not become less Jewish because they no longer entirely reflected vaudeville-era stereotypes.

In fact, the popularity of the Potash and Perlmutter plays derived precisely from the fact that the characters *were* recognizably Jewish. Erdman's argument that Jews essentially disappeared from popular culture when the

immigrant caricatures (popularized by Gentiles) fell out of favor is tanta-
mount to saying that images and representations of blacks vanished from popular culture with the end of the minstrel show.

This can be seen in the penultimate Potash and Perlmutter play, *Partners
Again*. This play is especially significant because it reunited the two irascible,
wise-cracking businessmen not as garment manufacturers but as the owners
of an automobile factory. As the play's premise makes clear, Jews were no
longer exclusively associated with the clothing industry in New York, despite
the fact that they had come to dominate all phases of that business. As
Deborah Dash Moore has found, Jews were moving into many different fields
for the first time in the 1920s, including building, contracting, importing, and
publishing, since universities and professional schools limited the number of
Jews who could join the professions.

The inherent joke in having Jews in the automobile industry was that the
captain of that industry, Henry Ford, was the most influential American anti-
Semite. Ford's newspaper, the *Dearborn Independent,* accused Jews of exerting
nefarious control over almost every realm of American life—from banking to
agriculture to the theatrical industry. Ford published attacks on Jews for
ninety-one consecutive weeks beginning with an article in 1920 entitled
"The International Jew: The World's Problem," which recapitulated the main
points of the *Protocols of the Elders of Zion*—the famous anti-Semitic tract first
published in English in London in 1920. Largely on the basis of this series,
the circulation of Ford's newspaper grew tenfold from 1920 to 1924.[62]

At its height, the *Dearborn Independent*'s readership approached that of the
New York Daily News, which had the largest circulation in America.[63] Indeed,
Ford's success as a newspaper publisher coincided with the most profitable
period in his automobile company's history. The historian David Halberstam
noted that 1922, coincidentally the same year that *Partners Again* opened on
Broadway, witnessed the arrival of the "high-water mark of Ford's domination
of the market," after which an expanding Chevrolet began to eat into Ford's
profits.[64]

Partners Again thus challenged the public's preconceptions of Jews, at the
same time as it bolstered Jews' pride in their emergence from the ghetto. What
could speak better to Jewish mobility, in both its geographic and economic
senses, than casting Jews as automobile manufacturers? The play showed that
Jews were, quite literally, on the move. And at a time when technology was
transforming American life and culture, it seemed natural that Jews (who were
viewed as possessing superior intelligence) should be inventing things and
selling their inventions.

Or perhaps Jews could be shown as inventors only if those inventions
were inherently comic, as in the "inventions" of Ed Wynn, mentioned in
chapter one. The hilariously intricate contraptions of Rube Goldberg were

also examples of inventing for its own sake, for the sheer pleasure of multi-
plying complexity. For Wynn and Goldberg, it was the ridiculousness of their
contrivances that characterized Jewish genius.

The only problem is that the automobiles that Abe and Mawruss manufacture in *Partners Again* do not actually work. The running joke in the play is
that the cars are duds; the first car they sell, dubbed the "Schenckman Six," is
such a clunker that it leads to numerous lawsuits against the firm.[65] They are
then fooled by a gang of confidence men into investing in a second car, the
"Climax Four," which lands them in trouble for stock fraud. Meanwhile, Abe
tries to discourage the budding romance between Hattie, his niece, and Dan,
a young non-Jewish mechanic—and, it turns out, a former pickpocket—who
has just started working for the firm. Abe's efforts backfire to the extent that
the couple promptly become engaged. Of course it is Dan, who is reformed
from crime, who saves the day by inventing a lucrative substitute for gasoline.

One of the most telling exchanges of dialogue between Abe and Mawruss
deals with the fact that they are no longer in the clothing business. They are
discussing Dan's criminal record:

ABE: He said the young feller was a pickpocket ten years ago. You was a garment operator 20 years ago, but you got over it, didn't you?

13. Alexander Carr (Mawruss Perlmutter, standing), Adele Rolland (Hattie), and Barney
Bernard (Abe Potash) go for a spin in Montague Glass's 1922 play, *Partners Again*. Cour-
tesy of Billy Rose Theatre Collection, New York Public Library for the Performing Arts,
Astor, Lenox and Tilden Foundations.

MAWRUSS: Abe, don't make any wisecracks. You know a garment operator ain't a pickpocket.

ABE: Sure, I know, but if a garment operator could improve himself, why couldn't a pickpocket?[66]

The joke is that Abe and Mawruss have "improved themselves" and made themselves more respectable by moving out of the garment industry. They have left it, with all its shady associations, behind. The humor of the play depended in large part on the changes they rang on the older Jewish stereotypes. The newspaper critics of the day, who almost universally praised the comedy, noted that Glass was taking a gamble in changing the setting for his characters' interactions while attempting to retain his successful comic formula.

The character of the Jewish inventor continued to be a popular one. For example, Mendel Marantz in David Freedman's *Mendel, Inc.* (1929) is so dreamy and averse to earning a living that his wife goes out to work and leaves him home to do the household chores. But Mendel resists the redefinition of his gender identity; he promptly invents a machine to do the housework that is so effective that it eventually makes him rich.

Finally, in Bella and Samuel Spewack's comedy *Poppa* (1928), the title character is a Jewish insurance salesman who runs for political office on a platform of providing modern conveniences—electric refrigerators, coin telephones (called "nickel slot machines"), and garbage burners—to each of the families in his district.[67]

Upon his appointment as alderman by Jake Harris, the corrupt district leader, he is promptly framed on bribery charges, jeopardizing his daughter's marriage to an uptown Jewish suitor. Harris threatens the landlords in the Bronx to get them to stop Pincus from making too many demands: "I says: Pinky's getting the folks around here all het up. They're learning a lot of things they can get up in the Bronx. Your tenants'll move out on you."[68] For Jewish residents to have the benefits of modern life is costly for the landlords; the idea is that Jews will move back to the Lower East Side if they can have these conveniences.

One of the most interesting aspects of *Poppa* is how acculturated this particular Jewish family is. Part of this is demonstrated by their patriotism; Act 2, following Pincus's political appointment, takes place on Abraham Lincoln's birthday; portraits of Lincoln and Washington hang on the walls, and the fire escapes are decorated with flags and bunting. The stage directions describe the set in terms of an "atmosphere of sudden Second Avenue elegance." The acculturated appearance extends to the characters' dress. The father, Pincus, is initially described as wearing a "sort of shabby overcoat with collar turned up, a soft hat, pencils are stuck in his pockets, and he is carrying a much worn-out brief case, in which he carries his various insurance articles and applications." He is thus the typical American working man. When he is appointed to political office, Pincus wears a "frock coat and silk hat" in addition to his overcoat, showing how much he has come up in the world. His wife impresses the neighbors by boasting that "all day the people come to my husband for advice—like he was a dentist."[69]

The family's pretensions to upward mobility are, however, difficult to sustain. When their daughter, Ruth, becomes engaged to an uptown Jewish boy, Philip Rosenthal, his well-to-do mother is appalled by the shabbiness of the Schwitzkys' apartment and the fact that Pincus does not earn any money. She is concerned that her son will have to support the entire Schwitzky family, even though Ruth—against everyone's objections—insists that she will keep working after she is married.

The plot against Pincus is ultimately frustrated through the use of technology, in this case a Dictaphone that the Schwitzkys' ne'er-do-well son, Herbert, has ordered through the mail. The Dictaphone, it turns out, was running while Harris was threatening Pincus and engineering the frame-up. The resolution is reminiscent of Dion Boucicault's 1860 play *The Octoroon,* in which the identity of a murderer is discovered through the use of a photograph, at a time when cameras had just been invented. Ironically, until it saves Pincus's career, the Dictaphone in *Poppa* is viewed by the family as just another kind of household appliance, similar to the other labor-saving devices that Pincus is attempting to introduce on the Lower East Side.

Critical response to *Poppa* was decidedly mixed, even in the Jewish press. While a writer for the *American Hebrew* praised the play's "universalism" and said that the play had "added an unforgettably commendable portrait to the gallery of sympathetic American Jews," the critic for *Der Tog* called the play a "cheap melodrama" and lambasted the principal actors for abandoning the Yiddish stage for Broadway.[70]

CAN A NON-JEW PLAY A JEW?

However Jewish identity itself might be represented and reinvented on stage, the idea still persisted in the minds of critics (and audiences) that Jewish characters had to be played by Jews. As Alexander Carr told *Theatre Magazine,* the Jewish comic "has only to be himself and he is excruciatingly funny."[71] But what did it mean for the Jew to "be himself?" As Jews began to lose their status as racial outsiders, it became problematic to find an essentialized quality to Jewishness.

Thus critics quickly fell back on the external manifestations of Jewishness in judging actors' performances in Jewish roles. As Arthur Hornblow wrote of the star of the Broadway version of *Bronx Express,* Charles Coburn, who was a Gentile, was "badly miscast." According to Hornblow, "Outwardly, Mr.

Coburn gives a genuine impression of a Jew—his beard and clothes are representative. But here the impression ends. He lacks all the Jewish mannerisms, his movements, voice and accent are all mechanical and superficial."[72]

Sometimes, however, non-Jewish actors were praised for their spot-on impersonations of Jews. For example, Howard Lang, an Irish actor, played the wrathful old Jewish cantor in the original 1925 Broadway production of *The Jazz Singer*. A feature writer for the English-language section of *Der Tog* described Lang as "bringing home to Jew and Gentile the pathetic strength of the Jewish nature, the strength of weakness." The article continues: "His eyes are Anglo-Saxon blue and his face, when seen without make-up, is pure Nordic. Sitting in his dressing-room, after the grease-paint has come off, his manner retains absolutely nothing of the Jewish. The old father whose heart is wracked by his successful son's apparent indifference to the Jewish faith disappears entirely, giving place to a soft-voiced, easy-going American actor, who looks as if he couldn't conceive any other use for a tallith [prayer shawl] than as a silk muffler."[73]

The debate came to a head with the stage version of *Humoresque*, based on a story by Fanny Hurst that had been turned into a film. Although the film had starred a Jewish actress in the role of the long-suffering Jewish mother who raises her son to be a world-famous violinist only to see him go off to war, a non-Jew, Laurette Taylor, was cast in the role for the play. Taylor had recently starred in both the play and film of *Peg O' My Heart,* a drama about a romance between an Irish boy and girl.

The debate in the press quickly centered on whether or not Taylor was playing a Jewish woman convincingly. Heywood Broun of the *New York World* reported that "Jews don't like to see a Gentile playing a Jewish role and that Gentiles don't like to see a Gentile playing a Jewish role. This makes it practically unanimous in New York except such patronage as may be picked up from out of town Mohammedans." But most reviewers were favorably impressed, although one complained that Taylor was too thin for the role whereas Vera Gordon in the film was "Yiddish from start to finish. She was stout, she was unmistakably of the race." A *Yiddishe mama*, it seemed, had to be overweight in order to be believable. Accompanying the article was a pencil drawing of Taylor in the role with the caption: "Can you picture the charming Laurette Taylor as a middle-aged and very Yiddish mother?"[74]

In general, the Jewish critics were more accepting of Taylor's performance than the non-Jewish critics were. Having a non-Jew playing a Jewish role suggested that the differences between Jews and non-Jews were less salient than non-Jews seemed to believe. This was flattering to Jews, who saw Taylor as a role model for the way that Jewish women should act, shedding their stereotypical behaviors for a more acculturated image. As the critic for the Yiddish daily *Der Tog* wrote in his review:

14. Non-Jewish actress Laurette Taylor as the "very Jewish mother" in Fannie Hurst's 1923 play, *Humoresque*. Courtesy of Billy Rose Theatre Collection, New York Public Library for the Performing Arts, Astor, Lenox and Tilden Foundations.

Plays about Jewish life are no longer new in the American theater. They have become fashionable. . . . In general, the Jews in *Humoresque* are real people—and thank God for that. One shouldn't ask for more. The main thing is that Fanny Hurst, or Laurette Taylor, has brought forth a new type of Jewish woman, that our own Jewish mothers must go and see. They will discover the fact, that a Jewish mother can be a woman, who does not wipe her nose on her apron, who does not curse and scream until you are deaf, and speaks in moderation and to the point.[75]

Taylor, for this critic, has actually helped to redefine what a Jewish woman can be—both on stage and in life. Rather than the stereotypical screaming, cursing shrewish loudmouth, a Jewish woman can learn to act in more socially acceptable ways. The review points to how ingrained these negative stereotypes of Jewish women had become, and suggests that the fantasy of "respectable"—i.e., Americanized—behavior was one to which many immigrant Jewish women aspired. But stereotypes of the Jewish mother still persisted; another critic, reviewing a Broadway performance by the Yiddish stage actress Clara Langsner, wrote that she is "so convincing a Jewish mother that it was often quite a surprise to hear her using English words."[76]

Jewish actors themselves often maintained that their Jewishness itself was an act, a put-on. As Harley Erdman has suggested, by distancing themselves from the characters that they played, Jewish actors could escape the typecasting that plagued the Hebrew comics. Equally important, they could win recognition for their talent and for the very real efforts that they expended in creating their characters.

It was thus common for Jewish stars to profess that they had to study immigrant Jewish mannerisms. While Fanny Brice disclosed in newspaper interviews that she had to travel to the Lower East Side in order to learn the accent and gestures of her Yiddish-inflected characters, Alexander Carr said that he got his "types" from Wall Street, learning by imitation how to perform a Jewish identity. "There are hundreds of Mawruss Perlmutters in Wall Street," he told the *Sunday News*. "They retain the dialect and mannerisms. . . . I studied several of them carefully before attempting the role." An immigrant Jewish actor whose father was a Russian rabbi, thus insisted that he had to "learn" how to be authentically Jewish. Carr's experience as a circus clown—*The Sun* joked that Carr, "played true to the traditions of clergymen's and rabbis' sons by running away to join a circus"—was evidently not sufficient training to make it as a comic on Broadway.[77]

Of the "Wall Street" type, Carr told another interviewer that "You can meet a Mawruss Perlmutter on Wall Street any day. He retains his Jewish heart even though he has attained American aggressiveness. He is a poet turned fighter; a sentimentalist driven into being a soldier in the battle of life." This

"Jewish heart" came, he asserted, from a history of oppression: "It is because their inheritance of suffering and pain and privation has given them the capacity for feeling; the ability to understand the pulsations of the human heart."[78]

Being Jewish thus meant, for Carr, having experienced persecution that hardened the "Jewish heart" in a way that prepared the Jew for the competitiveness of American culture. He could thus have it both ways—being Jewish was refigured as the ideal prelude to being American. This emphasis on aggressiveness was reflected in his performances; as one critic, Percy Hammond, pointed out, Carr played the "snarling, venomous, hostile contrast to Mr. Bernard's engaging Jew," although he "modifies his previous angry disregard for Potash with an acid forbearance."[79]

THE VALUE OF ETHNIC NAMES

These performance-like elements of ethnicity are abundantly present in *Abie's Irish Rose* as well, and they pertain to both the Irish and the Jews. Recall that Abie, a young veteran from the First World War, brings home an Irish Catholic nurse, Rose Mary, whom he has already secretly married, but he is afraid to incur his father's displeasure for marrying a non-Jew. The scene in Act I in which Abie introduces Rose Mary to his father makes hay out of the identifying features of ethnicity, especially ethnic names:

SOLOMON: Vell, tell me, vhere did you learn does Irish expressions? Sure!

ROSE MARY: (*very proudly*) From my father.

SOLOMON: (*now highly suspicious*) Hah! Iss dod so?

ABIE: (*interrupting hastily*) Why yes, Dad. He was once an actor.

SOLOMON: So? Vell vot is *his* name? Is it Mary too?

ROSE MARY: My father's name Mary?

SOLOMON: You just said your name was Rose *Mary.*

ABIE: (*interrupting hastily again*) His name is Solomon!

SOLOMON: Oh! Your name is Rose Mary Solomon?

ROSE MARY: (*very indignant*) Certainly not!

SOLOMON: (*quickly*) Oh, your father's *first* name is Solomon?

ABIE: (*quickly*) Yes! (ROSE MARY *looks at him—he is too fast for her—she gasps, so quickly has Abie retorted.*)

SOLOMON: Oh! Well, Solomon vhot? (Turns to ROSE MARY.)

ROSE MARY: Murphy—(SOLOMON *looks at her quickly;* ABIE *interrupts and finishes before* ROSE MARY *knows exactly what he is doing.*)

ABIE: (*quickly*) Miss Murpheski.

SOLOMON: Murpheski! say dod's a fine nize name! Now there you are. (ROSE MARY *is so taken aback by this interruption of Abie's she is speechless.*) At first I tought you vouldn't have a name like dod! You don'd look id.

ABIE: No, she doesn't does she?
SOLOMON: *(looking at* ROSE MARY) Faces are very deceiving! . . .[80]

Abie seems to draw Rose Mary into a kind of vaudeville routine in this scene, for which she is hilariously unprepared. Abie both takes pleasure in becoming involved with a forbidden lover, and seeks to domesticate her foreign-ness to gain parental approval. By presenting Rose Murphy as Rose Murpheski, Abie may even, on one level, be expressing his own preference that she be Jewish, as if changing her name made her so. On her part, Rose tells her father that she is marrying a man named Michael Magee, making for a scene of utter confusion in Act II when the two fathers meet.

This name-changing game is especially interesting given that many Jews during the 1920s did adopt less Jewish-sounding names in an effort to conceal their ethnic identity. Even the actor playing Solomon in *Abie's Irish Rose,* Alfred Weisman, changed his name during the play's run—to Alfred White. An article by Sidney Kluger in the *Brooklyn Jewish Chronicle* that was published during the play's run carried the amusing headline: "O Tempora! O Mores! And is 'Caine' Better Than 'Cohen' and Why," with the subhead "Voltaire's Comedie Re-Enacted as Cohens and Epsteins Seek Salvation By Changing Names."[81]

This meta-theatrical element of the comedy suggests a major reason that ethnic comedy was unsettling to mainstream observers; at a time of widespread animosity toward ethnic Americans, ethnicity was not a social category that could be as easily assigned as it appeared. A story in *Theatre Magazine* called "The Melting Plot" demonstrated what the magazine thought most theater-goers would find funny. Harry Shapiro (who speaks, rather oddly, with an accent that sounds more cockney than Yiddish) visits an upscale lawyer named Mr. Cheyney-Haverlie in order, for both professional and social reasons, to have his name changed to something that sounds less Jewish. After hearing a number of possibilities, including some especially prestigious hyphenated ones, Shapiro settles on Talbot Traymore, knowing that no one will mistake this ultra-WASPy moniker for a Jewish name.[82]

THE MOVEMENT OUT OF THE GHETTO

Moving out of the ghetto now became a theme in its own right in Broadway entertainment. Jews (who constituted 29 percent of the New York City population in the early 1920s) were indeed beginning to move from the lower class into the lower middle class. It is noteworthy that *Abie's Irish Rose,* which in an early typescript version was set in a squalid tenement area in "a part of the Lower East Side of years ago," opened on Broadway with a very different set: a spacious living room (adjacent to a conservatory) dominated by curving wood staircases and a large crystal chandelier.[83]

Rather than opening (as in the manuscript) with Solomon Levy standing "motionless in the doorway of his little store" with an attitude of "looking back into the past," the Broadway production is described in the Samuel French edition as set in "the home of a New York business man, a prosperous one." The chandelier is a reminder of the past only in the sense that it is described as "very ornate of the New York gas and electricity combined period."[84]

Thus, despite his Yiddish accent, crass comments, and occupation as a clothes peddler, Solomon Levy is introduced to Broadway audiences as a resident of an upper-middle-class apartment.[85] A huge reproduction of the set was used in a billboard advertisement for the production opposite the Concourse Plaza Hotel in the Bronx, in an area where tens of thousands of second-generation Jews were relocating in the early 1920s. The production wooed Bronx Jews by symbolically bringing the play to them, and showing them how much it mirrored their own experience and aspirations. The life-size figures in the huge diorama were shown in the positions of the characters for the Jewish wedding in the second act.[86]

Theater and reality sometimes became difficult to separate. Were second-generation Jews modeling their lives on what they saw on the stage, or was the stage simply reflecting the reality of Jewish acculturation and social mobility? Deborah Dash Moore has noted how closely the Art Deco–inspired apartment houses on the Grand Concourse, built and inhabited largely by Jews, resembled stage sets for Broadway productions. The lavish designs of these apartment houses, some of which have been preserved, demonstrate the desire of second-generation Jews to flatter their sense of having truly "arrived" in American culture.[87]

Moving out of ghetto tenements into more spacious surroundings in Harlem, Brooklyn, or the Grand Concourse was an important prerequisite for enhancing both quality of life and social class. Social historian Jenna Weissman Joselit has found that: "Beginning in the years preceding World War I and accelerating in its aftermath a growing number of upwardly mobile East European Jews and their children, the so-called 'second generation,' exchanged Lower East Side tenements for modern elevator apartments or private homes in the Bronx, Brooklyn or Manhattan. As much a social phenomenon as an individual one, moving away from the Lower East Side characterized an entire generation."[88]

But the second generation acculturated into American society by consuming cultural products in addition to material ones. Andrew Heinze has argued that the consumption of material goods was an important path to acculturation for American Jews in the late nineteenth and early twentieth centuries. How products were advertised and marketed, he writes, influenced Jewish consumers by playing on their desire to be viewed as, and view

15 Photo of diorama, displayed as advertisement above the Grand Concourse in the Bronx, of the set for second act wedding scene in Anne Nichols's 1922 play, *Abie's Irish Rose*. Courtesy of Billy Rose Theatre Collection, New York Public Library for the Performing Arts, Astor, Lenox and Tilden Foundations.

themselves as, Americans. According to Heinze, Jews "relied on their awareness of the symbolic potential of special products as they searched for a tangible American identity."[89] Although Heinze deals only incidentally with
popular culture, the theater was a sphere that held a great deal of "symbolic
potential" to flatter second-generation Jews' newfound social standing.

But second-generation Jews still felt ambivalent about upward mobility
when it seemed to threaten the cohesiveness of the Jewish community. The
movement away from the ghetto, as explored in chapter one, also meant a
departure from what seemed, in nostalgic retrospect, the most tightly-knit
community second-generation Jews had known.

Aaron Hoffman's *Two Blocks Away,* which opened on Broadway on
August 30, 1921, at the George M. Cohan Theatre, shows the negative con-
sequences for a kindly shoemaker when he inherits a large sum of money and
moves away from his Lower East Side neighborhood. John Corbin of the *New
York Times* wrote that the comedy was "frankly and shrewdly designed to meet
the public taste—to delight the same public that reveled in Mr. Hoffman's
Welcome Stranger."[90]

The shoemaker, Nate Pommerantz, was played by Barney Bernard, celebrated for his portrayals of Abe Potash in the *Potash and Perlmutter* series.
Bernard's character had formerly given charity to all who were in need, but
becomes mean and tight-fisted when he comes into a large inheritance.
Although a whole crowd gathers around him when the news of the inheritance is announced, Nate disdains his former friends, moves to a palatial apartment in what the stage directions say is an "aristocratic section" (probably
Gramercy Park), and concentrates on accumulating wealth. Nate's addiction
to prescription medicines is the sign that he has lost both his bodily vigor and
his powers of self-control. When, toward the end of the play he smashes a
mirror that shows him his now-intolerable reflection, he frees himself from
materialism, and he can resume his relationship with the beloved daughter he
has alienated.

The physical mirror that reflects the character's moral infirmities (a
device reminiscent, of course, of Oscar Wilde's novel *The Picture of Dorian
Gray*) is symbolic of the ways in which the stage itself reflected to the largely
Jewish audience—Bernard's "congregation"—its own culture. Pommerantz's
daughter, Jane, finally chooses the people of the Lower East Side over her
stubborn father, who wants to repudiate them. When she does so, the stage
direction says—for the sole time in the play—that she "faces the audience."
Jane declares that she is "not going to lose them, for money, or anything, or
anybody."[91] Pommerantz's decision to move away from the immigrant neighborhood to satisfy his own longings for upward social mobility is intended to
register as a kind of betrayal of his people.

Although the friends and neighbors might themselves be seen as interested only in Pommerantz's money, the play does not satirize them in any way; it only pokes holes in Pommerantz's pretensions and self-delusions. The smashing of the mirror marks Pommerantz's being recalled to his senses, but it also paradoxically restores the ruptured relationship between the character and his community. At the time, by providing a neat climax to the play, it helped the audience *avoid* reflecting on the ways in which it might actually be more loyal to the misguided Pommerantz than to the supposedly clear-thinking Pommerantz. At a time when Jews were acculturating into American society partly by their consumption of material goods, the idea of giving up physical comforts to reidentify with the ethnic group was a problematic one.

On a conscious level, however, the audience seemed to see the smashing of the mirror as a vindication and a triumph. The action was so climactic that it led to an interruption in the play: Hammond wrote that when Bernard smashed the mirror, "he was urged at that point to address the audience," which, according to Hammond, "he did with becoming modesty and eloquence."[92] The onstage action was so powerful that it somehow seemed to necessitate the actor stepping out of his role and consolidating his bond with the audience.

Jews and Consumer Culture

The seductive lure of American capitalism for Jewish immigrants and their families is explored even more explicitly in *The Bronx Express;* the play, most of which took place on a subway train, was a hit in its original, Yiddish incarnation but a flop on Broadway. Written by Osip Dymov, a Russian Jewish playwright who was best known for a play about the Old Country called *Yoshke Musikant, The Bronx Express* focused on the contest between traditional Jewish values and assimilated American "capitalist" values. The play uses many English words (transliterated into Yiddish in the playscript) to show the characters' attempts to absorb American culture.

The central character in *The Bronx Express* is Khatskl (later Harry) Hungerproud, an immigrant buttonmaker who has moved his family to a Jewish neighborhood in the Bronx called Bronx Park, but who continues to work at a factory on the Lower East Side. In the play's prologue, he is traveling home from work one evening when he meets an old friend, Yankl (now renamed Jake) Flames, on the subway. Flames tells him all about the world of manufacturing and high finance. Poking fun at Hungerproud's loyalty to family and faith, Flames points to the fictional characters who adorn the advertising posters for consumer products—Aunt Jemima (of Aunt Jemima Pancakes), the Nestlé Baby (of Nestlé Baby Foods), the Smith Brothers (of Smith Brothers Cough Drops), and so on. He tells Hungerproud how many millions of dollars these "people" have earned, and tries to entice Hunger-proud to sell himself, his wife, and the Jewish people for money.

In the first act, Flames comes to Hungerproud's home in Bronx Park, where he is eating Sabbath dinner. Flames persuades him to abandon his family for the "high windows" of Wall Street and Fifth Avenue. The second act takes place at the mansion of the "Mr. Pluto Corporation" (of Pluto Mineral Water, represented by a devil with a red tail), where Hungerproud meets the characters from the subway advertisements, who have magically come to life. He falls in love with Miss Murad, a dancing harem girl who represents Turkish cigarettes. The third act finds Hungerproud at a beach resort, Atlantic City, where he has married Miss Murad. Murad has given birth to the Nestlé Baby, whom he pushes in a carriage. Hungerproud's family shows up; his daughter is romanced by one of the Smith Brothers. But Hungerproud has pangs of conscience and tries to drown himself; he is saved by Flames. When Hungerproud's wife, Sara, shows up and accuses him of bigamy, he pleads to go back to his former life. As the Pluto Devil prepares to lynch him for his misdeeds, Hungerproud wakes up on the subway and realizes that everything has been a dream.

Dymov's play focuses on how both workers and products circulate in a modern capitalist economy. But by using figures of American commerce as evil spirits, *Bronx Express* contains fully as many demons and devils as the works of Yiddish drama that focused on the superstitions that held sway over the Jews in the Old Country—plays like Jacob Gordin's *God, Man and Devil* and David Pinski's *The Treasure*. Yet the play broke new ground in realism on the Yiddish stage in its exact reproduction of a car from the old White Plains Road line of the subway, which had a terminus in the Jewish neighborhood of Bronx Park. This realistic framework contrasted with the surrealistic quality of the work to produce a strong impression of a world out of kilter.

This can be seen most clearly in Boris Aronson's set and costume designs for a 1925 revival at the Unser Theatre in the Bronx. The ceiling of the subway train, with its hanging straps for riders to hold, remained on the set even as what surrounded it changed to reflect the places Hungerproud traveled to in his dream. The demonic figures of American commerce were leering, grinning gargoyles who looked like they had stepped out of a German expressionist film like *The Cabinet of Dr. Caligari*. In fact, Aronson's costume designs were so powerful that the star actor, Rudolph Schildkraut, complained that he had nothing to do; he was upstaged by his own costume![93] Still, by emphasizing the importance of packaging, for both people and products, Aronson's designs intensified the play's indictment of capitalism as a system based on surfaces and visual allure.

In Act 2, Hungerproud figures out a way to betray the Jews in the most effective way. In the original Yiddish play, retranslated recently by Nahma Sandrow, the text is as follows:

16. Photo of subway car and actors in Osip Dymov's 1922 play, *Bronx Express.* Courtesy of Billy Rose Theatre Collection, New York Public Library for the Performing Arts, Astor, Lenox and Tilden Foundations.

HUNGERPROUD: Make the Jews work on Yom Kippur. *(Thunderclap.)* Make an agreement with all the shops, all the factories, downtown, uptown, that day they pay the Jews double, triple, ten times. They'll work Yom Kippur too.

PLUTO: Jews love money.

HUNGERPROUD: Sure, Jews love money. This one has a sick child and has to buy medicine. That one has an old father or mother or just an old rebbe who can't work but wants to eat anyway, or a wife exhausted in the kitchen from hard work. Or relatives in misery back home. Yes, yes, Jews do love money. They'll work Yom Kippur too.

PLUTO: Go on, go on.

HUNGERPROUD: Yom Kippur breaks down, everything breaks down. No holidays, no religion, no tradition, one big pot of schmaltz. Everyone cooked in the same pot. The iron grinder grinds them all up together, with the Poles, Italians, Chinese, Japanese, Negroes—everything thrown in the iron wheels. Wheels and people—a machine with no holidays, no language, no traditions—a great mass of workers that works and buys, works and buys, and eats, and chews, and swallows. Two for a quarter, five for a dozen. The nicest, the best, delicious, you need it. Historical process, capital and labor.[94]

Pluto is so enraptured with the idea that he asks Hungerproud to sign over the rights to it; when Hungerproud refuses, he distracts him (by having Miss Murad dance a lustful dance) and "signs" by moving Hungerproud's hand over the paper. The betrayal of the Jews is complete. The linchpin of Jewish identity is seen as the Day of Atonement, when Jews are supposed to seek forgiveness for their sins.

The idea of the melting pot was not new, of course. It was the Anglo-Jewish writer Israel Zangwill whose play *The Melting Pot* (first performed in 1908 in Washington, D.C.; it later ran in Chicago and toured the country before coming to Broadway in 1909) popularized what became a very influential idea in American culture. The immigrant Jewish hero of that play, the violinist David Quixano, sees the melting pot as the crucible in which the hatreds and antagonisms of the Old World are burned away. (The image is of dross being refined into gold.) In Zangwill's play, the melting pot is an agent for the regeneration of mankind. Dymov's take on the metaphor is obviously quite different; he satirizes the melting pot as a big pot of "schmaltz," the chicken fat in which many traditional Eastern European Jewish foods were cooked. The idea that Yom Kippur, a holiday when Jews fast, is to be a day for a kind of infernal "cooking" only adds to the irony.[95]

Dymov's perspective is unabashedly socialistic. In his satire, Jews will become indistinguishable from other ethnic groups, and all Americans will become animalistic engines for consumption. The loss of religion will remove from Jews what makes them Jewish and detach from all Americans what makes them human. The soulless machine will destroy the souls of American workers.

Other (non-Yiddish) American plays of the 1920s employed expressionistic devices, like Elmer Rice's *The Adding Machine* (featuring the unforgettable character Mr. Zero) and Eugene O'Neill's *The Hairy Ape*. These plays blamed society for depriving the individual of his or her identity partly by detaching him or her from membership in a community. In fact, as Dymov recognized, the American industrial system makes the maintenance of a stable identity contingent on endless consumption, fueled by an insatiable need—instilled by advertisers—for new products. As Flames puts it, in trying to get Hungerproud to leave home and eat a (non-kosher) meal on Broadway, "When you eat just one meal there, you'll realize that all your life you've been hungry."

Most first- and second-generation Jews would have agreed; they valorized consumption. As the social historian Andrew Heinze has argued, American Jews acculturated into American society in the early part of the twentieth century by joining the consumer culture. Jews climbed into the lower middle class partly by buying the clothes, housewares, furnishings, musical instruments, and other symbols of middle-class life. An emphasis on consumption transformed even Jewish religious observance; ready access to higher quality food throughout the week made Sabbaths and holidays (when families traditionally ate special foods) seem more ordinary. Also, many Jews felt compelled to work on Saturdays in order to be able to support their families. The boundaries between sacred and profane began in critical ways to dissolve.

Bronx Express was translated by the author and by Samuel Golding for its Broadway production. It was produced by Charles Coburn, who also starred as Hungerproud. The original version had incorporated English words to show the characters in the process of assimilation; conversely, the English translation preserved a number of Yiddish expressions—mostly for humorous effect. For example, when Hungerproud meets the Wrigley Brothers, he exclaims: "*Gott in himmel! Rabena shelalom! Ich seh eppes bekantes!* I'm glad to meet you boys! How many times I chewed you."[96] The play seems to be poking fun at itself here, pointing to the ridiculousness of the situation.

In fact, the Broadway version takes itself much more lightly than the Yiddish one. When Hungerproud enters the Pluto mansion in Act 2, the new stage directions show him dressed in "sporty modern clothes slightly exaggerated in the latest fashion, patent leather shoes, purple silk stockings, a gardenia in his buttonhole, and a purple silk handkerchief showing from his coat pocket." Unlike in the Yiddish version, he is asking to be laughed at for his attempt to "Americanize" himself.

But just a few pages later, he is assailed by Flames not for being too American, but for being too Jewish. "You must forget your kykish ideas," Flames says. "They would laugh at you on Broadway." Perhaps it is no wonder, with such a contradictory image, that he character does not know if he is coming or going throughout so much of the play. Hungerproud continues to be insulted by him: "I have become a real American, a live wire, a regular guy—efficiency! And you are still a Bronx Jew."[97] Hungerproud may live in an apartment in the Bronx, but it is not the kind of upper-middle-class apartment that Solomon Levy inhabits in *Abie's Irish Rose*. It is closer to how the majority of second-generation Jews actually lived at the time, especially in the East Bronx (as opposed to the Art Deco buildings of the Grand Concourse, described above)—a step up from the ghetto tenements but not necessarily a fancy apartment house.

The voice of the past is Hungerproud's old teacher, Reb Kalman Lippe, who lives with him and who warns that he is not considering the true costs of Americanization: "Ah, Chatskel, you have forsaken everything—even Yom Kippur! And once that is forsaken, everything is forsaken! No holidays! No traditions! No memories!" The result, he tells Hungerproud, is that "You will see your son shine shoes in the streets and he will be whistling the Broadway melodies!"[98] As in *The Jazz Singer,* to sing American show tunes rather than Yiddish songs is presented as the ultimate form of assimilation.

In general, changes in the Broadway version seem to reflect the requirements of entertaining a broader audience beyond the Yiddish-speaking one. For example, Hungerproud's infidelity is dwelled upon at length; he has a long scene with his wife in which she asks him to throw Miss Murad down the stairs. (She is especially incensed by a revelation from Miss Murad that Hungerproud told her he "ruined a lot of women in the subway"—a feat that is difficult to imagine, but perhaps testifies to the associations the express train had with sexuality.) When he refuses, they decide to divorce, with Flames suggesting that he would like to marry Sarah. At this point, Sarah calls Miss Murad a "vampire, a Theda Bara," reflecting her knowledge of American culture. Later, in the last act, Hungerproud calls the crying Nestlé baby a "Caruso" and resists the blandishments of Sarah attempting to regain his affection by showing him how well she has learned to "shee-mee" to jazz music.[99] And in the discussion of the melting pot, Hungerproud resolves to eliminate not just Rosh Hashanah and Yom Kippur, but also Columbus Day, Good Friday, and St. Patrick's Day.

But the production was much less successful on Broadway than it had been in its original version. The mainstream critics were harsh: they found the play to be a bit of a mess. As Arthur Hornblow wrote in *Theatre Magazine*, *The Bronx Express* was an "unconvincing *pot-pourri* of melodrama, symbolism, musical comedy, brogue and vaudeville."[100] The play was clearly intended to be a comedy of some sort, but it was hardly a vaudeville-style Jewish entertainment. It thus confounded the critical categories used to judge Jewish comedy.

However, the critic for the Yiddish newspaper *Der Tog* (*The Day*) recommended the Broadway production highly, calling it "wholly amusing and surprising" and writing that the dream sequences in particular were "brought out more vividly on the English stage than on the Yiddish one" and that it was "richer and livelier" in spirit. He concluded that the play deserved to be seen, even by those who had taken great pleasure in the play's Yiddish version.[101] Critics for the Yiddish press thus did not automatically prefer the Yiddish version of a play over the English-language version, if they deemed the English-language one to be more stageworthy. They also seem to have taken pleasure in seeing Yiddish plays performed in English by well-known American actors, whether Jewish or not.

INTERMARRIAGE ON STAGE

But true integration into American society in economic and social terms raised the specter of the loosening of the ties to the Jewish community through marrying non-Jews. This was portrayed as a ridiculous fantasy in *Bronx Express,* but it quickly became more. Beginning with *Abie's Irish Rose,* intermarriage, particularly between the Jews and the Irish, became a staple of 1920s American Jewish theater and film.

Despite his Gentile appearance, Abie is presented as still very connected to the world of his fathers. Much of this, of course, has to do with his desire to please (or, at any rate, not displease) his father; this is why he cannot bring himself to tell Solomon that Rose Mary is not Jewish. His need to remain close to his father seems to indicate a desire to continue his ties to his father's religion and ethnicity as well. This is true on his wife's side; she has a similar relationship with her own father, and permits herself to be remarried by a priest just as Abie has permitted himself to be remarried by a rabbi. The couple shows respect for each other's religion, not a desire to abandon their individual religious and cultural identities. This seems most apparent at the end of the play, with one baby named after one grandfather and the second baby named after the other grandfather. Abie's insistence on kosher food, but willingness to have ham served to his wife's guests, is also a statement of balancing continued loyalty to Jewish tradition with respect for the differing customs of his wife's family and friends.

From Shylock's daughter's elopement with a Gentile in Shakespeare's *The Merchant of Venice,* to the intermarriage between the young violinist and his Gentile girlfriend in Israel Zangwill's *The Melting Pot,* Jews often intermarried on stage. But *Abie's Irish Rose* was the first play to combine vaudeville ethnic routines with an intermarriage plot to manufacture ethnic comedy. Intermarriage became so associated with Jewish comedy that Samuel Kuhn, critic for *The Jewish Forum,* noted in his review of Martha Stanley's *My Son* (1925) that although the play was about the Portuguese and New Englanders of Cape Cod, it "has a Jewish theme—intermarriage!"[102]

Comic treatment thus softened even the prickly theme of intermarriage; a review of the Utica, New York, production two years later hailed Nichols's play for the fact that "You are never asked to become tense and thoughtful over this intermarriage problem, nor to decide whether it is right or wrong." This did not prevent a lively debate in the Jewish community about intermarriage, but many Jews felt intermarriage did not threaten the survival of Judaism; Rabbi Nathan Krass of Temple Emanu-El in New York weighed in with the opinion that Jews could not shed their ethnic identity even if they wished to. In any case, the rate of Jewish out-marriage was extremely low, and remained so until the 1960s. As the sociologist Julius Drachsler found, in his study of marriage records in 1920, the rate of second-generation Jewish out-marriage was only about a tenth of the intermarriage rate for the children of immigrants in general (3.6 percent compared to 32 percent).[103]

Ironically, as Riv-Ellen Prell has pointed out in her analysis of the 1928 film version of *Abie's Irish Rose*, intermarriage in popular culture was idealized in a way that images of Jewish marriage never were; Jewish men and women were on a collision course with each other's societally produced expectations that compromised the success of their unions. Jews, qua Jews, were thus in danger of becoming victims to their own success in the marriage market. Prell's thesis is that Jewish men displaced both the anti-Semitism they encountered in American society and the burdensome expectations of material success that society used as a measure of masculinity onto Jewish women, whom they experienced as domineering, narcissistic, and preoccupied with gaining wealth and social status. "As Americans looked upon Jews as marginal, obsessed with money, uncivil, and unworthy of citizenship," she writes, "Jewish men and middle-class Jews projected those very accusations onto Jewish women and the working class."[104]

Nevertheless, it was through becoming accepted by the mainstream culture that Jews sought, paradoxically, to validate their ethnic distinctiveness. *Abie's Irish Rose* is a comedy not about assimilation, but about acculturation—conformity to cultural norms *without* utter loss of ethnic identity. Jenna Weissman Joselit has written that *Abie's Irish Rose* not only "validated the notion of intermarriage" but "dramatized the promise of America" in its suggestion that love conquers ethnic division.[105]

MIXING ETHNICITIES

Abie's Irish Rose spawned a host of imitators, both on stage and in film, which attempted to duplicate its success. One was Leon de Costa's musical comedy *Kosher Kitty Kelly,* which opened in June 1925. A more interesting, although much less popular work than *Abie's Irish Rose,* it was also later made into a film. The musical centers on an Irish girl, Kitty Kelly, who dates a Jewish boy named Morris Rosen while her friend, Rosie Feinbaum, has an Irish beau by the name of Pat O'Reilly. Rounding out the mix of ethnic characters is a Chinese man, Wang Lee, who speaks dreadful pidgin English. Rather than presenting a clash between immigrant fathers, the musical showed a conflict between the Jewish widow and Irish widow, each of whom disapproves of her daughter's choice. Interestingly, unlike *Abie's Irish Rose,* the story did not end in intermarriage; the Irish girl ended up with the Irish boy, and the Jewish girl with the Jewish boy.

Also unlike *Abie's Irish Rose,* none of the characters live in upscale apartment houses. But Morris Rosen is one of the first Jewish doctors in American Jewish drama; he just finished his medical training when the play begins. The décor of both mothers' apartments seems to betray no more than a lower-middle-class lifestyle; the same set is used for both, and is described in the stage directions as "showing bad taste in everything displayed. Each item seems to have been bought lately and in a different store."[106] But at a time when quotas on law and medical school admissions limited the number of

Jews permitted to study for such professions, Morris seems destined for a higher class position than most second-generation Jews.

Despite the proliferation of different ethnic characters in *Kosher Kitty Kelly,* the play seems to take place mostly in a Jewish milieu. This is especially apparent in the second act, which is set in Ginsburg's Delicatessen. The good-natured deli owner, Moses Ginsburg, his speech peppered with Yiddish expressions, doubles as a *shadchan,* or marriage broker. But, as many shop owners evidently did during Prohibition, he also sells bootleg liquor in the guise of milk. Ginsburg's store is a meeting point for the neighborhood; he seems to assume that his customers are Jewish and is surprised to learn that two visiting vaudevillians, Joe and Zella Barnes, are actually Greek. When Ginsburg is asked by Rosie's mother to help her find a Jewish boy for her daughter, Ginsburg tries to convince Rosie to give up her Irish boyfriend:

GINSBURG: It will never work. Perhaps he'll like you and you love him, but his folks won't like you and your folks won't like him, and that's the end.

ROSIE: But I'm not marrying his folks.

GINSBURG: But you must have their respect. You cannot afford to lose your mother's love, and that's what will happen. She is too old fashioned to change her ideas now, she has lived too long among her own to become used to new ideas.

ROSIE: But why shouldn't his folks love me?

GINSBURG: I heard once that some crazy cat nursed dog kittens, but it came out after that she did it only when people watched her. As soon as they turned, she scratched them! What a clever cat!

ROSIE: Mr. Ginsburg, your ideas are as old fashioned as my mother's. I'm not going to listen to you.

GINSBURG: But I could find you such a nice jewish [*sic*] boy who would love you to death.

ROSIE: I'm sure he would be the death of me. Mr. Ginsburg, I'm beginning to dislike our people more every day.

GINSBURG: You should be spanked for that, Rosie. Our people are fine people and can take care of themselves, and if other races don't want to mingle with ours, we can get along without them as well as they get along without us. It's fifty-fifty.[107]

Although Ginsburg pleads for Rosie to marry a Jew based on respect for her parents (with the words "Jew" and "Jewish" printed with lower-case "j"s throughout the script, in an apparent attempt by the playwright to democratize the various ethnicities), Rosie reveals the self-hating side of her Jewishness. Ginsburg immediately interprets her negative feelings about Jews to be internalized anti-Semitism, and expresses his own contempt toward anti-Semitic Gentiles. Ironically, Rosie is derogatory about Jewishness but Kitty

Kelly "affirms" it; a songwriter hears of Kitty's sobriquet and writes a song about her, paving the way to a stage career. Kitty can take pride in an ethnic label as long as the label is a joke; everyone knows that she is not really Jewish. The pleasure comes in the performance of the identity, not in the reality of it.

Despite the lack of intermarriage at the end of the play, the highly contrived conclusion still incorporates a symbolic double mix of ethnic identities. A fire in Rosie's mother's apartment, where Kitty's mother was visiting, badly scars both widows' faces. Morris volunteers to have some of his skin grafted onto Kitty's mother's face, while Pat volunteers to have some of his skin grafted onto Rosie's mother's face. As grateful as they are, the Irish mother is as concerned about her newfound "Jewishness" as the Jewish mother is about her involuntarily acquired "Irishness."[108] The grafted skin is viewed as a magical mask that changes its wearer's identity. Unlike the masks Jews wear on Purim, which disguise the wearer only in the context of the observation of the holiday (the wearing of the mask is paradoxically what *identifies* the celebrant, not what excuses him or her from the performance of the ritual), the skin grafts in *Kosher Kitty Kelly* partially but indelibly alter the women's ethnicities.

When Morris and Kitty come home late at night from a date, Lee leans out the window to complain, "Velly sleepy—Ilish makee noise allee time."[109] Although the Jewish and Irish characters constantly make fun of each other's speech, beliefs, and customs, they are united in looking down on the Chinese character. In fact, Lee is presented as both unassimilable into American society *and* a misfit in a Jewish neighborhood; he orders tea and "lice" from Ginsburg's Delicatessen. (He later realizes that gefilte fish is not as different from his native cuisine as he had anticipated.)

Nevertheless, the animosity between ethnic groups in the play goes far beyond *Abie's Irish Rose* in its virulence. Rosie's mother, Sarah, announces at one point that she is going to a "patriotic meeting—anti-Greek, anti-Catholic and anti-Irish," under the banner, "America for the jews." Wang Lee counters that he will "fool [the] foleign devils" that "makee noisee allee nightie" by lighting "punk" to smoke them out. His meeting is of the "tong," or Chinese Mafia, that he hopes will kill the foreigners and leave "Amellica" for the Chinese. As Ginsburg asks in exasperation, "Why can't you fellows be peaceful? The Irish dislike the jews—the jews the catholics—the chinks fight the japs—the protestants fight the Irish—It's just like a big fighting arena."[110] The ideal of ethnic tolerance that animated *Abie's Irish Rose* is ultimately absent from *Kosher Kitty Kelly,* even though the play ends with the characters coexisting in harmony.

As Michael Rogin suggests in *Blackface/White Noise,* Jews gained greater acceptance in American society partly by demonstrating their difference from

17. Deli owner Robert Leonard (Max Ginsburg) and customer Helen Shipman (Kitty Kelly) in Leon da Costa's 1925 musical, *Kosher Kitty Kelly*. Courtesy of Billy Rose Theatre Collection, New York Public Library for the Performing Arts, Astor, Lenox and Tilden Foundations.

an even lower social category—that which blacks belonged to. But although Jews were seen in nineteenth-century America as "Orientals," (Rogin points out that the first Yiddish theater in New York was called the Oriental), the "Semitic race" and the "Oriental race" were not viewed identically. Chinese immigrants had come to the United States beginning in the 1840s, where they became quickly identified with the transcontinental railroads that they helped to build.

But in New York, despite the presence of a Chinese community in what was called the "Five Points" section (which is present-day Chinatown), Asian immigrants constituted a much smaller percentage of the population than people of Irish, Jewish, and Italian descent. By the mid-1920s, the Chinese were in the benighted social position that these other ethnic groups were just climbing out of. Just as second-generation Jews found humor in the accents and Yiddish words that they themselves had eliminated from their speech, the Jewish and Irish characters in *Kosher Kitty Kelly* could take pleasure in making fun of a Chinese man who has not been successfully acculturated.

The reviews for the comedy were fairly negative, with the *New York World* complaining that it "sets to musical farce all the ancient wheezes about what the Irishman said to the Jew." The *New York Herald Tribune* was even harsher, saying that the "aimless incoherence of this bit of June imbecility was addressed to an illustration of the ways of the New York melting pot." The reviewer viewed de Costa as "thumbing his nose to Abie's Irish Rose, in that he caused the Irish to be married to the Irish and the Jews to the Jews, a pleasant dramatic surprise." But overall, he found the play to unfold in a "cadaverous environment" and found little to praise other than the fact that "there was a good horn-blower in the band, and the usher who showed me to my chair was shapely and courteous."[111] The Jewish publications seem to have ignored the play altogether, which is unsurprising since few of them reviewed *Abie's Irish Rose,* either.

In a sequel to *Kosher Kitty Kelly* entitled *Kitty Kelly's Kids,* de Costa has the daughter of Kitty and Pat, Nellie O'Reilly, marry a Jewish prizefighter named Toni (he uses an Italian name for what Nellie concedes are "business reasons"). Their wedding, along with a wedding between Nellie's brother, Mike, and an Irish girl, are both celebrated in what has now become Ginsburg's Kosher Night Club. ("Two Irish weddings in a kosher night club," quips the proprietor.) But the ethnic mixing goes beyond even the intermarriage; Mike O'Reilly has started a printing firm with a Jew named Morris Silverstein; they start by publishing a Jewish newspaper but end up with a combined Jewish-Irish paper, reading "Jewish Outlook" on the back and "Irish Freedom" on the front. ("In the printing business you can always look out for your type," puns Ginsburg.) The mixing of ethnicities seems so promiscuous that at one point Ginsburg jokes that he is attempting to become "engaged to a nice Schecho [sic]-Slovakian girl to make things complete. Ha! Melting Pot—Beef stew."[112]

JEWS IN THE WILD WEST

The impulse to overdo Jewish stereotypes also doomed the success of Fanny Brice's first foray into "straight" comedy, a vehicle called *Fanny* that was written for her by Willard Mack and David Belasco. The play was set on a ranch in the West, and Brice, playing the character of Fanny Fiebaum from the Lower East Side, played the romantic heroine. Traveling to Arizona as the companion of Leah Mendoza, the elderly sister of the recently deceased Jewish owner of the ranch, Fanny finds herself caught up in a mystery surrounding the disappearance of the deceased man's money. In *Fanny,* Brice did a kind of fish out of water act not dissimilar to the early 1990s television show *Northern Exposure,* about a young Jewish doctor in Alaska. As in *Kosher Kitty Kelly,* a Chinese character provides some of the comedy by his accent and ignorance of English. Jewish food is again the subject of humor. In this case, the Chinese character is actually the cook, High Low, who says things like: "You likee noodle soup—me fix good."[113] Fanny later praises High Low's *tzimmis,* or carrot pudding.

Fanny quickly realizes that things are not what they seem. Suspecting that one of the cowhands by the name of Joe is Jewish, she speaks Yiddish to him, calling him a *chazzer* (pig). When he fails to respond, Fanny complains to Leah that "It's queer. Something is phoney . . . or I am *mashuger* [crazy]. . . . I got a hunch that every one of them fellers in something they ain't. A Chinaman cooks kosher, and a Jew says he's a *goy* [non-Jew]."[114] Below the surface, Fanny perceives, the seemingly Gentile atmosphere of the ranch is pervaded with *Yiddishkayt*—the people she meets are much more Jewish than they seem. Her presence seems to activate the Jewishness of the people around her. When Jose turns out not only to be Jewish, but to be a detective in disguise, the victory for the Jewish characters is complete.

Nonetheless, what the producers called a "melodramatic comedy" was suited to Brice only in so far as it permitted her to reprise her immigrant Jewish vaudeville personas. In Act 2, she does a telephone routine similar to "Cohen on the Telephone," in which she places a telephone order, on a party line, with a drug store: "Vot? I won't tell you who is dis until you tell me who is dot. Will you please get off—you are on a busy wire—hello, operator—give me seven, two, Party J. Hello, is dis the drug store? Oh, the drug store is in the grocery store! Well, have you got camomile tea—cam—not camels, she don't smoke. Camomile tea for the stummick—sure, send it up, Miss Menoza, X.Y. ranch—how much will it cost to send it up here? Vot? Cancel it!"[115]

Despite her surroundings, Brice's character still acted as if she were back on the Lower East Side. A writer who interviewed Brice for *Der Tog* at the time that *Fanny* premiered wrote that when he saw her in her new role, she appeared "in every aspect like a Jewish shop girl, with a modest Jewish grace amidst the vulgarity of trade . . . a typical Jewish tenement house dweller who spends her days in the shop and her nights in a cheap cabaret."[116]

Her attempts to play a romantic heroine was disturbing to the critics, for whom she was typecast as a clown. To the critics, it was if a comic strip character had come to life and tried to act a serious role. It was bound to fall flat. As Gilbert Gabriel wrote in the *Sun, Fanny* "marks Miss Brice's enlistment among active Belasco forces. It is likewise her entry into legitimate drama. So they label it a 'melodramatic comedy,' sprinkle it with gunplay, mystery and Yiddish bywords—and it is none the less a vaudeville. . . . The seams of the plot must allow plenty of room for clowning, cluckling [sic] and Yeedling of Miss Brice's famous Music Box sort. They must give a Zionist tinge to an Arizona ranchland, must have Jewish lullabies crooned, Hester street burlesques strewn all over the great open spaces."[117]

Serious plays about Jewish life, with the notable exception of *Welcome Stranger,* were rarely set in locales outside New York. Brice is seen as "homesick" because she is viewed as outside her normal territory as a performer, in both physical and cultural terms. The idea that the Wild West would be colonized by Jews seemed absurd to many critics, despite the fact that Jews had been peddlers in the Western states for almost a century; many had built themselves up into successful businessmen, bankers, and manufacturers.[118] For

18. Fanny Brice in Willard Mack and David Belasco's 1926 play, *Fanny*. Courtesy of Billy Rose Theatre Collection, New York Public Library for the Performing Arts, Astor, Lenox and Tilden Foundations.

"Hester Street burlesques" to be "strewn all over the great open spaces" represented an explosion of *Yiddishkayt* from the confines of the Lower East Side to the rest of America. Like popular songs about "cowboy Jews" ("I'm a Yiddish Cowboy," "Yonkele the Cowboy Jew," etc.), the stereotypically weak and emasculated Jews were easily ridiculed by imagining them as cowboys.

Harry Hershfield's "Abie the Agent" reviewed *Fanny* in his theater column, accompanying it with a cartoon of an Indian in a headdress saying "Noo?" (a Yiddish word meaning "so?") and Abie replying, "You guys is positivel learning fast!" His review begins, "Listen, Minsk, I know why they laid the scenes of Fannie Brice's show in the West—they got to have them 'wide open spaces' for her to move her hands in! Because, when Fannkeleh starts doing her stuff, zones and borderlines mean nothing in her cavorting!" He allowed that "hearing Yiddish spoken in a Western cabin sounds strange at first to the average theatergoer, but 'unser' language will sound very homelike in Arizona in a few years if some of our moving picture magnates keep using that locale for their films." He predicted that "in three years, dozens of Yiddish characters will appear in Western dramas. Mister Belasco is ahead of his time, that's all."[119]

Hershfield was right that Jewish characters would no longer be seen only in plays set in New York, just as many New York Jews themselves relocated to other parts of the country. Indeed, by 1930 fewer than half lived in the New York area. But even faster than the physical movement of Jews into other parts of the country was the proliferation of representations of Jews in popular culture, especially, as Hershfield points out, in Hollywood film. Many of the plays discussed in this chapter had touring productions; *Abie's Irish Rose,* as mentioned above, broke box office records throughout the country, with dozens of touring companies. But theater was beginning to decline in popularity as Hollywood came to dominate popular culture. Jewish actors acquired a much wider audience, but one that was mostly composed of non-Jews. How Hollywood, by promoting a more positive image of Jews, caused them to become more accepted in American society, is the subject of the next and final chapter.

CHAPTER THREE

Jews in Silent Film

A SHORT STORY about Jews in Hollywood by the non-Jew-
ish writer George Randolph Chester appeared in the pages of the *Saturday
Evening Post* in 1923. Entitled "Isidor Iskovitch Presents," the tale was about
an aspiring young film producer named Izzy (the Isidor of the title) who,
through a series of clever moves, including marrying the granddaughter of a
Jewish banker, ultimately takes over his own studio.

Staged on Broadway in the fall of 1924, with a script by Lillian Trimble
Bradley and George Broadhurst, *Izzy* starred an Irish vaudeville comic named
Jimmy Hussey. The highlight of the show, according to the critics, was the
appearance of Izzy's five uncles (whose stereotypically Jewish businesses
included junk dealing, owning a delicatessen, pressing pants, and selling
secondhand furniture), each of whom helps finance his career. Just as all the
major movie "moguls" in Hollywood worked their way up from humble
origins, Izzy needed to transcend his blue-collar background in order to
achieve the American Dream.

Compared to his bearded uncles who spoke with heavy Yiddish accents,
the cleanshaven, relatively unaccented Izzy seems destined for success from
the outset. At a time when almost all the major studio heads were Jewish, it
made sense that a Jewish boy's highest aspiration would be to become not
president of the country but head of a movie production company. At the
same time, making films seemed to be not very different from the kinds of
occupations with which immigrant Jews tended to have been involved—the
film business seemed as odd and as vaguely disreputable as selling old clothes
or corned beef sandwiches.

But how were Jews to be represented on screen? It took a story in the
Jewish press to make a satirical comment on the new forms that Jewish screen
characters were taking. "The Amateur Actor," published in the *American Jewish
World* in 1926, focused on the trials and tribulations of a young Jewish college
student who is suddenly thrust into the role of a film actor. The student,
Joseph Selman, is interrupted while saying his afternoon prayers by a Gentile
friend named Ingalls who has been asked to conduct him to the dean's office
to meet with a film director. "Say, I would never take you for a Jew," Ingalls

exclaims. "You don't look like the Eastsiders I know. You look just like a moving picture hero. And yes—I think it's a moving picture man wants to see you."[1]

Waiting in the dean's office is Mr. Bennett, a producer from the Motiongraph Company (a fictional film production company). Bennett explains that his studio is "putting out some Jewish films" and, "for the sake of realism," seeks a "young Jew who can make a good appearance and who knows sufficient about Jewish life to act it out before the camera. From a first glance, you'll do."

Joe soon learns that the melodramatic film is called *The Rabbi,* and that he is to play the title role of the Jewish leader, clad in a small mustache and beard, "after the manner of a Frenchman." The four-reeler's plot focuses on a rabbi in a small town who dedicates himself to cleaning up vice but is almost foiled in his work by a traitor in his own congregation, whose daughter the rabbi is in love with, and who the villain pretends has been converted to Christianity.

In the course of rehearsals, Joe falls in love with his beautiful costar, Sybil Martin, but he is thrown into panic by the thought that she is not Jewish. He flees the set, but is eventually found by the actor, Carter Bannard, who plays the villian. When he explains why he left the set, Bannard laughs and tells him that Sybil Martin is "none other than little Sarah Marx, and her father is a rabbi around the corner." The two lovers are joyfully reunited in Harlem, and the story ends.

Joe, like thousands of real-life second-generation Jews, attends City College in Upper Manhattan. He is Jewish but does not look, according to his friend, like a Lower East Side type of Jew. To look like a Frenchman, with a short beard (like the rabbi in *Abie's Irish Rose*), made one seem distinguished, which connoted a level of acculturation. He was Jewish without being distastefully so, both to other Jews who were anxious about their own status as Americans, and to non-Jews who often looked down upon those who displayed overt signs of ethnic difference. How interesting that the producer in the story insists on having a Jewish actor play the Jewish character, as long as he does not look "too Jewish."

Just as in the Broadway plays of the era, the ability to intermarry symbolized movement into the wider society. Non-Jewish women became an object of fantasy. But it was not always clear who was Jewish and who was not. One is reminded of what a stagehand purportedly said to Moss Hart, scriptwriter of *Gentleman's Agreement* (1947), a film about a non-Jewish journalist (played by Gregory Peck) who pretends to be a Jew in order to write a magazine article about anti-Semitism: "I'll never be rude to a Jew again because he might turn out to be a Gentile."[2] For a Jew, loving a non-Jew is problematic, unless he or she turns out to be Jewish—allowing one to have it both ways by having the most desirable (read non-Jewish-looking) partner while still obeying cultural dictates to marry within the fold. The story thus centers on the actor's ambivalence about marrying a non-Jew, while the actor's story is mirrored by that of the character he plays, the rabbi who is in love with a woman whom he believes to have converted to Christianity.

Joe runs away from the set, betraying his costars and displaying his own inability to be a real film actor. Yet the film ends up being about Jews falling in love and marrying each other, despite all the confusions and mistaken identities that lead up to the ending. The story is grounded on the assumptions that Jewish life is interesting and significant for its own sake, and that Jews somehow need to marry other Jews. While the story almost founders on its own internal contradictions, it ends up with an implicit message about the importance of Jewish continuity.

There were literally dozens of films in the 1920s that had overt Jewish content and that gave a similar message. When the movies gradually supplanted the stage as the country's primary form of entertainment, the producers in Hollywood, almost all of whom happened to be Jewish, gained tremendous cultural power. The screen representations of Jews transformed the image of Jews in American culture. The producers of these films used the Jewish experience to speak to a nation of immigrants about universal themes of displacement, rootlessness, and cultural blending.

They spoke, perhaps, especially strongly to Jews. If, as Neal Gabler writes, movies were a "powerful socializing force" for immigrants, "acclimating them to American customs and traditions," they often did so by showing immigrants and their children struggling to reconcile both their ethnic and American identities.[3] Films about Jewish life like *Humoresque, His People,* and *Hungry Hearts,* rather than simply acting as an Americanizing force, likely served as a source of pride to Jews all across America who felt that their religion and culture were finally being taken seriously.

As the drama critic Julius Novick once wrote about a revival of *Fiddler on the Roof* with Zero Mostel, "It is tremendously validating to see your heritage up there on a stage; somehow, it confirms the fact that you exist, that you matter, that you belong to something, that your ways (even if you personally have given them up) have weight in the world."[4] How much more so to see your tradition on hundreds of film screens for all the world to see.

These films did not disguise the fact that Jews were still widely viewed as outsiders to mainstream America, but by showing the Jewish families' triumphs and tragedies they underlined the universality of the Jewish experience rather than its particularity. I am thus less interested in how the films were made, or the motivations of the filmmakers, than I am in how the films were received and what the broadening of the audience for Jewish material meant in terms of changing perceptions of Jews in American society.

Nevertheless, it is certainly significant that Jewish producers were responsible for the majority of these films. Jewish immigrants were drawn to the industry because of its newness and the relatively little capital it required. Unlike other businesses that were dominated by Gentiles, the fledgling moviemaking business drew in Jews from the outset. Jewish immigrants like Samuel Goldwyn, Marcus Loew, Louis B. Mayer, Bud Schulberg, Irving Thalberg, and the Warner brothers (Harry, Jack, Albert, and Sam) began to rent storefronts on the Lower East Side, in Harlem, and in other neighborhoods that happened to have high concentrations of Jews. When Carl Laemmle broke the monopoly of the Motion Picture Patents Company (a conglomerate that had been formed in 1908 to control the film industry), these Jewish immigrants formed their own independent film studios in Hollywood along the lines of Laemmle's Universal Pictures.

Not all of the producers who made films about Jewish life were themselves Jewish; the famous director D. W. Griffith of the American Mutoscope and Biograph Company made ten-minute shorts about Lower East Side life like *Romance of a Jewess* and *A Child of the Ghetto*. Darryl Zanuck, head of

19. Ike Lazarus (Harry Green) holding the ticker tape in Edward Sloman's 1930 film, *The Kibitzer*. Courtesy of Photofest.

production at 20th Century Fox, was also not Jewish, although he was often taken to be a Jew. And even of the Jewish filmmakers, not all were from New York: Jesse L. Lasky was born in San Francisco. But by the 1920s, when the film studios began to produce feature films of over an hour in length, the film industry was dominated by Jewish studio heads who hailed from the East. In addition, Lester Friedman notes that the bankers who provided the financing for the film studios were often German Jewish firms like Goldman Sachs for Warner Brothers, Kuhn and Loeb for Paramount, and S. W. Strauss for Universal. And Laemmle was himself of German-Jewish extraction; he was born in Laupheim in south western Germany.

German Jews had come to America in the mid-nineteenth century, before the massive waves of Eastern European Jewish immigration. German Jews had risen quickly to the top of the financial world in New York, dominating the banking houses. Their attitude toward the Eastern European Jews was typically disdainful; they were afraid of being tarred with the same brush as these unwashed and uneducated immigrants. The film industry did attract a considerable amount of anti-Semitism; as mentioned in the previous chapter, Henry Ford repeatedly attacked the Jewish "control" of Hollywood as having a deleterious effect on American values. (Many present-day anti-Semitic groups in America also reserve special venom for the supposed Jewish "control" of Hollywood, whatever that allegation means.) Ford published an article in his newspaper, *The Dearborn Independent* (the newspaper that he sent to all his automobile customers), that claimed that Jewish "control" of the film industry caused "trivializing and demoralizing influences."[5]

Veronica and Paul King, a husband-and-wife team of British historians who wrote widely about American culture, agreed. "From an art and a marvel," they lamented, the cinema "speedily became a business and an industry." This was all the fault, they believed, of the Jewish producers, who had turned their financial wizardry to the goal of weakening the moral fiber of the country.[6] Or as a British film journal complained in 1924, with thinly disguised anti-Semitism, "The typical American film reflects chiefly the mentality of many of the people who control the film industry, and these, for the most part, are as representative of real America as a Hottentot in gala dress is of Bond Street tailoring. Even the American public, the most insular in the world, is beginning to see that the mentality of many native producers may not be wholly a national asset."[7]

What were the Hollywood producers' attitude toward their Jewishness? Gabler argues that these men were eager to distance themselves from Judaism; they disdained their parents' traditional ways as barriers to success in America. According to Gabler, although "[g]uilt ran too deep for them to disavow Judaism entirely . . . Jews were to be seen and not heard."[8] But Gabler discusses very few films, and he slants his argument by ignoring most of the films that had explicit Jewish content.

It seems safer to assume that, like most American Jews, the moguls were ambivalent about being Jewish, rather than that they were utterly detached from their heritage. After all, Gabler quotes an unnamed producer who opined that the Jewish moguls were so good at making films because they "*were* the audience. They were the same people. They were not too far removed from those primitive feelings and attitudes" (emphasis in original).[9] This producer seems to be referring to the fact that many of the Jewish movie moguls came from modest circumstances and were familiar with urban life. But their Jewishness could hardly have been irrelevant to the ways in which they viewed the world, and the visions of the world that they created.

Furthermore, even if many of the Jewish movie producers in Hollywood were highly conflicted about their Jewish identity, they still gave tremendous sums to charity, usually Jewish charities. Gabler suggests that their largesse was a way of "buying respectability by doing what the respectable did."[10] And he paraphrases the writer Ben Hecht as speculating that giving money to Jewish charities may have been, for the moguls, a form of "penance" for their irreligiousness. But whatever the motivations, giving charity still tied them in an important way to the Jewish community.

For example, Adolph Zukor, who had merged Paramount with Famous Players–Lasky, assumed the chairmanship in 1925 of a $4 million campaign for the Federation for the Support of Jewish Philanthropies that coordinated the fund-raising activities of allied Jewish workers from many different trades, including jewelers, pawnbrokers, salesmen, and upholsterers.[11] Zukor may have been, in Gabler's words, the "Hungarian Jew transformed into the American gentleman," but he still maintained a public connection to his Jewish roots.[12]

It was also a great source of pride to other American Jews that the studio heads almost all had Jewish names. An article in the *American Hebrew* written by the powerful film censor, Will Hays, hailed the brotherhood of those who worked in the industry "without thought of class, race, or creed, under the broader ideals of true service to their country and to their fellow men." Still, he singled out Jews for special mention, noting that "American Jews have made great and lasting contributions to the development and to the conduct of the motion picture—and consequently to the happiness and welfare of the world."[13] And on the appointment of Joseph Levenson, a Jew, to the position of secretary of the New York State Moving Picture Commission, an article in the newspaper trumpeted that:

Nothing speaks more eloquently for the vitality and enterprising spirit of the American Jews than the commanding role they are playing in the moving picture industry. In this, the youngest of our industries and arts, which daily affects the lives of countless millions whom it entertains and instructs, the position of the Jews is supreme: They lead both as producers and exhibitors, as is shown by such familiar names as Zukor, Selznick, Lasky, Loew, Fox, Cohen, and Lesser, to mention but a few. Nor do they lag behind as artists, for it is no secret that many of our movie stars, for all their euphonious disguises, belong to the mighty tribe of Cohen, fiercest and most numerous among New York's hosts in the late war.[14]

As grandiose as this sounds, it bespeaks great excitement that Jews were so successful and influential. It claimed that Jews had a kind of energy and dynamism that was transforming American society and that even when Jews in the entertainment business changed their names, they were still objects of pride for the rest of the Jewish community.

Not that these films were entirely free of stereotypes. Far from it. As Hanna Jaffe, one of the only women to be involved in film production at the time, said about *Broken Hearts,* the film she produced with her husband, Louis Jaffe, films that purported to "mirror Jewish life," particularly those about Jewish immigrants, led to stereotypical portrayals that evidenced a "search for the melodramatic" rather than the "desire to present that life in its truth and entirety."[15]

Nevertheless, of the many Jewish-themed films produced in the 1920s, quite a few featured realistic Lower East Side Jewish families coping with issues of acculturation, intermarriage (sometimes between German and Eastern European Jews rather than between Jews and non-Jews), and generational conflict. The most famous of these is *The Jazz Singer.* But *The Jazz Singer,* I will argue, was groaningly out of tune with this genre of films about Jewish families, none of which glorified assimilation in the way *The Jazz Singer* did. And even *The Jazz Singer* only celebrates assimilation by virtue of its tacked-on ending, which does not appear in the original Broadway play. I will discuss *The Jazz Singer* briefly before moving on to the other, in many ways more realistic, films that are the subject of this chapter.

THE JAZZ SINGER'S TUNE

The Jazz Singer starred Al Jolson as a Lower East Side cantor's son, Jake Rabinowitz, who makes it big on Broadway as a blackface singer. The film was based on a story by Samson Raphaelson in *Everyman's Magazine* called "The Day of Atonement." The character was based, according to Raphaelson, on Jolson himself, whom he had seen performing in blackface.

The plot is well known. Jake's Orthodox father disowns him for his choice of career, which his father considers to be a betrayal of his family and people. Jake's opening night in a show occurs on the Jewish holiday of Yom Kippur, which he has presumably stopped observing. Jake's father falls deathly ill on the eve of the great Jewish holiday, and Jake's mother and the synagogue beadle, Mr. Yudelson, come to Jake's dressing room to beg him to assume his father's mantle. Jake agonizes between loyalty to his faith and the lure of fame. The film ends with the protagonist satisfying both his obligations; he leads services on Yom Kippur and then, sometime later, appears on Broadway, with both his mother and Mr. Yudelson (his father having died), sitting in the front row. He gets down on one knee to sing "Mammy," his paean to motherhood.

George Jessel, who starred in *The Jazz Singer* both on Broadway and in its touring versions throughout the country, was originally considered for the role. But Jessel demanded that his salary be doubled for the work involved in using the new Vitaphone technology, and Jolson was ultimately signed for the role. This mistake, Gabler points out, "ate at Jessel for the rest of his life," since the film became such a landmark.[16]

In an article published in *Theatre Magazine* in 1928, Jessel remarked that "since I owe my success in great measure to the Jewish public, and the Jewish public expects me to be loyal to it, I could not sincerely do the picture."[17] It is likely that this is partly a retrospective rationalization of Jessel's blunder. Still, it is nevertheless interesting that Jessel cast the message of the film as a betrayal of Jews in its endorsement of assimilation. Also interesting is the assumption of such a thing as a recognizable "Jewish public" with particular tastes and expectations, something that many of the Jewish-themed films of the decade attempted to exploit as they pursued the Jewish market.

The Jazz Singer has long occupied an important place in film history. Much has been made in recent years about the use of blackface in the film. Michael Rogin, who theorized that Jews assimilated into American society by performing in blackface, has been the most influential of these critics. Rogin argues that Jews changed their racial status in American society by distancing themselves from black people through the very act of parodying them on stage and screen.

Yet too much can be made of the blackface, which was not by any means done exclusively by Jewish performers; for example, *Uncle Tom's Cabin,* with its scenes of blackface, continued to be extremely popular well into the twentieth century, both on stage and on screen. Jolson is shown in the film as doing blackface simply because it was a way for his work to become commercially successful. In many ways, his character is a typical second-generation Jew who promises his mother that he will find a way to move her out of the Lower East Side tenement and into a middle-class neighborhood in the Bronx. As he tells her, in one of the few synchronized sound sequences, "Mama darlin', if I'm a success . . . we're gonna move up in the Bronx. A lot of nice green grass up there and a whole lot of people you know. There's the Ginsbergs, the Guttenbergs, and the Goldbergs. Oh, a whole lotta Bergs; I don't know 'em all."[18]

The evolving scholarship on blackface has tried to place its use in historical context to explain how minstrelsy functioned in American culture. In the wake of the crumbling of the partnership between Jews and blacks in the civil

20. May McAvoy (Sara Rabinowitz) and Al Jolson (Jakie Rabinowitz) in Alan Crosland's 1927 film, *The Jazz Singer.* Courtesy of Photofest.

rights movement of the 1960s, renewed attention has focused on the ways in which Jews and blacks interrelated throughout twentieth-century American history and popular culture. Cultural pluralism prizes the contributions that ethnic groups have made to each other's cultures; it blurs distinctions and thus ultimately deconstructs the very notion of a "pure" ethnic identity that is not a patchwork of different cultural influences. In this reading, Jews and blacks helped to construct each other's culture.

Rogin's thesis that Jews "became white" by blacking up[19]—essentially allying themselves with mainstream America in its fear and hatred of blacks— has inspired much debate about whether or not these Jewish performers were truly engaged more in showing contempt for African Americans than in demonstrating sympathy for them (as Michael Alexander has suggested).[20] But blackface found its way into a relatively small proportion of performances by Jews in the 1920s. If blackface helped Jews to acculturate into American society in some way, their entrance into the mainstream was furthered much more by their performances of Jewish characters, including in the few plays and films that included blackface scenes. The images that ultimately helped move Jews to a higher status in American culture were images of themselves, not images of a different ethnic group.

ASSIMILATION BLUES

The Jazz Singer resists easy categorization. The current trend in American Jewish history is to stress tendencies toward acculturation (i.e., the maintenance of ethnic identity despite the adoption of mainstream American values, particularly the privileging of economic success) above tendencies toward assimilation (i.e., the loss of ethnic identity). *The Jazz Singer* works less well in this context since it seems frankly assimilatory; it ends with the cantor's son performing on Broadway as if his career has supplanted the values of the ethnic community.

Nevertheless, critics have done backflips to try to avoid concluding that the ending is a gesture toward assimilation. For example, in the same breath the eminent scholar George Custen has written that "it is still possible for one to read the ending as ambiguous," and that "we are meant to think that Jake embraces show business to the *exclusion* of his former life."[21] Where is the ambiguity in that?

Even Michael Rogin seesaws back and forth; he states in one place in his book that the film "was promising that the son could have it all: Jewish past and American future, Jewish mother and gentile wife" and in another place that it "divides America between Old World parents and (so far as outward appearances are concerned) a fully assimilated second generation."[22] These provocative ideas open up more questions than answers. If the second generation was only assimilated in terms of its external appearance, then what does the ending of the film mean? And how does a "Jewish past" actually influence an "American future?" Or does it?

Custen finally seems to give up trying to reconcile the film's ending with the film's overall romanticization of Jewish ethnicity; he concludes that the ending is typical of the "ethnic dry cleaning most products underwent as they were transformed into movies."[23] His thesis is that films about Jewish life appealed to a wider audience than plays (or works of literature like short stories and novels) and thus had to sacrifice much of their ethnic flavor in order to be successful. Custen argues that "in its original form—full of Jewish ritual, phonetic yiddishisms, and references to the particularities of urban ghetto life—*The Jazz Singer* certainly appeared to be too parochially Jewish and even, perhaps, too city-based to make any faithful film version a hit outside New York." Custen adds that the studio "attempted to make the film less Jewish so it would be safe for its Christian national audience."[24]

Gabler writes about *The Jazz Singer* as focused on the relationship between a Judaism that is "identified with the desiccation and doom of the past" and show business that is "identified with the energy and excitement of the future." He says that the film "provided an extraordinarily revealing window on the dilemmas of the Hollywood Jews generally and of the Warners specifically."[25]

But if the Jewish moguls felt no conflict about disowning their Jewishness, then there would not have been a "dilemma" for the film to have supposedly captured so successfully. Gabler makes a lot of the split between Harry Warner (who, Gabler says, "paraded his Jewishness") and his brothers, Jack and Sam, who were much more assimilated. In fact, Gabler argues, the reason that Jessel was replaced with Jolson for the film version was that Jack and Sam "could never have identified with a strident professional Jew like Jessel," making it "almost inevitable . . . that they would ultimately cast a Jew as totally assimilated as they were." But then why make the film in the first place? Gabler is right that *The Jazz Singer* "acknowledges something that many of the Hollywood Jews themselves would acknowledge (though only privately, for fear it might seem to compromise their loyalty to America): Judaism somehow fructifies show business. It was one of the sources of their success in the movie business."[26]

When we look at other films, a constellation of questions emerges: Did Jewish-themed films (many of them based on the vaudeville routines and Broadway plays discussed in the first two chapters of this book) lose much of their ethnic flavor as their creators attempted to broaden their appeal for the wider audience outside New York City? Were non-Jews in particular less interested in seeing material with heavily Jewish subject matter? Was the mere suggestion of Jewishness (as in recent television shows like *Seinfeld*) enough to create endearing characters and plots without "overdoing" the ethnic content?

Jolson was already one of the biggest stars of his day by the time the film was released. He had starred in three musicals on Broadway—*Sinbad* (1918), *Bombo* (1921), and *Big Boy* (1925)—that were based around the same Negro character named Gus, whom he had first introduced in his vaudeville days. He had appeared in the Ziegfeld *Follies* of 1927.

He was also well known to be Jewish, to have been the son of a cantor, and even to have been the original inspiration of "The Day of Atonement," the short story by Samson Raphaelson upon which both the stage and film versions of *The Jazz Singer* were based. Yet he had performed almost no Jewish material up to this point. (He later did perform a Yiddish song called "A Chazend'l Oyfn Shabbos" [A Cantor on the Sabbath] in the 1931 play *Wonder Bar*.)

However, Jolson was viewed by many Jews as an ethnic hero. Interviewed in early 1927 by a Jewish newspaper, Jolson was asked repeatedly to reflect on his Jewishness and to prove his loyalty to Judaism. "When I entered," writes the journalist, Walter Ginsburg, Jolson was "hurriedly applying make-up to his strikingly Jewish features." He then gets Jolson to describe himself as a "100 percent Jew," to discuss the Jewishness of Houdini (who had recently died), to talk about the influence that his father's cantorial music may have had on his own musical career, and to express a "weakness" for Jewish cooking— potato latkes, knishes, and knaidlach (dumplings)—that led him habitually to seek out a Jewish restaurant when he arrived in a new city. To emphasize his Jewishness even more, Ginsburg describes Jolson's singing as containing "all the woes of Israel [and] all the pent-up emotions of the synagogue."[27]

Jolson was thus both a highly acculturated Jew who had little connection to Judaism and an important role model for Jews, many of whom did not want to believe that Jolson had fallen as far away from Jewish observance as he had. Many Jews wanted it both ways—to celebrate Jolson's success as a "true American" entertainer and also to keep him firmly ensconced within the Jewish fold.

TRANSCENDING THE LOWER EAST SIDE

The first feature film to depict tenement-dwelling Jews in sympathetic ways was *Humoresque,* released by Paramount in 1920. Paramount was headed by Adolf Zukor, a Hungarian Jew who, according to Gabler, was obsessed with transforming himself into a gentleman and who was thus the "ideal facilitator for the movies' similar transformation or, more accurately , the movies' synthesis between the new and the old, between the working class and the middle class."[28]

Humoresque is very much about the fluidity of class in America. It opens with scenes of the Lower East Side; a bearded Jew stands outside a tailor shop selling matches and other items from a pushcart. Trash spills into the streets, and children play in filthy alleys. Abraham Kantor sells brass goods in his shop—the shelves are filled with brass candelabras, lamps, urns, and samovars. Inside the Kantor residence, the children are dressed in rags, and their expressions are glum. The oldest, Mannie, has a twisted body and vacant look; he is mentally disabled.

It is little Leon's fifth birthday, and his father takes him to a secondhand store to pick out a birthday present. Although he has only one dollar to spend, Leon is drawn to a four-dollar violin. His father refuses to buy the violin, and Leon is inconsolable. When the father and son return home for dinner (the dinner table is graced with a seven-branched brass menorah), Leon's mother, Sarah, is ecstatic that her son wants a violin. She has always dreamed that one of her children would be a musical prodigy—a beautiful shot shows her with arms raised in prayer before the open ark in a synagogue, with the light pouring down on her at a forty-five-degree angle from a dusty window. She recalls that one of the other children had once had a violin, although Abraham had broken it in a fit of rage over the cost of the lessons. She runs out to the store to buy the four-dollar violin with her own savings, and gives it to Leon, who seems as if he already knows how to play it.

The time moves forward to Leon's adulthood, when he has become a world-famous violinist. There are shots of him performing for European royalty, and for huge concert audiences. But he also plays on the Lower East Side; at one recital he plays an instrumental version of the "Kol Nidrei," the great prayer for atonement sung on the evening of Yom Kippur. The audience goes wild; they demand one encore after another, including one of his specialties, Dvořák's "Humoresque." Leon is signed to a lucrative contract to play fifty concerts in the next year all across the country.

In the dressing room after the concert, Leon meets a childhood friend from the ghetto. She is Gina Berg (née Ginsberg), a famous opera singer. Their romance blossoms, but war is declared and the patriotic Leon decides to volunteer. Having traded his tuxedo and dress shoes for a uniform and boots, he comes to his family—now living in luxury in a fancy "uptown" apartment—to bid them goodbye. Sarah is heart-broken, and fears she will never see her son again. Gina is also there to confess her love for him.

Time passes. Leon's hand is injured in battle and he is sent home. He survives, but is depressed because he is physically unable to play the violin. Gina convinces him of her undying love, and he reaches for the instrument as the screen fades to black.

Humoresque sets out many of the themes of the ghetto films of the 1920s. It consciously evokes nostalgia for the Lower East Side, but also shows how the poverty and unsanitary living conditions of the ghetto made it a kind of purgatory between the European pogroms and the heavenly life of the middle and upper class. Still, Leon is most in his element, and has his most appreciative audience, when he plays on the Lower East Side.

The shots of the audience in the concert hall are especially revealing. The balcony seems to be entirely filled with old immigrant Jews—the women wear wigs and the men wear derby hats and beards. But the audience in the orchestra is composed of young people, fashionably attired and much less ethnically identifiable. The leap in social class that the Kantors make, the film implicitly suggests, mirrored to some extent the experience of many second-generation Jews. (The Kantors are shown at the end as so rich that they have seemingly skipped from the lower to the upper class—a move that many second-generation Jews must have fantasized about.)

Although *Humoresque* is not a documentary, many of the scenes were filmed on the Lower East Side, using local residents as extras. (By contrast, some of the other films that I will examine in this chapter, although set on the Lower East Side, were made entirely on Hollywood sets.) So the film preserves a certain historical "reality" despite the selectiveness, guided by a particular vision, that any creator of an artwork employs. In the time period before the First World War, not all Jewish immigrants on the Lower East Side looked like Abraham Kantor.

21. Vera Gordon (Mama Kantor) and Bobby Connelly (young Leon Cantor) in Frank Borzage's 1920 film, *Humoresque*. Courtesy of Billy Rose Theatre Collection, New York Public Library for the Performing Arts, Astor, Lenox and Tilden Foundations.

In fact, Kevin Brownlow was told by Frances Marion, who wrote the screenplay, that Zukor hated the film, even though his company had produced it. He reportedly told Marion that "If you want to show Jews, show Rothschilds, banks and beautiful things. It hurts us Jews—we don't all live in poor houses."[29] Even William Randoph Hearst, the publisher who helped finance the film, supposedly could not stand it. The film was released only because the

Criterion Theatre in New York needed a film to fill an open slot. But the film broke box office records and went on to win the first Gold Medal (a forerunner of the Oscar) from *Photoplay*.

David Levinsky, the hero of Abraham Cahan's famous novel *The Rise of David Levinsky,* was fairly typical in shedding his facial hair and Eastern European clothing almost immediately upon arrival in New York. Nor would all Jews who did look like stereotypical Jewish immigrants necessarily be poor, or be consigned to the balcony. The film thus simultaneously both perpetuates and deconstructs its own stereotypes; it shows lower-class Jews transforming themselves into upper-class Jews, but still being very identifiably Jewish. It shows lower- and middle-class Jews joining in celebrating the success of one of their own; the middle-class Jews maintain distance from their lower-class brethren but still participate in the same aesthetic experience.

Laurence Reid, the "critic" for *Motion Picture News,* a promotional magazine for the film industry, called *Humoresque* "one of the soundest, most human vital plays that has ever reached the screen" that "will move to the depths all who have imagination, feeling and sympathy no matter how repressed or neglected." He praised the film's "deep well of pathos," and what he saw as a total avoidance of "mawkish sentiment." He concluded that the six-reeler "is a picture with a soul."[30]

Nowadays, *Humoresque* seems both dated and trite. Kevin Brownlow argues that the "stunning success" of the film "proved that audiences did not want their realism unadulterated, when a little hokum could make even squalor and mental disease acceptable." *Humoresque,* according to Brownlow, "set the standard for future Hollywood films about the plight of the Jews. Virtually all the silent productions were affected by an overdose of sentimentality, in the hope of repeating Borzage's success."

Brownlow attributes the film's success to its theme of maternal love, which he says had not been examined much in film up to that point. As he points out, a film that "bombarded the emotions with scenes of maternal heartbreak—with a Jewish mother at that—could hardly have been more perfectly timed." Brownlow's reference to "timing" refers to the second generation rebelling against its parents; he speculates that *Humoresque* "exploited their suppressed sense of guilt while it (briefly) restored their parents' confidence."[31] As in the plays of Jewish life described in the previous chapter, the dynamics of parent-child relationships were at the heart of second-generation American Jewish film.

REJECTING THE PARENTS

Rejection of Jewish parents is front and center in *His People* (1925). The film's screenwriter, Alfred A. Cohn, scripted a number of other important silent films of the period that dealt with Jewish themes, including the original *Cohens*

and the Kellys, one of many film spin-offs of *Abie's Irish Rose.* He then went on
to write the screenplay for *The Jazz Singer.*

Cohn's *His People* is, in fact, strikingly similar to *The Jazz Singer;* its theme
is the rebellion of a son against his father's perceived Old World backward-
ness, and the son's ultimate acceptance of the importance of family unity. *His
People,* directed by Edward Sloman, features a magnificent performance by
the Yiddish stage and film actor Rudolph Schildkraut. Potamkin, typically,
laments that "so fine a player as Rudolph Schildkraut was used so ignobly,"
and compares the film to *The Jazz Singer,* which he calls "another 'cheap' and
spurious Jewish film."[32]

But *His People* holds up even today; the characters are complex and the
plot is genuinely moving. While *Hungry Hearts* depicts the Lower East Side as
mostly unappealing, even sordid—a place that Jews would understandingly
want to escape—*His People* presents a much more idealized, sentimental picture. The Jewish ghetto is almost a character in its own right, or an object of
worship, in the picture. The two sons need to rebel against their immigrant
parents, but it is their parents' values that ultimately win out. The older son,

22. Rudolph Schildkraut (David Cominsky) and Arthur Lubinsky (Morris Cominsky) in
Edward Sloman's 1925 film, *His People.* Courtesy of Billy Rose Theatre Collection, New
York Public Library for the Performing Arts, Astor, Lenox and Tilden Foundations.

Morris, attempts to reject his own origins, but the ghetto resists his attempts at repudiation. As in almost all films about the Lower East Side, the sense of neighborhood is very important. To reject one's parents is to sever one's ties to this entire community.

His People opens with location shots of the Lower East Side pushcarts on the street and elevated train going by. The neighborhood is depicted as bustling and full of life, with women shopping and children horsing around and causing mischief to the extent that they literally overturn an applecart. The director's sense of humor is apparent; he shows a recently bought fish squirming out of its owner's shopping basket and, unbeknownst to her, diving back into the water tank with the other fish. Little Sammy Cominsky is a neighborhood boy who sells newspapers; he gets into a fight with another boy that attracts the attention of a rich passerby. A prize is set for the fight, which Sammy wins, and he brings home a whole bag of groceries to his mother with his winnings. His family's apartment is small but tidy, with a window in one of the interior walls (an interesting feature in many of the Lower East Side tenements of the period; health regulations required a certain number of windows in each apartment, and landlords complied by installing these essentially useless windows). Adding to the local color is the fact that the family lives above a Jewish deli.

Ten years later, both Sammy and his older brother, Morris, are grown men. Morris is educated and pursuing a career in the law; Sammy lives by his brawn rather than by his wits. The elder Cominskys are introduced. The father, David, played by the Yiddish theater star Rudolph Schildkraut, wears a long coat, black hat, beard, and whiskers. His wife, played by Rosa Rosanova (the same actress who played the mother in *Hungry Hearts*) is the *yiddishe mama* par excellence—the overweight, nurturing, long-suffering type whose love for her children and husband gleams in her tired eyes. Both sons seem equally uninterested in the Sabbath evening ritual; while his father is blessing the challah bread, Sammy gets up from the table to lean out of the window and talk to his Irish girlfriend in a neighboring apartment. Sammy and the Irish girl then leave together to go out on a date while Morris heads uptown to pursue a social life outside the ghetto. The parents are left sadly bereft of their children on the Sabbath, which is traditionally a time for families to spend together both in worship and in play.

While the Cominskys are sitting in the summer heat on the street outside their apartment, one of their friends shows them an advertisement with Sammy's picture on it. Sammy has taken an Irish monicker, "Battling Rooney," and become a boxer. Although his mother secretly visits him, bringing him warm socks ("All he needs is a good sock," the manager tells her, a remark that she humorously misinterprets), his father disowns him. The father's favorite is clearly his first-born, Morris, for whom he will sacrifice anything. Even though Morris moves to an apartment on the Upper West Side, upsetting both his parents, his father still remains devoted to him.

Morris repays their affection with dishonesty. He tells the wealthy German Jewish banker whose daughter he is romancing that he is an orphan, so he will not have to face the shame of having his humble origins exposed. He returns home only to beg money from his parents; he tells them that he must have a new dress suit in order to succeed in his career. His father, who has no money, tells Morris to wait; he goes out in a blinding snowstorm to pawn his long black coat. The pawnbroker refuses to give him more than a few dollars for the coat, but when he learns the nature of his customer's errand, he offers to trade him a dress suit for the coat. The father is delighted, and he agrees to the deal. He heads back to the apartment in the snow, but slips in the street, where he is rescued by a man whom he does not recognize but who turns out to be his younger son, Sammy. Ironically, and painfully for Sammy, his father compares his rescuer to his son Morris, his own "good boy."

Morris is impatiently waiting for his father to return with the money while his mother is angry with her husband for jeopardizing his frail health. When his father returns with the suit, Morris is disappointed. Upon leaving the apartment house, he tosses the suit in the nearest trashcan. Meanwhile, his father is coughing and sneezing; he has caught pneumonia from the misguided adventure. Morris receives an urgent telegram asking him to visit his sick father, but he caves in to the demands of his girlfriend to spend time with her instead. Sammy comes, but his father's eyesight is failing and he gives his final blessing to his younger son, thinking he is Morris. Sammy is again heartbroken by his father's favoritism.

David is told by his doctor that the only way he can preserve his health is to move to a warmer climate. Sammy convinces the boxing promoters to allow him to participate in a major bout, with a $1,000 prize. When he sees a notice of his elder son's engagement in the newspaper, David heads for the engagement party to see for himself. At the same time, Sammy's Irish girlfriend, pretending that they are going to a movie, takes Rosa to the boxing match. Although Sammy is being trounced, his mother's cries and inspiration allow him to rise up and triumph over his adversary. But David has less luck in his errand. He arrives at the Steins' Fifth Avenue mansion and makes a pathetic figure in the midst of the high-class celebration. Morris, to save himself from humiliation, tells the gathering that he has never seen this old man before. His father is stunned; he blames the mistake on his failing eyesight and is shown out the door.

When he arrives at the subway, David runs into his wife, son, and son's girlfriend. Sammy is outraged at his brother's behavior, and he takes a taxi to the Steins' mansion. He forces his way in and confronts his brother, who is now no longer able to maintain the pretense. Sammy physically drags his brother back to the Lower East Side and throws him onto the floor in their parents' living room. Morris begs his father's forgiveness, and the parents and children are reconciled to one another.

The Cominskys' apartment, located above a delicatessen, is similar to the family's apartment in *Hungry Hearts*. It has the interesting interior wall common in many tenement flats. But it is another window, looking out on another tenement, that symbolizes the Cominskys' connection with the outside world. As theorists who have written about the voyeuristic nature of the movie-going experience have noted, windows are extremely important symbols in films; the movie screen is itself a kind of window onto another world.

It is important that the Cominskys have both types of windows, one that is perhaps more like a mirror and symbolizes self-involvement and sectarianism, and one that links them to the Irish family in the apartment across the way. The community that the Cominskys inhabit is not only a Jewish one; it is presented as a mixed Jewish-Irish milieu, in which the Irish family is their closest friends. It is especially interesting, given the amazing popularity of 1920s plays and films about intermarriage in which the Jewish and Irish families are at loggerheads, that neither family shows any opposition to the interfaith romance between the Jewish son and the Irish daughter.

While it is clearly distressing to the Cominskys that their son gets up from the Sabbath table to lean out of the window and talk to his girlfriend, there is no conflict in the film that centers on the relationship. More problematic, by far, is the son's decision to take up prizefighting; his taking of an Irish name in order to succeed at this sport seems almost beside the point. However, the son's performing an Irish identity seems to indicate the same kind of interchangability between Jewishness and Irishness that was evident in the vaudeville performances and Broadway plays described in earlier parts of this book.

One contemporary critic called *His People* the story of "one of the most poignantly pitiful phases of our modern American city life," and a "compelling realistic picture of [the Jews'] huddled quarters, where, instead of flaming liberty and the horn of plenty, these 'chosen people' are harassed by customs they do not understand and their spirits broken by privation and want."[33] Laurence Moore has written that immigrants and other "religious outsiders" actually "invented [their] Americanness" through expressing their sense of marginalization, but I would add that Jews also "invented their Americanness" in the opposite way, by demonstrating, through popular culture, how similar they were to everyone else.[34]

SYMPATHY FOR IMMIGRANTS

There were many factors that contributed to greater sympathy for immigrants in the 1920s, despite the rise of Nativism and the government's gradual constriction of the flow of immigration. There were tremendous changes in American society in the first three decades of the twentieth century. In 1900, two-thirds of the American population lived in rural areas or in small towns. For the most part, they distrusted strangers, and viewed cities as cesspools of crime, disease, prostitution, and the ills of industrialization. They had little experience with immigrants of any kind and almost no contact with Jews.

But by 1930, more than half the American population was living in towns or cities of 2,500 or more. Much of the growth of American cities occurred in the 1920s, as people moved to the cities seeking employment. New York's population increased by 23 percent during the decade, while Chicago's jumped by 25 percent, Detroit's leapt by 57 percent, and Los Angeles's more than doubled. Since almost all immigrants and their children still lived in cities, or at least in metropolitan areas, there was probably much more contact in the 1920s between foreigners and "native" Americans than had been true in the past. Films that dealt with the problems of urban life, including the difficulty of relating to people from very different backgrounds, were thus likely to meet with a sympathetic reception from those who were themselves in the process of adjusting to the urban milieu.

Even the immigration restrictions passed by the federal government may have paradoxically improved perceptions of immigrants already living in America. Gilman Ostrander has argued that the National Origins Act of 1924 was "enormously beneficial to the recent immigrant groups against whose former countrymen it was directed."[35] Ostrander speculates that once the doors to new immigrants were closed, many Americans were relieved that the "invasion" had ended and began to cast a more benign eye upon the immigrants already here. Also, the immigrants themselves felt especially entitled to be in America, and perceived themselves as equal to other Americans.

The failure of Prohibition may have also contributed to a warmer attitude toward immigrants. Although many Americans had initially supported the criminalization of the sale of alcohol, the ban proved to be virtually unenforceable and people took great pleasure in subverting it. Bootleggers and owners of speakeasies tended to be immigrants and they, according to Ostrander, "became minor heroes to the people they served."[36] Although Irish immigrants were particularly identified with saloon-keeping, many of the most famous gangsters who ran crime syndicates were Jewish, and their exploits became romanticized in the newspapers.

The dozens of films produced in the mid- and late 1920s about Jewish-Irish intermarriage—with titles like *Sweet Rosie O'Grady* (1926), *For the Love of Mike* (1927), and *Clancy's Kosher Wedding* (1927)—were no exception to this trend. The success of *Abie's Irish Rose* and its stage progeny like *Kosher Kitty Kelly* (also made into a film in 1925) provided a fertile source for material. (Ironically, given the much larger potential audience, *Abie's Irish Rose* was

23. Advertisement for Arvid E. Gillstrom's 1927 film, *Clancy's Kosher Wedding*. From the collection of Ted Merwin.

much more successful on the stage than in either of its two film incarnations—the mostly silent one in 1928 and the remake in 1946.) Jews and Irish were shown in these films as remarkably similar in their process of adjustment to American society.

Patricia Erens sees these films' focus on intermarriage as in fact celebrating the ability of the Jews to "climb ahead" by "taking in a member of another group."[37] But the films also showed the Irish falling in love with the clever, kind-hearted young Jewish heroes and heroines, and thus showed Jews as overall generally caring rather than calculating—the kind of person one would not mind having as a son-in-law or daughter-in-law.[38]

Jews came to stand in these films for Americans in general. Hollywood promoted the inclusion of Jews within American society by presenting Jews, despite their exotic flavor, as essentially just like everyone else. In other words, these films paradoxically became universal in theme by emphasizing the ethnic particularity of their characters and settings. I see these films as not about the "capitulation" (to use Perlmutter's term) of Jewish culture to American society, but about the adaptation of Jewish culture to American society.

THE POWER OF FILM

Much of the transformation of attitudes toward Jews in particular occurred through the power of the film medium itself. Through its ability to create an entirely self-contained fictional world, film promoted a level of identification with Jews beyond that which the theater and vaudeville could achieve. Movie audiences empathized with the travails of Jewish immigrants depicted on the screen. That the characters were Jewish may even have been beside the point. In her dissertation on the reception of 1920s silent film, Kathryn Fuller found one woman who remembered seeing the film *Humoresque* and aspired to become a violinist like the Jewish boy in the film. (Fuller takes this, oddly, as evidence of "contradictory messages about gender roles, with whose ambiguities even young girls were forced to wrestle.")[39] The character's Jewishness seems to have been irrelevant for this particular viewer.

Notwithstanding Fuller's unpublished dissertation on the making of a national film audience, which includes a chapter on the rise of the motion picture "fan," there has been little scholarly work on the reception of silent films, and almost none on silent films about immigrants. Lester Friedman and Patricia Erens have both written books on the depictions of Jews in film; both books contain chapters on the silent era, but they are mostly concerned with cataloging the films and describing their plots. And Kevin Brownlow, in his fine work on early American film that contains a section on Jewish silent film, focuses primarily on the making of the films, not about the ways in which they functioned in American culture.

Friedman and Erens have both emphasized the similarity between a typical Jewish character in a 1920s film comedy and a "Hebrew" performer from the vaudeville stage (both were costumed in rumpled clothes and bowler hats; both gesticulated wildly and were obsessed with money, etc.). This was true of many of the films of the decade, especially the intermarriage comedies based on *Abie's Irish Rose*. But there were also a significant number of silent films that went far beyond the typical humor of the vaudeville routines in their humanization of Jewish immigrants. In their focus on the Jewish characters' conflicts with their children, desire for a better life for their families, and difficulties fitting into American society, this whole genre of Jewish-themed silent films portrayed Jews in much more realistic ways than the vaudeville stage had ever done.

Contemporary theories of ethnicity have collapsed the distinction between ethnic and "non-ethnic," and see everyone (including white Protestants) as belonging to one or more ethnic groups. Although this was hardly the prevailing view in the 1920s, when both immigrants and native blacks were still demonized in many ways in American society, there were also subtle, more positive shifts in attitudes toward foreigners and their children.

Hollywood films may have, in Ruth Perlmutter's words, "validated the dominant culture," but the mainstream culture was itself in the process of change, moving toward greater reflection of diversity.

Slightly more than half (58.5 percent) of the American population in 1920 was both white and children of American-born parents. Immigrants and children of immigrants together comprised about 30 percent of the population.[40] Historians have emphasized the prejudices that Americans held against immigrants; in the words of Geoffrey Perrett, they were viewed by "true" Americans as lacking in the "quick wits, the self-reliance, the energy and mechanical aptitude of the native born."[41] Nevertheless, films about Jews showed them as possessing pluck and courage and drive—the virtues that all Americans were supposed to have in a rapidly expanding industrial economy with seemingly unlimited economic opportunities.

Despite the vigor of the Nativist movement and the continuing presence of widespread anti-Semitism, Jews began in films of the 1920s to appear as complex and sympathetic people with real human problems and with, for the most part, a rich, attractive, and viable culture. Although Lester Friedman has described these films as promoting the "cherished vision of America as a vast melting pot of ethnic groups who discard their individual heritages to form one people," the melting pot concept was already outdated by the 1920s.[42] Friedman is right that the films "attempt to make Americans less nervous about Jews and Jews more conscious of themselves as Americans," but this is not incompatible in any way with the communication of pride about Jewish ethnicity. Rather than, as Thomas Cripps would have it, an "icon of the ritual of Americanization," the silent-movie Jew was an icon of the maintenance of Jewish ethnicity.[43]

According to Friedman, the films appealed especially to immigrants who "recognized screen versions of familiar aspects of [their] own experience."[44] But it was not just immigrants, but Americans in general, who could identify with the Jewish characters in the silent films. In fact, films needed to appeal to a national audience in order to be profitable, whether or not they dealt with specific ethnic minorities.

MARKETING JEWISH FILM

Scholars of American Jewish history have emphasized the ways in which Jews acculturated into American society by buying consumer products. As Andrew Heinze has written, adapting Thorstein Veblen's theory of "conspicuous consumption" to Jewish immigrant buying patterns, Jews "relied on their awareness of the symbolic potential of special products as they searched for a tangible American identity."[45] Similarly, Jenna Weissman Joselit views shopping as "a tangible instrument of integration and Americanization" for Jewish immigrants and their children.[46]

But what happened when Jewishness itself became a kind of commodity, not just for Jews but for Americans in general? Film, while not tangible in any sense like the consumer products that Heinze and Joselit discuss, was also a kind of product that could yield handsome profits to the studio, exhibitors, and everyone who worked on it.

In the 1920s, there were many trade publications for the film industry that recommended how exhibitors could maximize their profits through window displays, mailings to prospective customers, and advertising in local newspapers.

First, however, the studios had to get the theater owners to rent the films in the first place, often through the use of salesmen who visited the owners. In the *Exhibitors Herald,* each film was listed along with quotes from satisfied theater owners from all over the United States and Canada who had shown the film. The intermarriage comedy *The Cohens and the Kellys,* for example, was recommended by no fewer than twenty different exhibitors. For example, the owner of the Reel Joy Cinema in King City, California, called the film "a positive knockout here. The best pleased crowd I have had in three months and it drew well. Get behind this one, as it ought to go over anywhere. Raised my price and no kicks." Or as an owner in Montpelier, Idaho, put it, "They are still laughing and talking about the Jews and the Irish."

But it did not go over so well everywhere, as evidenced by other quotes, which, while still praising the feature to the heavens, admitted that the film was a disappointment at the box office. As the owner of the Rex Cinema in Newport, Washington, disclosed in a remarkable non sequitur, "Brothers, it's a sure winner. Didn't do very good on it, but the conditions of my town are such that I just got general patronage." Or as the owner of the Eminence Cinema in Eminence, Kentucky, put it, "One of the most enjoyable pictures I've had the good fortune to run, and one of the poorest box office receipts I've had the misfortune to count. Patterned after *Abie's Irish Rose* of stage fame. It would be hard to tell who secured the biggest hit, the Jewish family or the Irish family. By all means run it."[47] How the other poor exhibitors were supposed to make sense of these contradictory statements is hard to say, but they demonstrate that ethnic comedy was not as universally well received as Universal Studios, in this case, would have liked to believe. Still, *The Cohens and the Kellys* was successful enough to spawn no fewer than six sequels between 1928 and 1933.

The only scholarly work on how the studios marketed films with Jewish content is in Henry Jenkins's book on early talkies, *What Made Pistachio Nuts?* In analyzing how the vaudeville aesthetic was transferred to film, Jenkins examines the stage and film career of Eddie Cantor. He writes that in live performance Cantor had "relied heavily upon his Jewishness as an appeal to the city's ethnically diverse audience." But when Cantor began to appear in talking films, like *Palmy Days* (1931), *Kid Millions* (1934), and *Strike Me Pink,* Jenkins argues, the studios decided to "deny or shift attention from the question of Cantor's ethnicity."[48]

The reason for this, according to Jenkins, can be found in the intolerant climate of the 1920s; he paraphrases Irving Howe about the ways in which Jewish performers dropped their ethnic personas in order to become successful outside New York. But Jenkins begins his chapter by analyzing earlier films of Cantor's like *Glorifying the American Girl* (1929) and *Whoopee* (1930), both of which did contain heavily Jewish material. *Glorifying the American Girl,* for example, incorporates Cantor's famous "Moe the Tailor" sketch from his vaudeville performances—perhaps his most explicitly Jewish routine.

It also makes little sense for Jenkins to refer to a "chilling climate" when discussing the ways in which Jewish-themed films were marketed.[49] Cantor's films of the 1920s were not denatured of their Jewish content; by contrast, they revel in it. Mark Winokur sees this as a constituent element of Cantor's style that continues into his 1930s talking films. He writes that Cantor's films "tend to call attention to Cantor's ethnicity and, more interestingly, to conflate the ethnic with the national identity." In fact, Winokur suggests, "the ethnic character Cantor plays tends to affirm not just the possibility of ethnic durability, but the defining of the American as ethnic."[50]

This is akin to what Oscar Handlin noted in the introduction to his seminal work of American history, *The Uprooted,* when he said that he had set out to write about the place of immigrants in American history and realized that immigrants *were* American history.[51] We live in an era in which we are often reminded that, except perhaps for American Indians, we are all relatively recent arrivals on this continent. This redefines the "American" not as the antithesis of the ethnic but as its equivalent; it eliminates the difference between insider and outsider.

The studios actively encouraged this shifting of conceptual boundaries. They marketed their Jewish-themed films in ways that not just piqued the curiosity of non-Jews about aspects of Jewish language and culture, but suggested that non-Jews could participate in that culture on equal terms. They also emphasized the extent to which both Jews and non-Jews shared a common consumer culture. And they sought to duplicate the success of stage hits by turning them into profitable films. As the publicity for the 1923 screen version of *Potash and Perlmutter*—retitled *Dr. Sunshine* when it ran in Great Britain—trumpeted, the play had been seen for nine years on Broadway, nine years in story format in the *Saturday Evening Post,* nine years on tour, five years in London, three years in Berlin, and three years in Petrograd. "It has been laughed at in 20 languages," one hyperbolic advertisement, in the shape of a film strip, declared. This made the film "the greatest laughmaker [that] stage, screen or story has ever known."

An ethnic-sounding title was more of a problem for film publicity. In the case of *The Kibitzer*, it was turned into an asset. *The Kibitzer* was a Broadway play written by Edward G. Robinson and newspaperman Jo Swerling that premiered on February 18, 1929. Robinson starred as Lazarus, the owner of a cigar store on Amsterdam Avenue who gives unwelcome advice to the card players who gather nightly in his store to play pinochle. Although his daughter is engaged to a soda clerk in a drug store, she is also the object of the romantic attention of a son of a wealthy industrialist, James Livingston.

Lazarus pays Livingston a visit to tell him that their respective offspring are planning to elope; he uncovers the fact that the millionaire's butler is masquerading as his son, and planning to steal valuable bonds. As a reward, Livingston gives Lazarus half the profits from any future rise in 10,000 shares of steel company stock. (In other words, Lazarus will only make a profit if the stock price goes up.) Lazarus sells part of his shares to his creditors, installs a stock ticker machine in his store, and exults as the stock price rises. Then the stock plummets, and Lazarus is wiped out. However, he turns out not to have lost the money after all; his half-wit brother Yankel, who speaks no English other than "Yes—sure—certainly," happens to have answered the phone at the crucial moment and unwittingly given the broker the order to sell. All ends happily in this extremely contrived plot.

When the film version was made in 1930, the leading role was cast not with Robinson, who was not yet well known to film audiences, but with a Jewish comedy actor named Harry Green (né Henry Blitzer), who had practiced law before going on the stage, appearing in ten Broadway plays and other talking films before doing *The Kibitzer.* Other well-known performers appeared in the early talkie, including the Yiddish stage actor Tenen Holtz and the vaudeville star Eddie Kane. But Paramount's ad campaign focused not just on the actors, but on the film's Yiddish title, which, in its original sense, means an annoying and intrusive person or meddler.

The word actually derives from the German word *kiebitz,* which means literally a "plover or lapwing," but in German slang took on a meaning of a "meddlesome or annoying onlooker at a game." Only later in the 1930s did the word begin to take on connotations, that are common nowadays, of simply chatting or gossiping.[52]

As the studio's "Press Sheet," a circular designed to give movie theaters ideas about how to promote Paramount films, suggested, "To millions of persons this word as yet means nothing. That's why it is a wow title, for a full meaning of the term is only realized after the public has seen the picture." In this quote, "the public" is assumed to be a non-Jewish public that will be puzzled by the Yiddish term; there is no reference to the Jewish audience. (Interestingly, when the film was released in the United Kingdom, the title was changed to *The Busybody*.)

24. Publicity material for the 1930 film *The Kibitzer*. Courtesy of the Academy for Motion Picture Arts and Sciences.

Nevertheless, the studio's publicity experts predicted that the film "will make the American people kibitzer-conscious." They advised theater owners to arouse the public's curiosity about the meaning of the term. The sample press releases, newspaper advertisements, lobby posters, and window cards depicted in the Press Sheet all make fun of the kibitzer's pretense to knowledge and expertise.[53] The studio advised that theaters run contests for the best definitions of the term and then publish selected definitions—especially those from famous people.[54] Finally, the studio suggested that the theaters give out "Kibitzer Union membership cards." These cards would "certify" that the bearer is entitled to "butt-in on any conversation," correct the mistakes of card, golf, and billiard players, "help losers to cry," and perform other unnecessary and irritating services.

By soliciting humorous definitions of the term, and permitting practically any definition of the Yiddish word that anyone suggested, the studio's publicity department was playfully demystifying Jewish culture. Rather than making non-Jews feel excluded, Jewish culture could embrace them. By contrast, the 1927 program for *The Jazz Singer* at the Strand Movie Theater in New York contained a glossary that defined the Yiddish and Hebrew terms used in the film, thus implicitly pointing to the distance between the world of the film and the world that most of the audience inhabited, but also attempting to overcome it.

The ethnic element could also be simply a foil for commercialism, as in the promotion of *Abie's Irish Rose* by Paramount's "Special Exploitation Service." Unlike *The Kibitzer,* for which the studio traded on the title's unfamiliarity, the title *Abie's Irish Rose* was expected to be instantly recognizable to most Americans, given the extraordinary popularity of Anne Nichols's play—both on Broadway and in the many touring productions. The mock newspaper advertisements and posters reproduced in the circular invariably pointed out that 18 million people (a wildly inflated number) had seen the play, and even called it "The Most Perfect Play Ever Written." (The film was "perfect," it seems, mostly in terms of the way it lent itself to money-making movie tie-ins.) The "exploitation suggestions" included putting large displays of roses in theater windows, sponsoring essay contests on the reasons for the play's popularity, and selling copies of the music used in the film (including a song called "Rosemary") in the theater lobbies.

Publicity was tailored to each city where the film played. In addition to radio and newspaper coverage (with ads and stories placed both in Jewish newspapers and general papers—the Jewish newspapers were furnished an ad in Yiddish), heralds (advertising flyers with photographs) were placed in taxicabs.

In Pittsburgh, for example, a boy and girl playing Abie and Rosemary—clad in their wedding attire—went on a newlyweds' "shopping tour," and were photographed buying appliances, furniture, and other products for their

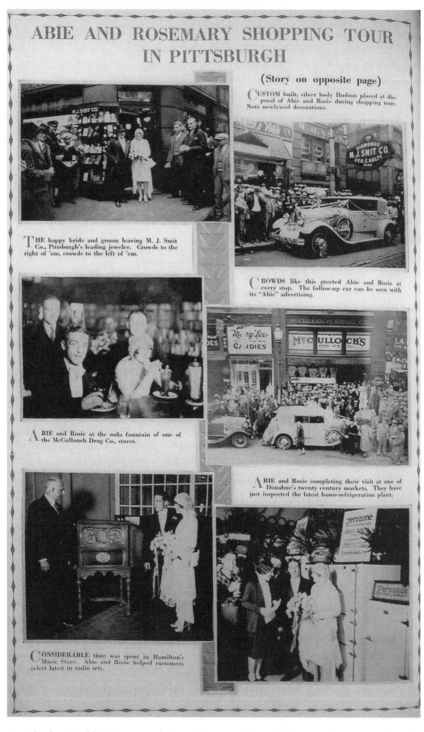

ABIE AND ROSEMARY SHOPPING TOUR IN PITTSBURGH

(Story on opposite page)

CUSTOM built, silver body Hudson placed at disposal of Abie and Rosie during shopping tour. Note newlywed decorations.

THE happy bride and groom leaving M. J. Smit Co., Pittsburgh's leading jeweler. Crowds to the right of 'em, crowds to the left of 'em.

CROWDS like this greeted Abie and Rosie at every stop. The follow-up car can be seen with its "Abie" advertising.

ABIE and Rosie at the soda fountain of one of the McCullouch Drug Co., stores.

ABIE and Rosie completing their visit at one of Donahue's twenty century markets. They have just inspected the latest home-refrigeration plant.

CONSIDERABLE time was spent in Hamilton's Music Store. Abie and Rosie helped customers select latest in radio sets.

25. Charles "Buddy" Rogers and Mary Brian as Abie and Rosemary impersonating the newlyweds making a shopping trip in Pittsburgh in the publicity material for Victor Fleming's 1928 film, *Abie's Irish Rose*. Courtesy of the Academy for Motion Picture Arts and Sciences.

"home." (Mock wedding announcement cards were distributed, stating that the couple would be "at home" to callers on particular dates, and giving the movie theater's address as their "home.") In Cincinnati, the couple's names were used to hawk everything from lamps to porcelain gas ranges to shoes— all by having the happy couple "appear" at the different stores. Although the bride and groom were Irish and Jewish, respectively, they became a model "American" couple in their consumption of household goods.

Publicity campaigns for other films emphasized Jewish food. Since many of the Jewish-themed films were at least partially set in Jewish delicatessens, the studios could exploit the fact that some traditional Jewish foods were popular among non-Jews. *Film Daily* suggested to the exhibitors of *Private Izzy Murphy* (a film about a young Jewish delicatessen owner, played by George Jessel, who sets up shop in an Irish neighborhood), "Here's your chance to give local delicatessen stores a chance to benefit by a tie up with 'Private Izzy Murphy.' Get the stores to display prominent announcements of the picture mentioning that 'Murphy's' delicatessen serves laughs as well as cold cuts."[55]

How well did these publicity techniques work? Unfortunately, measuring the actual size of the audience that viewed a specific film is difficult, if not impossible. As Donald Crafton has found in his research on the reception of *The Jazz Singer,* producers had many ways of inflating the numbers of tickets "sold," including distributing both free tickets and discount passes. In the case of *The Jazz Singer,* Crafton concludes that these practices helped make the film seem like a bigger "hit" than it actually was in box office terms.[56]

However, gauging a film's reception in terms of the warmth of the audience's response is even trickier than measuring that film's success in financial terms. Even a film review, however knowledgeable and experienced the critic may be as compared to the average viewer, can represent only his or her individual perspective. As Janet Staiger has pointed out, the "unspoken mass of [audience members] deserves as much attention as does the popular press—if not more."[57] How the audience greeted these films is notoriously difficult to discern. Even reviews in the ethnic press are not reliable evidence of an entire ethnic group's response to a cultural product. As Crafton points out, the audience for the reviewer's periodical and the film's audience may overlap but are not identical; the review becomes a kind of secondary cultural product that speaks to an audience of its own.

AUDIENCE RESPONSE

Film reviews show us how particular viewers both responded to films and influenced others to respond. They capture attitudes and feelings that we can assume were not limited to the people who wrote them. As a critic for the *New York Times* wrote of *Hungry Hearts,* "the people of the story, their customs, habits, ways of living and variety of character and appearance, are brought to the screen, definitely, genuinely, memorably. . . . [T]he spectator feels himself carried into the life of which the persons in the play are an integral part."[58] Film has the power to make its viewers feel swept away by the film-going experience; this was no less true of the silent films about Jewish life on the Lower East Side.

Film, much more than theater, fosters fantasies that the viewer is actually involved in the action and situations depicted. Lary May has argued that "Going to a movie meant more than merely watching the screen. It was a total experience that immersed the fans directly in the life they saw in celluloid."[59] Much more than in the theater, this "immersion" created tremendous empathy for the ethnic characters; as the reviewer of *Hungry Hearts* for *Picture Play* exulted, "The life of the Jewish family is your life as you sit and watch the screen. You are as much a part of it as your teeth are part of you."[60]

Although Kevin Brownlow has speculated that *His People,* produced by Universal Pictures, was "aimed, as were virtually all their films, at the audience of small-town America," it seems obvious that the urban Jewish audiences were also a prime target. Of course, the response to the film by Jews may have been largely based on the way they perceived their own culture being portrayed for the Gentile audience. As Sam B. Jacobson, a film critic for a Los Angeles Jewish newspaper, wrote, "This is the first time that a film has so vividly portrayed the lives and environment of the Jewry in a metropolis. . . . Edward Sloman is responsible for one of the finest pictures ever made. He has done, with *His People,* more to eradicate with one blow prejudice and racial hatred than any other agency has accomplished."[61]

After all, Americans liked to congratulate themselves on the civilizing influence life in America had on immigrants. As another review of *Hungry Hearts* put it, "The advantages which immigrants derive from this Land of the Free are always popular with our patriotic audiences. Even though we vote for restrictions at Ellis Island, we like to think of ourselves as big-hearted hospitable folk, who welcome oppressed aliens with open arms and teach them how to wear Kollege Kut Klothes." If immigrants remained in poverty even after they arrived in America, this myth would be eroded. The review pretends to mock the film for "dar[ing] to insinuate that some of the immigrants are just as badly off as they were at home . . . [which] is rank heresy."[62]

THE JEWISH AUDIENCE

Immigrant audiences often needed help in understanding the films. A little-studied phenomenon is that of the moving picture "lecturer," who interpreted the film to the audience. In an innovation by the producer Marcus Loew, hundreds of people were trained to supplement silent films with explanations of the action, invented dialogue, and even singing. Loew soon discontinued the practice, but Jewish audiences in New York clung to the idea.

In 1920, an article in the *New York Times* reported that only five lecturers still remained in New York—all five of them on the Lower East Side. Many of those in the audience, the article noted, did not speak English; they "are here to learn the 'Yankee' language." It is in the movie house that the immigrants "learn English words that they dare not ask the younger generation for fear of being laughed at. . . . Now and then the voice coming through the megaphone drops a Yiddish phrase, and then there are wide manifestations of delight."[63]

Nevertheless, according to one of these lecturers, Harry Levine, his skills were in demand because going to the movies was an intellectually challenging experience for a Yiddish-speaking audience. Levine theorized—perhaps somewhat tongue in cheek—that the amount of ice cream, chocolates, chewing gum, peanuts, and grapes consumed during the film corresponded to the difficulty the Yiddish-speaking audience experienced in trying to decipher the English-language titles.

Harry Sabath Bodin, writing in the *American Hebrew* about *Hungry Hearts,* called the English titles done by Montague Glass (author of *Potash and Perlmutter*) "reservoirs of risibility" in the literacy of their translation from Yiddish to English. But the titles could only "afford amusement with their quaint humor," as Bodin puts it, to an audience that could understand Yiddish.[64]

His People, like *The Jazz Singer,* elevates religious ritual to a central place. It was precisely these rituals that Sam B. Jacobson, a film critic for a Los Angeles Jewish newspaper, exulted over in his review. Writing that *His People* is "the first time that a film has so vividly portrayed the lives and environment of the Jewry in a metropolis," he went on to ask, "Can't you see the little Cominsky family as the old father pronounces 'kiddush' with his 'brosha' over the wine and the final 'moitze' over the bread? Not once does he omit to kiss the 'mezuzah' as he leaves or enters his home. And true to his traditions, he blesses his first born when he believes that he is on his dying bed."[65]

Perhaps for a Gentile audience, the use of these Jewish rituals was powerful partly because they seemed so mysterious. For example, one reviewer gushed that "[n]o truer picture of the Ghetto, and more human, has ever been produced" and that "[n]one of the details of Orthodox Jewish life has been overlooked. The Mazuza, for instance, which is the Ten Commandments, is fastened on the door frame just above a man's head, is there; whenever the father enters, he put his fingers on the Mazuza and then on his lips."[66] This is inaccurate; the *mezuzah* contains the first two paragraphs of a passage from the Hebrew Bible called the Sh'ma, which is the Jewish credo of God's essential unity. But the reviewer was not alone in getting the details of Jewish observance wrong; no one who worked on the picture seemed to have noticed that it hung on the wrong side of the door frame! It was the specificity, if not the accuracy, of the Jewish rituals that underlay the seeming "authenticity" of the Jewish life presented in *His People*.[67] In the 1928 silent film version of *Abie's Irish Rose,* Jean Hersholt, playing the Jewish father, even wore *tefillin*—the long black straps tied to boxes containing parchments with Biblical texts that observant Jewish men wrap around their arms and foreheads during weekday morning prayer. This is very likely the only time this particular Jewish ritual was ever shown on the silent film screen.

Whatever their appeal to non-Jews, films about Jewish life were produced at least partly with Jewish audiences in mind. Jews had been a prime audience for film since the turn of the century. Judith Thissen has studied the exhibition of Yiddish films on the Lower East Side and concludes that these films helped to socialize Jewish immigrants into the manners and mores of American culture.[68] Some research has been done on the class composition of early-twentieth-century film audiences in New York; Robert Allen and Ben Singer have debated whether or not the nickelodeon audience included a significant number of middle-class patrons. However, there has been no research yet published on either the class or ethnic composition of audiences for 1920s feature films—both inside and outside New York.[69]

Jews had been disproportionately represented among early film audiences in America, and they built up a habit of cinema attendance. According to Robert Allen, out of 120 movie houses in Manhattan in 1908, 42 were

26. Jean Hersholt (Solomon Levy) laying *tefillin* (black boxes containing biblical verses) in Victor Fleming's 1928 film, *Abie's Irish Rose*. Courtesy of Photofest.

located on the Bowery on the Lower East Side; there were seven times as many movie theaters in Jewish neighborhoods than in other areas.[70] By the late 1920s, there were 28,000 movie theaters in the United States, more than half of which were in the major cities in New York, Illinois, Pennsylvania, Ohio, and California—the same cities with the largest numbers of Jews and other immigrants. As an article in the *Exhibitor's Trade Review* about *Hungry Hearts* predicted, the film "should appeal favorably to all nationalities because of its simplicity and strength. It ought to prove a good box office investment for any exhibitor and in theatres catering to Jewish patrons there can be no doubt as to its heavy earning capacity."[71]

Nevertheless, the Jewish audience was increasingly viewed as merely a segment of the overall American public. According to Miriam Hansen, Jewish-themed films "became a standard sideline for certain producers (Laemmle, for example) through the 1920s, by which time the targeted group was part of a multiethnic mass audience."[72] This seems borne out by a review of Frank Capra's *The Younger Generation.* The reviewer for *Variety* concluded that Capra's film, coming on the heels of so many other films about immigrant Jewish life, was yet "another insincere attempt to sell sympathetic syrup to the Jewish public."[73]

NOSTALGIA FOR THE GHETTO

The desire to prolong the association of Jewish life with the Lower East Side reflected, I would argue, a sense that the memories of the immigrant neighborhood were a crucial common denominator of both the immigrant and second-generation Jewish experience. In addition to the important "local color" that setting films in the teeming ghetto provided, the films exploited both the fears and fantasies that accompanied increasing acculturation on the part of the second generation. As they moved farther and farther away, in both geographic and cultural terms, from the world of the ghetto, the members of the second generation were pulled back into it, in symbolic terms, through their viewing of these films. In the words of Hasia Diner, the story of the Lower East Side, as preserved in popular culture and memory, "reflected in microcosm the broad outlines of the metanarrative of the Jewish past."[74] The Lower East Side thus came to stand for the Jewish immigrant experience itself; it reflected not just the Jewish immigrant experience in America, but the many periods in which Jews had to begin anew in a strange land.

As in the Jewish-themed Broadway comedies of the era, the silent films also often had a kind of "multicultural" flavor. If one looks for example at the set of *Rose of the Tenements,* a 1926 film about an Italian orphan girl raised by Jewish immigrant parents on the Lower East Side, one sees crowded scenes of pushcarts and shoppers of different ethnicities in front of tenements housing a Jewish-owned shoe store, a Chinese laundry, and a delicatessen. Jewish-Irish

27. Set for Phil Rosen's 1926 film, *Rose of the Tenements*. Courtesy of Photofest.

comedies about intermarriage were just as prevalent on screen as they had been on Broadway. Some were converted from stage plays and some, like *Clancy's Kosher Wedding* and the seven films in the *Cohens and the Kellys* series (made between 1926 and 1933), were based on original scripts.

Nostalgia, as historians have come to recognize, is an active process, in which the past is continuously remade according to the values of the present. By the 1920s, as Beth Wenger has written, the ghetto began to figure in the construction of second-generation Jewish identity. "The development of nostalgia for immigrant life was no retreat from the modernization and acculturation of Jews," she argues, "but rather an integral part of the ongoing reconstruction of Jewish consciousness in an American context."[75]

But nostalgia for an idealized past, and the deep-seated ambivalence about the future that it suggested, was not limited to Jews. Lawrence Levine has written that the "central paradox" of American history is a "belief in progress coupled with a dread of change; an urge towards the historical future combined with a longing for the irretrievable past; a deeply ingrained belief in America's unfolding destiny and a haunting conviction that the nation was in a state of decline."[76] The giddiness of Jazz Age life thus masked a kind of panic and desperation.

Levine's fruitful take on the 1920s is that despite the mood of excitement and optimism that characterized the Jazz Age, Americans feared that their values were slipping away. But despite the fact that this emphasis on traditionalism often intensified prejudice toward "aliens" and blacks, non-Jews could empathize with the contradictory attitudes toward the past that the Jewish-themed films encapsulated. The films about Jewish life seemed both forward-looking and backward-looking at the same time, celebrating the future but keeping an eye fixed on the past. The Jewish characters in the films typically shared the same need for reassurance as most Americans who, in Levine's words, "found it far easier to come to terms with the new if it could be surrounded somehow by the aura of the old." New technologies (including the automobile, radio, and film itself) were both delightful and disorienting in their power to transform modern society.

In hindsight, then, the Lower East Side appears as a kind of staging ground, a place where Jews prepared to launch themselves for their true immigration. As Diner has written, the Lower East Side was "that metaphoric middle ground where Jews dwelled among themselves while waiting for permission to enter the real America."[77] And yet, as the films amply demonstrate, the life of the Lower East Side was richly textured in its own right; Mario Maffi has written that "even in Hollywood's silent era, the multi-faceted life of the quarter, with its texture of lives, dreams and illusions, was a constant feature."[78] Many of these films were shot, at least in part, on the Lower East Side, where they made ample use of the neighborhood's local color—the pushcarts, tenements, and "exotically" dressed inhabitants.

Films about Jewish life thus permitted both Jewish producers and Jewish audiences to experience a kind of vicarious homecoming, but one that ultimately justified their movement away from the grinding poverty those homes represented. By honoring in this way their parents' material sacrifices for the sake of their children, the second generation could assuage its guilt over having essentially left its parents behind in its movement toward acculturation into American society. Romanticizing the ghetto helped the second generation in some measure to transcend it.

The filmmakers elevated the Lower East Side to its mythic status, while at the same time they plumbed the Jewish audience's potent wellsprings of memory and emotion.[79] The films were rich in melodrama: landlords exploiting destitute tenants, children betraying their parents, parents disowning their children, siblings warring among themselves. At a time when, according to Beth Wenger, merchants and government officials on the Lower East Side were creating the image of "a packaged, safe, and colorfully exotic Jewish culture" in order to attract business from second-generation Jews, the films depicted the neighborhood as remarkably dirty and dangerous. Although the city and neighborhood association were rehabilitating tenement buildings, reducing the number of pushcart peddlers, and cleaning the streets, the films of the 1920s presented an image of the ghetto as the second-generation Jews had experienced it as children.[80] As Bodin wrote in the *American Hebrew* regarding *Hungry Hearts,* the settings "are so judiciously chosen that no one who knows the lower east side of New York could find fault with a single scene."[81]

The plot in almost all of these films is of an immigrant family striking it rich and moving north from the ghetto to a fashionable upper-class neighborhood—something that almost never happened in reality. For example, in the Warner Brothers film *Millionaires* (1926), starring George Sidney and Vera Gordon, a Jewish couple moves from Hester Street to a forty-room mansion on Riverside Drive. Only in one, *Hungry Hearts,* does the family make a more realistic move to a house in the suburbs.[82] In some (*The Cohens and the Kellys, April Fools*), it is the immigrant fathers who suddenly become rich, either through chance or through dint of hard work and business acumen; in others (*Humoresque, The Younger Generation*), it is the son's success that makes possible the family's economic rise. But in film after film, the sudden contrast is shown between tenement life on the Lower East Side and the high life of the upper class.

That Neighborhood Feeling

The sense of neighborhood is extremely important in these films, as is the idealized sense of community. When Leon, the world-famous violinist in *Humoresque,* comes back to the Lower East Side to play for an audience of his "own people," he is expressing a sense of pride in his origins.

In other films, the Lower East Side was shown rather less appealingly, as a neighborhood in which Jews exploited one another for financial gain. For example, in *April Fools,* an immigrant umbrella maker, played by Alexander Carr (of *Potash and Perlmutter* fame), falls into the clutches of a business and romantic rival, who ultimately extorts from him all his possessions. However, in the end the umbrella maker wins the hand of the local delicatessen owner. And in *Hungry Hearts,* an immigrant mother played by Rosa Rosanova paints her kitchen a sparkling white, only to have the venal Jewish landlord raise the rent. In her rage she attacks the kitchen walls with a meat cleaver (literally "breaking down the ghetto walls," as Lester Friedman has astutely observed) and is arrested by the police. But when her case comes up in court, the judge frees her and lambastes the landlord for his greed. While *Hungry Hearts* has a happy ending, the ghetto is viewed as a place that one needs to escape from in order to preserve one's sanity. When the family ultimately moves to the suburbs, thanks to help from their daughter's husband (a lawyer who used to work for the landlord), they seem to have achieved their middle-class dream at last.

The desire to become middle class unites the characters in many of these films, as is especially apparent through their attitudes toward clothing. The Jewish characters tend to have a large emotional investment in clothing as a marker of American identity. In *His People,* the elder son, Morris, demands a new suit from his father, saying that he needs it for his job as a lawyer. The penniless father pawns his heavy winter coat (one of his few remaining possessions from Eastern Europe), trading it for a suit for his son. But the son tosses the secondhand suit in the garbage. The gap between the father's and son's different notions of the clothes that "real Americans" wear is painfully clear.

Similarly, in *Hungry Hearts,* the daughter, Sara, tells her father to earn money so that she can have work clothes for her job in a shirtwaist factory. She is encouraged in this by the factory owner, Mindel, who tells her she can transform herself from a "nobody" to a "somebody" by changing her "greenhorn" clothes for a more "American" outfit. Her father later gets the idea that his wife, Hanneh, should also have some fancier clothes; he buys her a ridiculously inappropriate hat with a feather—"like Mrs. Vanderbilt's, three years ago." Hanneh's expression when she wears it is priceless; she is pleased by his attentions but bewildered by his buying something so useless in the ghetto. But the couple's fantasies about the hat (a potential prop, perhaps, in their sexual activities) marks in a particularly poignant way the gap between their material possessions and the lifestyle to which they aspire.

Moving On Up

However, these films suggest that the price for economic success is often high, in that it entails the loss of the ethnic community. This is the basic theme of *The Cohens and the Kellys,* the series of six Jewish-Irish film comedies that starred the Jewish comic George Sidney and Irish comic Charlie Murray. The original film, as mentioned earlier, was clearly inspired by *Abie's Irish Rose.* It was based more explicitly, however, on Aaron Hoffman's play *Two Blocks Away,* a drama that I discussed in chapter two. In the first installment, a conniving, unkempt Jewish shop-owner suddenly inherits a fortune and moves his family to Park Avenue. But he is not happy, especially because his intermarried daughter remains on the Lower East Side. He moves back when his daughter has a child, and when he finds out that the money belongs to the Irishman rather than to him.

Similarly, *The Younger Generation* is a film about a successful second-generation Jew who moves his family to a mansion on Fifth Avenue. But his elderly father, Julius, complaining that he is "cold all the time" and that he "hasn't been warm since we left Delancey Street," ventures back to the old neighborhood for comfort and solace. (The critic for *Motion Picture News* joked that the character "longs for the old bearded cronies who speak his language.")[83]

The filmmakers exploited the power of the medium to show the characters' suddenly transformed circumstances and places of residence; in one frame the characters are living in a hovel, in the next they are living on Park Avenue. At a time when most Americans were enjoying the fruits of the post–World War I economic boom, these films gratified the widespread fantasy that sudden riches could come even to people who seemed least likely to succeed. If immigrants, who were hampered by their unfamiliarity with the English language and with American manners, could make it big, the prospects for "ordinary" Americans seemed almost unlimited.

These fantasies were promoted by the entire film-going experience, not just by what was presented on the screen. Lary May has written about the exotic theater "palaces" that opened throughout the country in the second and third decades of the twentieth century; he notes that theater owners furnished their theaters with opulent decors, including grand staircases, large gilt-framed mirrors (suggesting the movie screen itself), and elaborate façades. May quotes one observer's impression that these "Million Dollar" cinemas offered patrons "a gilded mansion for the weekly invasion of those who lived in stuffy apartments, a gorgeous canopy to spread over a cramped and limited life."[84] When patrons entered the theater and viewed themselves in the ornate mirrors, May suggests, they could imagine that they were themselves the stars of the films.

Indeed, since Jews were associated with the Orient, the more exotic these theaters became, the more they appeared to some observers to manifest "Jewish" qualities. As the British author Eric Linklater described Grauman's Chinese Theater in his popular satire, *Juan in America,* the famous theater was built "with grotesque extravagance. This was the Hebraic conception of a Chinese pagoda. Signs of a Semitic renascence were frequent indeed, more especially in interior decoration, where there was such a willful splendour of carved flowers and pomegranates, knopfs, palm trees overlaid with gold, pillars of brass and golden hinges, as would have made Solomon's house of Lebanon look bare as a barn. This Jewish exuberance jostled with Spanish and Indian styles."[85]

As discussed earlier, in the section on marketing the films, movies became a commodity like other American consumer products. And as Douglas Gomery has pointed out, the movie palaces were built in the shopping districts of middle-class neighborhoods, making an implicit link between moviegoing and other forms of capitalist consumption.[86] The luxurious cinema interiors promoted fantasies of instant upward mobility, much as the Broadway set for *Abie's Irish Rose* did. According to Richard Butsch, these theaters "recapitulated on a larger scale the palaces of [early] vaudeville," in which even the working class had been welcome.[87]

CONFLICT BETWEEN PARENTS AND CHILDREN

The content of the films about Jewish immigrants discussed in this chapter also spoke to one of the inherent promises of American capitalism, that children could be expected to do better economically than their parents had done. The desire of parents to see their children succeed was not entirely self-less; it derived partly from the parents' need to be taken care of in their old age. Children were expected to have an abundant sense of gratitude for their parents' sacrifices on their behalf. But some of the films showed the opposite: the children acting out their sense of shame about their immigrant parents, even to the point of publicly humiliating and disowning them. Kevin Brownlow has suggested that *Humoresque* was popular among Jewish audiences because it "exploited" the second generation's "suppressed sense of guilt" at having rebelled against its parents, while at the same time it reassured the immigrant parents that their children were not necessarily lost to them.

Both *His People* and *The Younger Generation* show the dangers of sons getting too big for their britches in this way, forgetting the respect they owe their fathers. The most poignant moments in *His People* and *The Younger Generation* occur when sons turn their backs on their fathers, refusing to be associated with them. (The opposite, of course, occurs in *The Jazz Singer*; it is the father who cuts his ties with his son.) In *His People*, Morris pretends not to recognize his father when he comes to his son's engagement party (to which the immigrant parents have not been invited, the son having told his fiancé's family that he is an orphan). In *The Younger Generation* it is the scene in which the son, also named Morris, pretends that his father, laden with packages, is a servant; he lambastes him in front of the guests for not using the servants' entrance.

Furthermore, in *The Younger Generation,* it is the son who believes his parents should be grateful to him, rather than the other way around. "If it wasn't for me," Morris tells them, "you'd still be rotting down on Delancey Street. But I'm going to make real people out of you, whether you like it or not." Julius has become totally emasculated by his own son, who gives orders to the butler that his father cannot have his clothes until after his bath. "What will Morris say, you staying in bed all day?" asks Mama. "I'm sick from what Morris says," he responds. "I wish I was back on the East Side!" Mama rejoins, "How could Morris get into society—with his father on the East Side?" According to his mother, Morris is measured not by his own accomplishments, but by who his father is, and where his father lives. But the mother is mistaken; the real problem is Morris's own sense of self, which seems compromised by his parents' poverty.

But Morris is unable to see this; he congratulates himself on having done his parents a tremendous favor by rescuing them from the ghetto. He confers upon them meaningless luxury and utter disempowerment. As Birdie accuses her brother, "Who buried [papa] in this cold Italian tomb and make him look like an antique?" Morris, who has risen from junk salesman to art dealer, has turned his own parents into objets d'art. They are reduced, metaphorically, to decorations, to frozen statues. By "burying" or imprisoning his parents, Morris is able to wreak a kind of subconscious revenge—showing them what he lacked in his own childhood, he turns them into dependent children whom he can order around. They become just like items in his inventory. When his father still manages to embarrass him by bringing objects from the Lower East Side back to the mansion, Morris is infuriated. After all, his new home is defined by the objects it contains; by infecting one habitat with the artifacts of the other the distinction between the two places collapses.

FATHERS AND SONS

The son's sense of masculinity, in both cases, seems to depend on his ability to humiliate his own father. In a national culture that feminized immigrant Jewish men, the sons appeared to need not to contradict the stereotypes, but to show that they were somehow immune from them. By moving upward in social class, they could detach from themselves the kinds of societal labels that stuck so persistently to their fathers. Interestingly, the younger son in *His People* is less caught up in an Oedipal conflict with his father; he expresses his masculinity by becoming a prizefighter. Nevertheless, his sobriquet, Battling Rooney, suggests that he must pretend to be Irish rather than Jewish in order to project the proper image in the boxing ring.

The son's success thus often threatens to reduce the father to irrelevance. His resentment toward his son is perhaps rooted most powerfully in jealousy of his son's success. In *The Jazz Singer*, Jakie returns to his parents' apartment as an adult and promises his mother (in one of the few talking sequences in the film) that he will give her the money to move from the Lower East Side to the Bronx. By doing so, however, he would symbolically castrate his own father, whose role it is to make such decisions for the family. The contest is between the two men over control of the family. Still, Jakie ultimately bows to his father's wishes in returning to the synagogue. Similarly, in *His People* the rebellious son ultimately learns that his father is boss, and that he must respect him.

Many historians who have written on the 1920s have emphasized the popularization in America of Sigmund Freud's theories during the decade. The popularity of Freud's ideas has been viewed as contributing to the liberalization of attitudes toward sexuality during the period, and helping to give rise to the image of the flapper in popular culture.[88] But although scholars have described the ways in which films of the period reflected changing sexual mores, they have not emphasized the ways in which the films also presented family conflicts that Americans could understand in Freudian terms. Americans could embrace the representations of ethnic characters portrayed in the Jewish-themed films because they depicted family relationships that seemed universal.

THE JEWISH MOTHER REDUX

For example, the mother in the Jewish-themed films was invariably played by one of two actresses, Rosa Rosanova or Vera Gordon. The mother's influence over her son often dominated the plot, as in *The Jazz Singer,* where it seems as if Jake's mother is actually his primary love interest. The son and father battle for the mother's attention. Thus although the mother is often cast as the mediator of the father-son conflict, she also often seems to some degree responsible for the conflict in the first place by favoring her son over her husband. When the mother berates her husband for his lack of economic success in contrast to his son, she fans the flame of the Oedipal conflict between the two men.

The Jewish mother in these films is thus not quite the feminist icon that many would like to see. For example, Sharon Pucker Rivo has argued that "[a]fter World War I the image of Jewish women [in film] was transformed to that of capable, strong and independent mothers and daughters."[89] But the immigrant mothers in the Jewish-themed films of the 1920s seem actually to be relatively disempowered; they tend to live vicariously through their sons. In both *Humoresque* and *The Younger Generation,* the mother expresses her frustration with the family's poverty by continually insulting the father's inability to succeed in business; she holds up to him their son as a model. But by doing so, she has imperiled her son's sense of self; without a father to provide a kind of bridge to the real world, he has little sense of himself as a man.

Leon in *Humoresque* detaches himself from his mother in stages. His decision to go off to war, even before being drafted, is her worst nightmare, and does in fact result in his injury. He chooses his duty to "Uncle Sam" above his career and, in a sense, above his loyalty to his mother. And the end of the film (unlike in the short story, which ends with his enlistment) shows that it is not Leon's mother who can keep his music alive, but his fiancée. Leon has traded one Jewish woman for another, and although the effect of this on his mother is not really seen, this represents his final independence from her control. Although the film is about an extraordinarily nurturing mother, it is also about an extraordinarily controlling one. But the mother-son relationship still seemed to have elements of universality, at least at the time the film was produced. Laurence Reid called *Humoresque* "a picture with a soul" that "will move to the depths all who have imagination, feeling and sympathy no matter how repressed or neglected."[90]

28. Rosa Rosanova (Rose Cominsky) feeds Rudolph Schildkraut (David Cominsky) in Edward Sloman's 1925 film, *His People*. Courtesy of Billy Rose Theatre Collection, New York Public Library for the Performing Arts, Astor, Lenox and Tilden Foundations.

The mother is also typically unable to avoid the rupture in the father-son relationship. For example, in *The Jazz Singer,* she tries to make peace between the two men, to no avail. (In *His People,* she succeeds in stopping her husband from beating their younger son since it is the eve of the Sabbath, but she can do nothing to prevent their elder son from both taking advantage of and disrespecting his father.) While in some ways the films reinforced the stereotype of the *yiddishe mama* (the overbearing, excessively nurturing but also extremely controlling figure), in other ways they showed Jewish mothers as helpless and dependent.

Unable to take charge of her own fate, the Jewish mother inevitably became an object of pity. In an article on Jewish mothers in the *American Hebrew,* Zelda Popkin pointed to the centrality of the Jewish mother in popular culture; she remarked that the figure appears in "all films and fiction about Jews—recall *Humoresque.*" But Popkin opined that this "loquacious, family-loving, full bosomed maternal type" paradoxically remains an "alien" while she "rears Americans." In Popkin's words, "She must create a new generation in strange surroundings—watch it grow up and away from her—and then, her duty done, melt into the drab background, from which she emerged often as much of an alien as ever." The immigrant mother, in other words, is heroically self-sacrificing; she is perennially left behind as her children acculturate into American society. She has sacrificed herself to their Americanization. They have outgrown her and her culture.

Popkin thus called the Jewish mother "a much sentimentalized but strange and pathetic figure in American life." She remarked that the Jewish mother appears both in Yiddish theater—"perennially wearing the robe of tragedy"—and in "all films and fiction about Jews." She pointed out that the paradox of the Jewish mother is that although she is a foreigner, an "alien," she must "rear Americans."

The Jewish mother, Popkin added, is "timidly emerging from the shawl-and-sheitel [wig] stage of American evolution," when Jewish mothers were said to have "sewed their infants into flannels for the Winter, used bathtubs to store the Winter's coal and gave their babies herring tails for pacifiers." But their lack of education in modern methods of child-raising, Popkin believed, often redounded to the benefit of their infants. According to the New York City health commissioner, Royal S. Copeland, who was also quoted in the article, the fact that Jewish mothers breast-fed their babies accounted for a lower rate of infant mortality in the Lower East Side than on the ritzy Upper East Side.

Also quoted in the piece is a Mrs. Thomson, who headed a tuberculosis clinic in Brownsville, and who, despite being a Scotswoman, "speaks better Yiddish than her 'patients' speak English." Mrs. Thomson theorized that important differences existed between two different categories of Jewish mothers—the foreign-born and the American-born. The immigrant mother, she had observed, "cares above all for her babes. Herself, her home, her husband are relegated to things of minor consequence." Her children's diet is particularly well-regulated; "Little Benny or Beckie no longer get pennies for lollypops or soda. They must buy baked sweet potatoes or an apple or a 'malted.'" In contrast, the "Americanized" mother, concerned that her home be respectable, "divides her time between her home and her babies."

One important factor in the health of the children of immigrant mothers, according to Mrs. Thomson, is that they spend most of their time outdoors, out of the "reeking, suffocating, dank, airless" tenements. And those families that moved uptown during the postwar economic boom remained uptown even when wages fell, taking on boarders in order to pay the rent. But "space didn't matter, for she kept the sunshine and the fresh air."[91]

Although second-generation Jewish men in these films need, in good Freudian style, to define themselves in opposition to their fathers, the mother-son relationship is central to many of these films. In contrast to *Abie's Irish Rose,* in which no mothers are present (the only older woman in the play is the wife of the couple next door, who is purely a figure of comedy), the mother serves an important role in many of these films as mediator of the father-son conflict (as in *The Jazz Singer* and *His People*) or to provide a kind of sentimentalized, self-sacrificing nurturance otherwise denied Jewish men in a hostile society. The *yiddishe mama,* who invariably favored her sons over her daughters, often also seemed closer to her sons than to her own husband. This stereotype was not just reflected in Jewish popular culture; it was fed and reinforced by it.

The self-sacrificing element of the Jewish mother stereotype is prevalent in all the films. Perhaps the most fully realized Jewish mother character is that of Amelia Rosen (Mary Alden), the delicatessen owner in *April Fools,* a film about a discharged pants presser, Jacob Goodman (Alexander Carr, of *Potash and Perlmutter* fame) in a Lower East Side garment factory. Goodman starts out by selling umbrellas to Yiddish theater patrons and ends up opening a successful umbrella "hospital," or repair store. He competes with his business rival, Samuel Appelbaum (Snitz Edwards) for the hand of Amelia, who favors Goodman and also looks after Goodman's young daughter, Irma (Baby Peggy). But when Appelbaum spreads a rumor that Goodman's interest in Amelia is solely pecuniary in nature, she withdraws her affection. To make matters worse, Appelbaum's adopted son, Joe (Pat Moore), steals valuable bonds from his father's banking house and leaves Leon Steinfeld, Irma's fiancée who is also Appelbaum's nephew, to take the rap. Steinfeld thus shows up at his wedding with the police ready to arrest him, and Appelbaum extorts from Goodman all of his possessions in order to drop the charges. A penniless Goodman goes back to hawking umbrellas on the street, where he is spotted by Amelia; the film ends as they are presumably preparing to celebrate their own long-delayed nuptials.

But the Jewish mother could also be controlling. Brownlow points out that *Humoresque* was one of the first silent films of any type to focus on the mother-son relationship. He writes that a film that "bombarded the emotions with scenes of maternal heartbreak—with a Jewish mother at that—could not have been more perfectly timed." His insightful explanation for the film's popularity among Jewish audiences is that while it "exploited" the second generation's "suppressed sense of guilt" at having rebelled against its parents, it also reassured those same parents that their children were not lost to them.

Leon lives out his mother's dream—not necessarily his own—in becoming a violinist. In fact, it seems quite possible that his mother has played a large role in inducing him to make the career choice that he does. It seems quite impossible for him to decide *not* to pursue it. But the process of his becoming a musician is not shown in either the short story or the film. Also, when Leon plays for the Lower East Side audience, the immigrants in the audience all seem to be stand-ins for his parents; Leon wants to please his parents the most.

Or is it the filmmakers who want to please the audience, giving them a view of Jews as fitting perfectly into the evolving American scene? Neil Gabler has argued that the ending of *The Jazz Singer* sidesteps the issue of Jake's primary loyalty. He argues that the film "swiftly and painlessly, dissolves the problem altogether." For Gabler, this is emblematic of the Jewish movie moguls' use of Hollywood to give themselves a kind of symbolic rebirth. He cites Jack Warner's marriage to a Catholic woman as "a symbol of the same old battle: the young assimilated American Jew defying the authority of the past to establish the supremacy of the future ... between obligations and aspirations, between the old and the new, between Judaism and America." Gabler calls this "a kind of paradigm of the tensions of assimilation generally, just as *The Jazz Singer* was its clearest, most paradigmatic artistic expression."[92]

The film was remade twice, in 1952 and in 1980. (It was also done as a radio version in 1936 and 1947, and as a television movie in 1959; the television version starred Jerry Lewis, who sang the "Kol Nidrei" in blackface!) The 1952 film version, starring Danny Thomas, moved the story to an affluent suburb of Philadelphia, and barely sidestepped the issue of intermarriage by having Jack's love interest, played by Peggy Lee, say that she had not been to a Passover seder since she left home. In the 1980 version, starring the pop star Neil Diamond, he openly marries a woman named Molly Bell, played by Lucie Arnaz. (The cantor is played by Laurence Olivier.) As Whitfield has pointed out, it is she who becomes the voice of Jack's Jewish conscience; by insisting that he not lose his ethnic identity, she "demonstrates how baseless the ancient Jewish anxieties about intermarriage really are."[93]

Whitfield views the original film as itself helping to advance the assimilation of Jews into American society. In its distance from Jewish tradition, Whitfield calls the film a "parable of modernization, a sign of the eclipse of the sacred, a testament to what the sociologist Max Weber labelled 'the disenchantment of the world.'" Whitfield argues that it was Jolson's very success and the "pride and identification that he fostered" that "helped to erode [the Jewish] community. . . . By proving that they could make it in America, the popular entertainers and the businessmen behind them made the distinctive subculture of the immigrants seem parochial, stunted and doomed." Whitfield concludes that, "By articulating our [Jews'] common dreams and in permeating much of our experience, [popular culture] also homogenized our lives and helped to shatter the context of the particular."[94]

Yet Jews did not want their Jewishness to be "eclipsed" or "shattered." They wanted to find ways to integrate the different parts of their identities so they could live happily both as Jews and as Americans. Jewishness, far from antiquated and disposable, appeared in silent films as, for the most part, viable, vibrant, and enduring. Although the children of Jewish immigrants are not shown as clinging to the faith and the folkways of their parents, they are also quite pointedly not shown as entirely rejecting the culture that gave birth to them. While they may have physically moved away from the Lower East Side, they still felt a strong pull from the immigrant sensibility; they lived out their lives in this tension between their parents' culture and the new American culture that they were helping to shape. It is this ambivalence that haunts all the Jewish-themed films of the 1920s.

Still, the films had Jewish subject matter. They showed Jewish families, which even while coping with these issues of acculturation, were Jewish families nonetheless. And at a time when economic and political opportunities for Jews were still quite limited and anti-Semitism was still quite strong, they spoke to Jews' need both to romanticize the past and to imagine a brighter future.

Thus, although the changing images of Jews in American film did have an effect on the place of Jews in American culture, it was not simply to

29. Publicity material for the 1930 film *The Kibitzer*, showing different expressions of Ike Lazarus (Harry Green). Courtesy of Photofest.

collapse the distinctions between Jews and other Americans. Jewish identity was thus reinforced at the moment of its seeming destabilization, reinvigorated at the moment of its seeming dissolution.

I'd like to close this chapter with a look back at the vaudeville comic turned film star, Harry Green. As part of the marketing campaign for the film version of *The Kibitzer,* Green was photographed doing six different facial expressions, as if to teach people how to "kibitz." The first photo, according to the caption, shows Green's face lighting up as he discovers an opportunity to engage in kibitzing. The second one shows him assuming his position behind the chair of the "victim." The third one shows him turning up his nose at a play. The fourth one shows him thinking aloud about how he would play the card differently. The fifth one shows him reacting in shock that the "victim" is acting differently from the way he has proposed. The sixth one shows him delighting, as the card player presumably makes a big blunder, in being vindicated in having been right all along.

In essence, Green is giving the American public a window into Jewish culture. Now it is Jews who can "teach" both Jews and non-Jews how to be Jewish, in a sense. Jewish culture has been validated and made into not just an object of scorn and ridicule, but something that can give pleasure to all. Unlike in the photo discussed earlier in this chapter, where Green's tie is askew and he is not wearing a jacket, in this set of images he is neatly attired in jacket, with his tie pulled up to his neck. His triumph in the last image is the success of Jews in general in clambering up to a more dignified position in American society. While most of their appearances in popular culture have been as comic figures, show business Jews have still dignified themselves, transcending many of the vaudeville stereotypes that kept them from seeming like true Americans. In the process of elevating themselves, they changed America.

Conclusion

In a recent article in *The New Yorker* about the film comedian Harold Ramis, Tad Friend wrote that "The secret of American commercial success is to hijack a subculture and ransom it to the mainstream." He went on to explain that "What Elvis did for rock and Eminem did for rap, Harold Ramis did for attitude: he mass-marketed the sixties to the seventies and eighties."[1]

While words like "highjacking" and "ransom" seem more connected to the world of terrorism and fear that we now inhabit than to early-twentieth-century popular culture, this does seem like an apt way to talk about Jewish culture in the 1920s. One generation's stereotypes, visual images, and verbal tics were repackaged for the pleasure of another generation. American Jewish culture became a cross-generational conversation in which all Americans, whatever their ethnicity, could participate.

Indeed, what would early-twentieth-century popular culture have looked like without Jews? In all the "lively arts" enumerated by Gilbert Seldes, Jews played a major and defining role. A tremendous amount has been written about Jews in popular culture, from showbiz biographies of Jewish entertainers to books on Jewish blackface performers, film producers, playwrights, and television stars. Among the questions asked by this body of work are: What makes Jewish culture Jewish? Does a Jewish creator automatically and inevitably create a Jewish work? If so, where does the Jewishness of it reside?

By contrast, this book has focused less on Jewishness as a construct than as the representation of a specific group of American Jews, the second-generation Jews who lived in New York, during a single decade, the 1920s. This is a much narrower focus, but it has enabled me to isolate what I view as the point in time in which Jewish entertainment, broadly defined, not just reached a pinnacle of popularity among both Jews and non-Jews, but had a significant effect on the ways in which Jews were viewed both by themselves and by other Americans.

Jewish entertainment was both nostalgic and future-oriented; it referred back to the immigrant life of the ghetto and forward to the diminishing boundaries between Jews and other American groups. In vaudeville, Jewish entertainers were both sympathetic and self-denigrating, self-aggrandizing and self-parodying, exultant and confused—all of which fed gloriously into their comedy.

On Broadway, a string of comedies flattered the second generation's upward mobility as they moved to the outer boroughs and into the lower middle class. In silent film, Jews were seen as coping with the same basic struggles, and having the same aspirations, as other Americans. But Jewish popular culture was targeted at both Jews and non-Jews; while Jews could feel proud about having truly "arrived" in American culture, non-Jews could feel connected to the universal aspects of the Jewish experience.

The extent to which these representations and images shored up Jewish ethnicity is a difficult question. It may be a central tenet of the growing field of Performance Studies that, as Harley Erdman has pithily put it, performances "shape material and cultural reality," but it is notoriously difficult to establish the cause-and-effect relationship. The fact that Jewish stereotypes have changed over time seems clear, and I have tried to trace some of the changes. Nevertheless, one of the most interesting aspects of the older, essentially anti-Semitic Jewish stereotypes is their persistence into the second-generation culture rather than their outright disappearance, as Erdman and others had speculated would happen. Second-generation Jews needed these caricatures in order to flatter themselves that they had moved beyond them.

But what were the new, second-generation Jewish stereotypes that first coexisted with the immigrant stereotypes on stage and screen, and were gradually to replace them? What was left when the immigrant mannerisms, dialect, and clothing were replaced with a more "up-to-date" and "Americanized" appearance? What were the characteristic beliefs, feelings, and attitudes that were characteristically "Jewish" for the second generation? And what were the differences between Jewish men and Jewish women in this regard? I have tried to get at this in discussing the differences between the Jewish male and Jewish female stereotypes of the second generation, but the question remains a difficult one. Perhaps it was the very fact of their grappling with issues of Jewish identity and continuity that made Jewish characters Jewish. For the second generation, this process of producing and consuming representations was itself a constituent element in the formation of the new second-generation Jewish ethnicity.

Furthermore, to the extent that New York Jewish culture was especially meaningful to Jews themselves, this focus provides for a sustained exploration of the ways in which Jews redefined the meaning of Jewishness through both a sense of longing for their origins (both personal and historical) and a sense of pride in having moved up in the world. Among their heroes and role models were not just Jewish athletes and Jewish politicians, but Jewish entertainers.

Minority groups need celebrities from their group; their success is viewed, by extension, as the group's success as a whole. By showing how far members from the group can rise, the whole group is elevated both in their own eyes and in the eyes of the majority.

Yet if this study grows to some extent out of a kind of intellectualized nostalgia for Jewish life in the 1920s, which, I cannot help fantasizing (since I was born decades later) was fuller, richer, and more saturated with Jewish culture than the present era, then it is partly because Jews in the 1920s were themselves looking back to an earlier period to which they remained powerfully though ambivalently attached.

Perhaps most important, this study has looked at how historical and sociological changes in the Jewish community were reflected on stage and screen. This study thus bridges various realms that are not often brought together. Other than in Irving Howe's *World of Our Fathers,* one looks in vain, in historical studies of New York Jews in various periods, for much about popular culture in those periods. Those books that do mention popular culture are usually content to talk about *The Jazz Singer* or *Fiddler on the Roof* and let it go at that. But popular culture has defined the lives of Jews, by reflecting back to them recognizable images and representations of their lives—that is to say, their attitudes, fears, fantasies, and, above all, their pride in becoming American. Yet books on Jewish popular culture rarely take a sociological approach to their subject, analyzing instead the content of Jewish humor, Jewish art, or Jewish music.

THE GREAT DEPRESSION

The Great Depression essentially brought the Golden Age of Jewish entertainment that I have chronicled in this study to an end. The ethnic joie de vivre that characterized Jewish popular entertainment gave way to somberness and introspection that lasted through the 1930s. Crude ethnic stereotypes began to fall out of favor; negative Jewish stereotypes particularly declined in the wake of the Holocaust. The heady, giddy celebratory aura of American life in the Jazz Age began to dissipate. As if emerging from an alcoholic stupor, Americans began to sober up, look around, and take stock.

The appetite for crude ethnic comedy, so prevalent in the 1920s, was greatly diminished. The Yiddish theater company known as ARTEF staged agit-prop theater and demonstrations to bring attention to the ravages of the Depression. The Federal Theatre Project, formed by the Works Progress Administration, incorporated a Yiddish unit that staged both vaudeville shows and comic plays by authors like Sholem Aleichem and David Pinski. But the signal achievement of the decade was the formation of the Group Theater, created by Harold Clurman, Cheryl Crawford, and Lee Strasberg in conscious imitation of the Moscow Art Theatre, a company that subordinated individual acting to the overall effect of the ensemble, just as the Depression in some respects fostered a sense of community among those who suffered economic setbacks.

The greatest production of the Group Theater was Clifford Odets's *Awake and Sing!*, which portrayed an extended Jewish family living in the Bronx, the members of which, in the playwright's words, "share a fundamental activity: a struggle for life amidst petty conditions." Among the petty conditions are, of course, the Depression, which, as Beth Wenger has written in her study of New York Jews in the 1930s, "represents an aberration from the overall pattern of twentieth century Jewish mobility," even though, according to Wenger, they were comparatively better off than other minority groups, having risen into white-collar employment.[2] But Jews, like all Americans, were greatly affected by the Depression.

Jews thus experienced, along with other Americans, a significant loss of both financial security and overall morale. Tensions between various factions of the Jewish community emerged, as the Depression affected different Jewish neighborhoods differently, exacerbating the poverty that existed on the Lower East Side and in Brownsville, while having a much lesser effect on more prosperous Jewish neighborhoods such as the West Bronx (along the Grand Concourse) and the Upper West Side.

In *Awake and Sing!*, which seems clearly set in the East Bronx, the epicenter of radical Jewish politics, a rich uncle, Uncle Morty, lords it over the younger members of the family, who have to work hard for a living. The patriarch, Jacob, is an ardent socialist who sees the war dead as "workers and farmers who murdered each other in uniform for the greater glory of capitalism."[3] As even young Ralph seems to understand, "life is not printed on dollar bills." The play is a searing critique of capitalism; as Steven Whitfield has written, American Jewish dramatists have often turned for subjects to the "corrosive effects of business and to the resulting enfeeblement of the family and the ravaged ties of community."[4]

But in *Awake and Sing!*, the Bergers seem to be very much part of the overall community that is suffering from the Depression. If the "ties of community" are breaking down, it is the ties to the Jewish community. Unlike Odets's original version, which had been titled *I've Got the Blues* and had contained numerous Yiddish expressions, biblical allusions, and explicit Jewish references, *Awake and Sing!* barely mentions Jews, Judaism, or Jewishness. Yet, as the critic Julius Novick has put it, the Bergers are "explicitly, riotously Jewish."

Its effect on the Jewish audience was immense. Alfred Kazin has written of *Awake and Sing!* that the playwright's words were a "lyric uplifting of blunt Jewish speech, boiling over and explosive. . . . Everyone on that stage was furious, kicking, alive." The playwright, he added, "pulled us out of self-pity.

Everything so long choked up in twenty thousand damp hallways and on all those rumpled summer sheets, everything still smelling of the cold shadowed sand littered with banana peels under the boardwalk at Coney Island . . . was now out in the open, at last, and we laughed."[5]

It was the verisimilitude of the work that so captivated Kazin, which went beyond the kinds of Jewish stereotypes that he was used to seeing on the stage. Something of the reality of Jewish life, of its true vibrancy and tension, was finally realized onstage. And not just realized, but validated, as if Jews could be the subject of tragedy and not just melodrama; the greatest thrill for Kazin was "Sitting in the Belasco, watching my mother and father and uncles and aunts occupying the stage in *Awake and Sing!* by as much right as if they were Hamlet and Lear."[6]

Outside of New York, however, many in the entertainment industry, particularly in film, saw the need for Jews to reduce overtly ethnic characterizations. Henry Jenkins has studied the changes in Eddie Cantor's screen persona through the course of his career, finding that Cantor had to tone down the overtly Jewish content and style of his performances in order to succeed with the national audience.

Jenkins notes a progression from the heavy ethnic content of the earlier films (such as *Glorifying the American Girl,* which contains the "Belt in the Back" routine) to later films like *Kid from Spain, Kid Millions,* and *Strike Me Pink,* in which, according to Jenkins, using a term borrowed from Irving Howe, Cantor was "de-Semitized." Jenkins writes that, "While the question of ethnic identity was a central concern of urban immigrant audiences and thus prime field for the construction of jokes aimed at that group, it did not prove amusing in the hinterlands, which either found the issue irrelevant or threatening."[7]

Even the later film *Glorifying the American Girl,* Jenkins suggests, "treated Cantor's ethnicity as one more exotic aspect of the New York show world."[8] Along with Michael Rogin and Andrea Most, Jenkins focuses more on Cantor's 1930 film *Whoopee,* in which Cantor plays an Indian chief with Jewish mannerisms and references, as an example of Jewish ethnicity being to some extent deemphasized or superseded by a more universal framework. As John F. McClymer has pointed out, Cantor's neurasthenic persona in *Whoopee* is much more stereotypically WASP than Jew since, McClymer writes, "underneath the layers of ethnic and racial meaning lies, not a stereotype, but the recognition of common humanity. That is why the scene struck both Jews and gentiles alike as hilarious."[9]

Yet we have seen that there were a number of heavily Jewish-themed films produced in the 1920s that were geared to national audiences. So it was hardly a question of there never having been a national audience for Jewish material. Not all Jewish comedians had chosen to do explicitly Jewish comedy; the Marx Brothers, for example, had always eschewed it. But Jenkins argues that those who could not be "normalized" or "repositioned," such as Fanny Brice, were, at least in the 1930s, "rejected by Hollywood and forced to try to regain a place on the stage."

This is not entirely true even of Brice, though, since she made a film in 1930 called *Be Yourself* in which she played a rather stereotypical Jewish woman whose husband was played by Harry Green, the Jewish dialect comedian discussed in the last chapter. And even the films in which Jewishness was downplayed, Jenkins has found, were often marketed through the Yiddish press in order to attract a Jewish audience. Did Jewish stars and filmmakers project their own ambivalence about their Jewish identity onto non-Jewish audiences, or were the audiences already ambivalent toward Jews in some way? It is more difficult to tell than Jenkins would have us believe.

Moving to the Suburbs

Things changed even more for the third generation. When Jews began to move in large numbers to the suburbs in the years following the Second World War, they generally left their aged parents behind. As the sociologist Samuel Heilman has written, "Grandma and Grandpa stayed behind in the city, in the apartment blocks in the old neighborhood. Indeed, the flow of Sunday traffic between the suburbs of Long Island and the old neighborhoods of the Bronx in New York City became a kind of choreography of the residential pattern."[10]

The suburbanization of New York Jews led to a loss of ethnic cohesion; as Eli Lederhendler has put it, "As the New York (white) middle class made its way up and out of the city's neighborhoods, inevitably the Jewish, second-generation cohort was less able to define (much less perpetuate) the group-mediated urban ethic that had defined it."[11] The entertainment choices of second- and third-generation Jews began to diverge from each other.

One needed to visit the grandparents in the city in order to watch Milton Berle, Victor Borge, and Red Buttons on television; suburban television sets were somehow disabled from tuning into these kinds of vaudeville-type Jewish performers. As George Lipsitz has written of 1950s television shows like *The Goldbergs* (about a Jewish family), *The Honeymooners* (about an Irish family), and *Life with Luigi* (about an Italian family), television shows "presented ethnic families in working-class urban neighborhoods at the precise historical moment when a rising standard of living, urban renewal and suburbanization contributed to declines in ethnic and class identity."[12]

Not to say that Jewishness entirely disappeared from popular culture. But third-generation Jews were more drawn to the comedy of Sid Caesar, renowned for his ridiculous foreign accents, and to Mickey Katz's Yiddish parodies of pop songs. As George Robinson has written of Katz, his music was the "plastic detritus of '50s America, the musical equivalent of formica and tuna casseroles, of 'Danish' modern and 'French' provincial . . . a matzah ball in the eye of popular culture."[13]

In the early 1960s the song parodies of Allan Sherman topped the charts. Sherman took familiar folk songs, Jewish wedding songs, and even operatic pieces and put new lyrics to them about Jewish suburban life. When John F. Kennedy was reportedly caught singing "Sarah Jackman" (based on "Frère Jacques"), Sherman's stardom was assured.

The number of plays and films about Jewish life dropped precipitously. Those that did feature Jewish characters often changed or whitewashed their ethnicity, as in the 1946 remake of *Humoresque,* starring John Garfield and Joan Crawford, with a script by Clifford Odets and Zachary Gold, in which almost all traces of Jewishness are obliterated, including changing the violinist's name from Leon Kantor to Paul Boray.

But it was the 1946 remake of *Abie's Irish Rose* that, many scholars have suggested, led to real changes in the depiction of Jews onscreen. Produced by Bing Crosby in an effort to speak to the same postwar spirit of unity that made the 1920s play and film so popular, the remake was widely denounced for its use of offensive stereotypes. As Joseph Foster editorialized in *New Masses,* the film "goes beyond bad taste and painful stage jokes." He added that the film is about Jewish characters who "have escaped the ghetto into substantial houses and morning coats, yet shriek at the mention of ham and the sight of Christmas trees, confuse Christmas bells with fire alarms and . . . use every threadbare gesture of the stage Jew."[14]

The result was the formation by the National Jewish Community Relations Council (an umbrella organization of major Jewish organizations) of the Motion Picture Project, designed as a way of "developing the potentialities of motion pictures as a medium for fostering good human relations." But their attitude was primarily defensive, with a mandate to "deal with problems arising from defamatory and stereotypical characters of minority groups, primarily Jewish."[15]

While Felicia Herman has argued that the various Jewish community relations agencies had a "strong, effective Jewish voice" that succeeded in preventing degrading depictions of Jews in film, it seems that the changing position of Jews in society had more of an effect on moderating prejudice than any steps taken by these organizations.[16] Compare, for example, the recent controversy over Mel Gibson's *The Passion of the Christ,* in which Jewish organizations, fearful of an outbreak of anti-Semitism, appealed to Gibson, with very limited success, to change the film. But no anti-Semitic incidents were reported as a result of the film; indeed, surveys showed that it did not change attitudes toward Jews in American society.[17]

Lester Friedman has argued that while films in the 1940s did often show Jewish characters fighting and dying in war, both the 1930s and 1950s were decades in which few films were made that featured Jewish characters. "Fifties filmmakers," he writes, dusted off old stereotypes and retreated to worn-out clichés, placing their Jewish characters into bloated biblical epics, conventional war sagas, sanitary biographies, and syrupy melodramas."[18]

However, the Jewish films of the 1920s had also been "syrupy" and melodramatic. The difference is that, in David Weinberg's words, Jews had become a "socially acceptable minority."[19] Jews have been embraced by American society, which is increasingly comfortable having them in its midst, while most Jews are uncomfortable with their own tradition, about which they know little.

What would it look like to apply this combined approach to other periods of American Jewish life? How would our understanding of Jewish life in the 1960s, for example, change if we looked at a wide range of Jewish cultural products from that decade, beyond just *Fiddler on the Roof*, which is not set in America and does not represent American Jewish life. What if we looked at a Broadway show from the 1960s, like *The Education of H*Y*M*A*N K*A*P*L*A*N*, the music of humorist Allan Sherman ("Hello Muddah, Hello Faddah") and a film from the 1960s, like *Goodbye, Columbus*, and analyzed them not just in terms of their representation of Jewish characters but in the sociological terms set out in, for example, Samuel Heilman's *Portrait of American Jews: The Second Half of the Twentieth Century*, which shows the effects of suburbanization on Jewish identity? We might learn much about the Jewish experience in that decade that is inaccessible if looking through only one lens.

In many ways, this book has been motivated by Robert Warshow's insight that the "images of this group" in popular culture bear a relationship to the group's lived experience, to the places they reside and the consciousness of their social class. Interestingly, as they became more accepted in American society, New York Jews actually became less comfortable with explicit Jewish content in the popular culture they created. This is partly because ethnic stereotypes became distasteful to Americans in general, so it was difficult for ethnic groups themselves to feel positively toward them.

INSIDER/OUTSIDER

This insider/outsider dynamic is the central paradox of early-twentieth-century American Jewish culture. In some ways, yes, Jewish pop culture existed in a kind of world of its own, in which Jews made shorthand references, told in-jokes, and used a code to which non-Jews had no access. This was what frustrated so many non-Jewish theater and film critics, who had a difficult time evaluating something that seemed to exclude them. On the other hand, the most interesting dimension of Jewish pop culture from this period was the fact that it *was* so amazingly popular, in some cases, like *Abie's Irish Rose,* touring not just around the country but around the world, reaching millions in an era long before American pop culture developed a truly global reach.

Jews lived in such high residential concentration in the outerborough neighborhoods that, as Jonathan Sarna has written, they "inhabited a largely self-contained subculture, a parallel universe that shared many of the trappings of the larger society while standing apart from it." Rather than religiously based, their Jewishness was "characterized less by religious observance than by ethnicity, propinquity and culture."[20] But what were the outlines of this culture? This study has pointed to the performing arts as a central component of that culture. For just as New York Jews lived, to a large degree, in their own neighborhoods, worked for Jewish employers, and maintained almost exclusively Jewish social networks, they created and consumed entertainment that was heavily Jewish-themed.

Nevertheless, they took the subway back to Manhattan from their Bronx and Brooklyn neighborhoods, and they hardly limited their trips only to the Lower East Side. As much as Broadway was filled with Jewish producers, playwrights, theater critics, and songwriters, the majority of those who worked on Broadway were not Jewish. Thus, even in the entertainment field, Jews participated in the life of the city to a much greater extent than their immigrant parents ever had. As in other parts of the country, where the owner of a Jewish store often served a mostly non-Jewish clientele, there were many second-generation Jews whose businesses were directed to mostly non-Jewish customers. Even Jewish delicatessens served many non-Jewish patrons. And in Harlem, Jewish store owners and African American shoppers encountered each other in ways that they probably never would have in midtown; they would not even have been found next to each other in movie or Broadway theater seats.

Not to mention that Jewish entertainers leapt to stardom on the strength of an audience that was not just composed of Jews. In *Glorifying the American Girl,* the clip of Eddie Cantor in the tailor shop is shown right after a clearly non-Jewish couple in the audience for the Ziegfeld *Follies,* shown among a sea of well-dressed patrons, talk about how excited they are that Cantor is about to appear. The film thus shows non-Jews looking at Jews, suggesting that non-Jews embraced Jewish entertainment. Did they find it exotic or just amusing? Did it allow them to express sympathy, as I suggest in the chapter on film, or indulge anti-Semitic feelings?

Consumers have different responses, and individuals often have a mix of different reactions. One cannot even assume that individual Jews felt a certain way—prideful, disdainful, or anything in between—when they viewed Jewish-themed entertainment. But when a large market develops for a product, one can assume that there is a host of reasons for that product's success. People must be drawn to it for some reason; it must be fulfilling some need or desire.

Perhaps because they teetered on the edge of acceptance into American society, the second generation did have a tendency to want to live in a world of their own, especially when it came to the entertainment they preferred. How else to explain the phenomenon of the Catskills, the mountain range in Upstate New York where second-generation Jews created an entire alternate universe of entertainment? When the streets of New York became unbearably hot every summer, second-generation Jews almost universally headed "up the mountains," as my grandmother used to say, where they would swim, play golf and tennis, eat incredible amounts of food, and take in a show every evening.

As Myrna Katz Frommer and Harvey Frommer have written, in the Catskills, "hired entertainers bridged the transition from the Old World to the New with a repertoire of both Yiddish and American songs and inside humor." The audiences and entertainers were both almost exclusively Jewish. It is difficult to underestimate the importance of the Catskills as a training ground for comedians; according to the Frommers, their "shtik, delivered in the nasal cadences of New York Jewish speech, may have debuted on the vaudeville circuit and in Coney Island saloons. But they were nursed and nurtured and cut their teeth in Catskill resorts."[21]

Jews in the 1920s could not assimilate into American society; they were barely even accepted into it. The Jewish movie producers were phenomenally successful not by joining the American mainstream but by their very exclusion from it. The place of Jews in American society is very different today from what it was in the 1920s. The themes of Jewish-American culture in the interwar era play very differently today. While intermarriage is still a source of humor, it has become a fact of life generally accepted, other than by the Orthodox, as the price paid for living in an open society. It is thus less a source of generational conflict, either on stage or in life.

A more common theme in American Jewish culture is the presence of non-Jews in Jewish life; witness the current off-Broadway play *Jewtopia,* which came to New York after a long run in Los Angeles, about a non-Jewish man who enlists his Jewish friend's aid in finding a Jewish wife. (Both male stars, who wrote the script, happen to be Jewish.) But this is not surprising at a time when the pop star Madonna has embraced Jewish mysticism to the extent that she uses Jewish symbols and rituals in her music videos and concerts.

While Jews remain concentrated in a relatively small number of American cities (with New York, Los Angeles, and Miami–Fort Lauderdale the largest

Jewish communities), the overall size of the American Jewish population declines every year. Yet, according to the National Foundation for Jewish Culture, the number of new Jewish films, books, songs, and other cultural products means that we are in a "Golden Age of Jewish Culture unlike any in the four thousand year history of the Jewish people."[22] But one needs to make a distinction between high and low culture; writers like Nathan Englander, Allegra Goodman, Myra Goldberg, and Jonathan Safran Foer are reaching a different audience than comics like Adam Sandler and Ben Stiller. One would need to compare the Jewish writers of today to the Jewish writers of the 1920s (e.g., Ludwig Lewisohn and Samuel Ornitz) rather than to the comedians and film stars.

Still, there is no denying that Jewish culture is enormously popular, even if, as Jon Stratton has found, it is not necessarily read as Jewish; the characters on the long-running television show *Seinfeld* were widely seen not as Jewish but just as New Yorkers. What is missed, however, is that the roots of this explosion of Jewish culture go back to the 1920s, when a secular Jewish identity was beginning to emerge, and when Jews first chose to express their Jewish identity in cultural forms. Much of this new Jewish culture seems shallow in its most popular forms (e.g., Adam Sandler's Chanukah songs). But it is hardly less deep in many respects than the Jewish pop culture of the 1920s, particularly the humor, which was so heavily based on crude Jewish stereotypes. In many ways, actually, it is deeper, based on biblical themes, Eastern European Jewish influences, and mystical elements. Also, as has been insufficiently recognized, this is in many respects a youth culture; many Jewish artists are in their twenties and thirties.

The routines of Fanny Brice and Eddie Cantor were funny both because they helped their second-generation audiences laugh at themselves, which was pleasurable in a self-deprecating way, but also because they spoke to the second generation's genuine difficulties in finding a stable, coherent, unified sense of self in American society. Some have described contemporary American Jews as still struggling with the same issues that, I have argued, characterized the second generation's ambivalence about their Jewishness. As Norman Kleeblatt, the curator of the 1996 exhibit at New York's Jewish Museum, *Too Jewish,* argues in the exhibit catalog, these third and fourth generation artists are "the first generation to have grown up watching their American and Jewish reflections on the television screen. . . . [T]hey have reaped the contentious rewards of assimilation and Americanization, while nevertheless experiencing marginalization, alienation and the subtle anti-Semitism that still permeates American culture."[23] Kleeblatt argues that the confusion that American Jewish artists feel about their Jewishness is itself the constitutive element in their Jewish-themed work.

A larger danger, however, is that many American Jews have little or no knowledge of their heritage, and thus nothing to grapple with or feel confused about. This means that Jewish tradition is occasionally even portrayed in unintentionally negative ways on television. One episode of *Friends* showed Ross (a Jewish character on the show) in an armadillo costume, trying to explain to his son the meaning of Chanukah, while Chandler (a non-Jewish character) was garbed in a Santa Claus suit. Although it is unlikely that the creators of the show intended this, having the Jew marked as alien and ugly (and a target for derision) recapitulated long-standing anti-Semitic stereotypes about the Jew's body. It is thus not surprising that Ross only gives a one-sentence explanation of Chanukah (having to do with the Maccabees) and that although the episode ends with the lighting of the Chanukah menorah, Chanukah seems paltry and poorly understood in comparison with Christmas.

As Jews have journeyed farther and farther from the Lower East Side, they have thus found themselves with less and less upon which to base a viable ethnic identity. Even the fondness that many American Jews retain for traditional Jewish foods is not sufficient to sustain Jewish identity, despite what has been dubbed the "gastronomic" Jew—the Jew whose Jewish identity is expressed only through the consumption of Jewish food.

The proliferation of "kosher-style" delicatessens in posh urban neighborhoods, like Artie's on New York's Upper West Side, points to the oddly half-hearted quality of their patrons' nostalgic desire for the foods of their childhood. The menus of these restaurants include bacon and ham, and meat sandwiches are made with cheese (a violation of the kosher laws that prohibit the serving of meat and dairy products at the same meal). Furthermore, as traditionally Jewish foods like bagels have entered the mainstream American diet, it has become increasingly difficult to ground a distinct minority ethnic identity simply on consumption of these foods.

THE AUDIENCE FOR JEWISH CULTURE

Much of the focus of this study has been on the audience. Studies of audiences are notoriously difficult, even when one tries to study the contemporary audience for a play. (Most audience studies nowadays are focused on trying to determine the class composition of the audience, in order to allow advertisers to target their theater program ads more effectively.)

Still, since they were first attracted to Broadway in the 1920s, Jews (who tend to have higher levels of education and greater affluence than the general population) have been a mainstay of the Broadway theater audience. In fact, one of the reasons often given for the decline of Broadway drama is the decrease in the number of Jewish patrons. As Michael Goldstein has written, "many of Broadway's problems are sociological, too large for the theater to confront as a business institution" such as "the departure of thousands of suburban Jews, who have traditionally been among Broadway's biggest audience constituencies, for destinations Floridian."[24]

Nevertheless, some plays and musicals still seem to cater to this audience. It has been often said that Broadway drama would decline when the bulk of the Jewish audience inevitably retired to South Florida. But although the number of nonmusical plays of any kind has plummeted since the 1920s, the two or three new plays that open each season on Broadway often do include a play of Jewish interest.

But plays with Jewish content and characters, for all their popularity with Jewish audiences, cannot make a profit by attracting only Jews; witness the runaway success of Mel Brooks's musical *The Producers,* based on his 1960s film of the same name. *The Producers* is the story of a Jewish theatrical producer and his accountant who perpetrate a scam by raising far more money than they need to put on an atrociously bad (and in deliberately bad taste) musical about Hitler. But their plan to keep the extra money after the musical flops are confounded when the play becomes a hilarious hit. Interestingly, the lead was originated by a non-Jew, Nathan Lane.[25] But non-Jewish actors are not always successful playing Jews; the tall, rugged television actor Tom Selleck was not particularly convincing to either critics or audiences when he played the rumpled, unemployed writer Murray Burns in 2004's revival of Herb Gardner's comedy *A Thousand Clowns.*

Perhaps the boldest experiment in having non-Jews play Jewish roles was undertaken a few years by the National Asian Theater Company, an off-Broadway Asian American troupe that generally produces revivals of classic plays. Their choice was William Finn and James Lapine's *Falsettoland,* a dark, slightly cartoonish Broadway musical about a very nontraditional Jewish family planning their son's bar mitzvah at a time when the father's non-Jewish homosexual lover, Whizzer, is dying of AIDS. (The parents are divorced; the mother is remarried to her former psychiatrist, who has become the boy's stepfather.)

As unusual as it was to see Asian American actors throwing around Yiddish terms and talking about Jewish food (one of the family's next-door neighbors is a lesbian kosher caterer), the nontraditional casting underscored the universality of the musical's themes. The climax comes when the son celebrates his bar mitzvah in the dying Whizzer's hospital room, and the father learns that he himself is probably infected as well. The bar mitzvah ceremony marks the son's true coming of age as he realizes his debt to Whizzer; it also helps to unite and strengthen the family in the face of their grief. The presence of community is also very strong, unlike in most current Jewish-themed entertainment. Almost all Jewish characters on television shows are inter-married. As Kera Bolonik pointed out, the wedding between Grace Adler (Debra Messing) and Marvin "Leo" Markus (Harry Connick, Jr.) on *Will and Grace* was the first wedding between a Jewish man and a Jewish woman ever on a prime-time sitcom. *Abie's Irish Rose* situations are now the norm, rather than the exception.[26]

In fact, most contemporary Jewish-themed plays and musicals are gener-ally unconcerned with examining Jewish themes. As the chief theater critic for a New York Jewish newspaper, *The Jewish Week,* I have seen remarkably few plays that focus on issues like intermarriage, the place of women and homosexuals in religious worship, the waning of Jewish identity, and the revival of Jewish mysticism. Perhaps the only truly "hot" topic is the Holo-caust; last year there was a spate of plays that reassessed the meaning of the Holocaust in Jewish memory and life.

Most contemporary Jewish artists seem to have little nostalgia for the immigrant Jewish experience in America, and have thus apparently escaped the pull of the ghetto culture so evident in the work of earlier generations of Jewish artists and entertainers. Nostalgic Jewish theater survives, like the musicalized adaptation of *The Jazz Singer* at the Jewish Repertory Theatre in 2003. But the production ended with Jack Robin back on Broadway but without blackface—the production actually eschewed the use of blackface altogether—singing "April Showers" in a sing-a-long with the audience. The whole conclusion seemed to me, like the ending of the 1927 film, a kind of ritual transcendence of the particularistic claims of Jewish tradition.

American Yiddish entertainment is limited to the annual production by the Folksbiene, the sole remaining Yiddish theater in New York; a recent pro-duction was a bilingual Yiddish-English adaptation of Itzik Manger's Bible tales, originally written in Yiddish. But this theater has trouble drawing an audience, even though they offer simultaneous translation into both English and Russian, the latter because much of their audience is drawn from recent Russian Jewish immigrants. A review of Allan Sherman songs that ran at the same time in New York garnered a much larger audience.

Nevertheless, the meaning of the Lower East Side in American Jewish culture has been the subject of remarkably intense interest among scholars in recent years. A recent issue of *American Jewish History* was devoted to reinter-pretations of the landmark 1976 study of the American Jewish ghetto, Irving Howe's *World of Our Fathers,* in an effort to understand its success in putting the Lower East Side back on the map of Jewish Studies. Howe's book was published at the height of both the country's bicentennial celebration and the renewed pride in American subcultures promoted by the popularity of *Roots,* the television documentary about the African American experience. The spate of conferences and books about the Lower East Side in the last few years testifies to an ongoing interest in the place of the Lower East Side in the collective American Jewish consciousness.

I hope that this book will point the way to future research in the field of ethnic popular culture, and Jewish popular culture in particular. Much more needs to be understood about the relationship between acculturation and popular culture. Does ethnic popular culture resist acculturation or advance it? Can it do both in the same moment? Who produces ethnic popular culture, and how does it function within the economic and political power structure?

Moreover, how does seeing a "real" member of an ethnic group differ from seeing an actor playing a member of that ethnic group on the stage or in film or television? I have argued that this process is different in different media; the directness of live performance creates a bond between actor and audience that is missing in film. (Vaudeville entertainers tended to exaggerate the characteristics of the ethnic characters they were playing in order to get a laugh; even Jewish comics thus remained somewhat caught in the tradition of the non-Jewish comics who had traded on the audience's anti-Semitism in presenting extremely caricatured portraits of Jews.)

I hope this book will encourage other scholars to investigate the role of popular culture in advancing the acculturation of different ethnic groups into American society, and to examine other forms of popular culture, from visual art to music to material culture. What are the roots of these popular culture forms and images in ethnic history? What visions of society, and of the particular ethnic group's place in it, are communicated by these pop culture icons? How has ethnic identification been commodified; how do we buy and sell our ethnic identities?

I began this book by recounting a memory of my grandmother reading a catalog from a company called The Source for Everything Jewish. Indeed, perhaps popular culture is not just the reflection of our ethnic identities, but to some extent its wellspring. May the fountain of Jewish culture never run dry.

NOTES

INTRODUCTION

1. Charles Hardy, "A Brief History of Ethnicity in the Comics," http://lrrc3.sas.upenn.edu/popcult/cartoons/COMICS.HTM.
2. Gilbert Seldes, *The 7 Lively Arts* (New York: Sagamore Press, 1924).
3. George Lipsitz, *Time Passages: Collective Memory and American Popular Culture* (Minneapolis: University of Minnesota Press, 1990), 13.
4. Ibid., 17.
5. Elizabeth Crocker, "'Some Say it With a Brick': George Herriman's *Krazy Kat*," http://www.iath.virginia.edu/crocker/
6. See Seth Korelitz, "From Religion to Culture, From Race to Ethnicity," *American Jewish History* 85; "Americanization," *Harvard Encyclopedia of American Ethnic Groups* (Cambridge, MA: Harvard University Press, 1980), 571–598.
7. Theodore Sleszynski, "The Second Generation of Immigrants in the Assimilative Process," in John J. Appel, ed., *The New Immigration* (New York: Pitman Publishing, 1971), 102–108.
8. Will Herberg, *Protestant-Catholic-Jew: An Essay in American Religious Sociology* (Garden City, NY: Anchor Books, 1960).
9. Harley Erdman, *Staging the Jew: The Performance of an American Ethnicity, 1860–1920* (New Brunswick, NJ: Rutgers University Press, 1997), 160.
10. Ellen Schiff, ed., *Awake and Singing: Six Great American Jewish Plays* (New York: Applause Books, 2004), 49, fn 25.
11. Edward D. Coleman, *The Jew in English Drama: An Annotated Bibliography* (New York: Ktav Publishing House, 1968).
12. Henry L. Feingold, *A Time for Searching: Entering the Mainstream, 1920–1945* Volume IV in Feingold, ed., *The Jewish People in America* (Baltimore: Johns Hopkins University Press, 1992), 60.
13. Deborah Dash Moore, *At Home in America: Second Generation New York Jews* (New York: Columbia University Press, 1981), 3–4; 21.
14. Robert Warshow, "Clifford Odets: Poet of the Jewish Middle Class," in *The Immediate Experience* (Boston: Harvard University Press, 2002), 56.
15. Moses Rischin, *The Promised City: New York's Jews, 1870–1914* (Cambridge, MA: Harvard University Press, 1962), 93.
16. Moore, *At Home,* 19.
17. Lloyd Ultan and Barbara Unger, *Bronx Accent: A Literary and Pictorial History of the Borough* (New Brunswick, NJ: Rutgers University Press, 2000), 78.
18. A similar dynamic was underway during this period in London, where second-generation Jews moved out of the immigrant neighborhood of the East End into the suburbs in the northern and northwestern parts of the city. See David Cesarani, "A Funny Thing Happened on the Way to the Suburbs: Social Change in Anglo-Jewry Between the Wars, 1914–1945," *Jewish Culture and History* 1, 1 (1998): 5–26.

19. Zalmen Yoffeh, "The Passing of the East Side," *The Menorah Journal* (December 1929): 275.

20. Some Yiddish newspapers published English-language sections for the benefit of their readers who knew the language. Bernard Postal, "Over the Bridge to Bensonhurst," *Der Tog (The Day)*, English Section (June 10, 1928). Postal opined that Bensonhurst, "the heir of Brownsville, the East Side, and the Bronx, is becoming all Jewish, in fact another Brownsville."

21. Park and Burgess, *The City* (Chicago: University of Chicago Press, 1925), 58–59.

22. Sherry Gorelick, *City College and the Jewish Poor* (New Brunswick, NJ: Rutgers University Press, 1981), 115. See also Thomas Kessner, *The Golden Door: Italian and Jewish Immigrant Mobility in New York City, 1880–1915* (New York: Oxford University Press, 1977), 77–99.

23. Ultan and Unger, *Bronx Accent,* 78.

24. Gorelick, *City College,* 123. Gorelick emphasizes, however, that although increasing numbers of Jews were attending college, their numbers were still quite low, and the dropout rate was extremely high; Gorelick calculates that fewer than two dozen Jewish men actually graduated from CCNY in 1913, at a time when there were almost a million Jews living in New York!

25. Moore, *At Home,* 4.

26. Feingold, *A Time for Searching,* 93.

27. Jeffrey S. Gurock, "Jewish Commitment and Continuity in Interwar Brooklyn," in Ilana Abramovitch and Seán Galvin, eds., *Jews of Brooklyn* (Hanover, NH: Brandeis University Press, 2002), 232.

28. David Nasaw, *Going Out: The Rise and Fall of Public Amusements* (New York: Basic Books, 1993), 4.

29. Mark Slobin, *Tenement Songs: The Popular Music of the Jewish Immigrants* (Champaign, 1995), 199.

30. Beth Wenger, "Introduction: Remembering the Lower East Side—A Conversation" in Hasia R. Diner, Jeffrey Shandler, and Beth Wenger, eds., *Remembering the Lower East Side: American Jewish Reflections* (Bloomington: Indiana University Press, 2000), 2.

31. Beth Wenger, "The Invention of the Lower East Side," *American Jewish History* 85 (March 1997): 4. See also Jenna Weissman Joselit, "Telling Tales: Or, How a Slum Became a Shrine," *Jewish Social Studies*, 54–61.

32. Jenna Weissman Joselit, *The Wonders of America: Reinventing Jewish Culture, 1880–1950* (New York: Hill and Wang, 1994), 4. See also Andrew R. Heinze, *Adapting to Abundance: Jewish Immigrants, Mass Consumption, and the Search for American Identity* (New York: Columbia University Press, 1990).

33. Michael G. Corenthal, *Cohen on the Telephone: A History of Jewish Recorded Humor and Popular Music, 1892–1942* (Milwaukee: Yesterday's Memories, 1984), 7.

34. Paul Buhle, *From the Lower East Side to Hollywood: Jews in American Popular Culture* (New York: Verso Books, 2004), 3.

35. Ibid., 21.

36. Chandra Mukerji and Michael Schudson, "Introduction" to Mukerji and Schudson, eds., *Rethinking Popular Culture* (Berkeley: University of California Press), 1.

37. Mukerji and Schudson, "Introduction," 3.

38. John Higham, *Strangers in the Land: Patterns of American Nativism, 1860–1925* (New Brunswick, NJ: Rutgers University Press, 2002), 267. As Ann Douglas has written, the "drastic fluctuations, the sudden shifts from boom periods into sometimes tenacious depressions, downturns accompanied by massive layoffs and sometimes violent agitation, ever more visible in America's full-fledged, more or less unregulated capitalist economy, erased the traditional image of the immigrant as part of an unending supply of docile, industrious, cheap, and quickly Americanized labor

and raised in its place the alarming specter of an unemployed, ill-educated and angry mob of foreigners with no real stake in the American enterprise, with no knowledge of its Anglo-Saxon values and traditions . . ." *Terrible Honesty: Mongrel Manhattan in the 1920s* (New York: Farrar, Straus and Giroux, 1995), 305.

39. Joan Hoff Wilson, "Introduction: How Normal Was Normalcy?" in *The Twenties: The Critical Issues* , ed. by Joan Hoff Wilson (Boston: Little, Brown and Co., 1972), xxiii.

40. See Albert Lee, *Henry Ford and the Jews* (New York: Stein and Day, 1980).

41. Andrea Most, *Making Americans: Jews and the Broadway Musical* (Cambridge, MA: Harvard University Press, 2004), 25; 26.

42. Henry Popkin, "The Vanishing Jew of Our Popular Culture," *Commentary* (July 1952): 46.

43. Steven J. Whitfield, *In Search of American Jewish Culture* (Hanover, NH: University Press of New England, 1999), 19.

44. Abel Green and Joe Laurie, Jr., *Showbiz: From Vaude to Video* (New York: Henry Holt & Co., 1951), 7.

45. Mario Maffi, *Gateway to the Promised Land: Ethnic Cultures on New York's Lower East Side* (New York: New York University Press, 1995), 237.

46. Hutchins Hapgood, *The Spirit of the Ghetto* (New York Schocken Books, 1966), 137.

47. J. Hoberman, *Bridge of Light: Yiddish Film Between Two Worlds* (Philadelphia: Temple University Press, 1995), 151–167.

48. Schiff, *Awake and Singing,* 20–21.

49. A. Mukdoni, "Trouble in the Yiddish Theater," *The Jewish Digest* (November 1940): 65.

50. See Adina Cimet, "Ambivalence Acknowledged: Jewish Identities and Language Strategies in Contemporary Mexico," in Luis Roniger and Tamar Herzog, ed., *The Collective and the Public in Latin America: Cultural Identities and Political Order* (Portland, OR: Sussex Academic Press, 2000), 273–284.

51. David Hollinger, *Postethnic America: Beyond Multiculturalism* (New York: Basic Books, 1995).

52. Werner Sollors, *Beyond Ethnicity: Consent and Descent in American Culture* (New York: Oxford University Press, 1986).

53. William Boelhower, *Through a Glass Darkly: Ethnic Semiosis in American Literature* (Venezia: Edizioni Helvetica, 1984).

54. Whitfield, *In Search,* 237.

CHAPTER I   JEWS ON THE VAUDEVILLE STAGE

1. Harry Jolson, as told to Alban Emley, *Mistah Jolson* (Hollywood, CA: House-Warven, 1952), 45.

2. Harley Erdman, *Staging the Jew : The Performance of an American Ethnicity, 1860–1920* (New Brunswick, NJ: Rutgers University Press, 1997); Paul Antonie Distler, "The Rise and Fall of the Racial Comics in American Vaudeville" (Ph.D. diss., Tulane University, 1963); Esther Romeyn, "My Other/My Self: Impersonation, Masquerade and the Theater of Identity in Turn-of-the-Century New York City" (Ph.D. diss, University of Minnesota, 1998).

3. Stephan Kanfer, *Groucho: The Life and Times of Julius Henry Marx* (New York: Alfred A. Knopf, 2000), 375.

4. Arthur Asa Berger, *Jewish Jesters: A Study in American Popular Comedy* (Cresskill, NJ: Hampton Press, 2001), 27–34.

5. Herbert Goldman, *Jolson: The Legend Comes to Life* (New York: Oxford University Press, 1988), 229.

6. Goldman, *Jolson,* 302.

7. Douglas Gilbert, *American Vaudeville: Its Life and Times* (New York: Dover Publications, 1940), 4.

8. Gilbert, *American Vaudeville,* 62.

9. Quoted in James H. Dormon, "American Popular Culture and the New Immigration Ethnics: The Vaudeville Stage and the Process of Ethnic Ascription," *Amerikastudien/American Studies* (Heidelberg, Germany) 36, 2 (1991): 183.

10. Louise A. Mayo, *The Ambivalent Image: Nineteenth Century America's Perception of the Jew* (Cranbury, NJ: Associated University Presses, 1988), 90.

11. Erdman, *Staging the Jew,* 102. It is interesting that two important later American Jewish playwrights, Arthur Miller and David Mamet, both created characters of salesmen who have presumably turned from the former into the latter. In both *Death of a Salesman* and *Glengarry Glen Ross*, the gift of gab has deserted the main characters, leading in each case to a dramatic and painful end to their careers. See Richard Brucher, "Pernicious Nostalgia in *Glengarry Glen Ross*," in Leslie Kane, ed., *David Mamet's Glengarry Glen Ross: Text and Performance* (New York: Garland Publishing, 1996), 211–225.

12. Joe Laurie, Jr., *Vaudeville: From the Honky-Tonks to the Palace* (New York: Henry Holt, 1953).

13. Gilbert, *American Vaudeville,* 291.

14. Robert W. Snyder, *Voice of the City: Vaudeville and Popular Culture in New York* (New York: Oxford University Press, 1989), 111.

15. Lou Breau and Billy Hueston, "He Knows His Groc'ries" (New York: Edward B. Marks Music Company, 1926).

16. "Inter-Marriage is Her Incentive to Write for Stage," *American* (October 1922). Clipping in Billy Rose Theatre Collection, Lincoln Center, New York.

17. Ibid.

18. According to David Nasaw, black vaudevillians "could only parody 'darkies,' and occasionally the Chinese." Only in black theaters could they don whiteface. David Nasaw, *Going Out: The Rise and Fall of Public Amusements* (New York: BasicBooks, 1993), 57.

19. Felix Isman, *Weber and Fields* (New York: Boni and Liverright, 1924), 51. See also Edmond and L. Marc Fields, *From the Bowery to Broadway: Lew Fields and the Roots of American Popular Theatre.* (New York: Oxford University Press, 1993).

20. Jolson, *Mistah Jolson,* 83–84.

21. Erdman, *Staging the Jew,* 159.

22. See Tyson Freeman, "The 1980s (Too) Easy Money Fuels a New Building Boom!" *National Real Estate Investor* (September 30, 1999).

23. Edward D. Coleman, *The Jew in English Drama* (New York: The New York Public Library and Ktav Publishing House, 1968). Based on his own collection of recordings, Michael G. Corenthal says that the stereotype died out by the mid-1930s. He attributes this partly to the nature of the radio medium, which, he says, "required a more sustaining situation comedy type format not as agreeable to the gimmick comedians of vaudeville." Michael G. Corenthal, *Cohen on the Telephone: A History of Jewish Recorded Humor and Popular Music, 1892–1942* (Milwaukee, WI: Yesterday's Memories, 1984), 7.

24. Arthur Leroy Kaiser, *Hey! Teacher! A Humorous Entertainment (in two acts)* (Chicago: Dramatic Publishing Company, 1928).

25. Albert Byers, "Abie Eats" (Franklin, OH: Eldridge Entertainment House, 1927). Oysters are, of course, prohibited by Jewish dietary laws. Abie is clearly not a religious Jew, even though he is given stereotypical Jewish traits.

26. For a listing of these, and other Jewish comedy recordings from the period, see Corenthal, *Cohen on the Telephone,* 49–52.

27. Ed Wynn, "Wynn Explains Methods Used by Comedians," *New York Herald Tribune* (October 30, 1927), 4. Billy Rose Theatre Collection.

28. Martin J. Porter, "Funny Reasons Why Wynn Gives Radio the Air," unidentified paper, Billy Rose Theatre Collection.

29. Gilbert Seldes, *The 7 Lively Arts* (New York: Sagamore Books, 1924), 171.

30. Henry Montor, "Jewishness—and the Box Office: Why Broadway Stars are More Jewish Than Ever." *American Jewish World* (St. Paul and Minneapolis) (June 25, 1926), 1.

31. Ibid.

32. Seldes, *7 Lively Arts*, 175.

33. Michael Kammen, *The 7 Lively Arts: Gilbert Seldes and the Transformation of Cultural Criticism in the United States* (New York: Oxford University Press, 1996), 20; 105–110.

34. Seldes, *7 Lively Arts*, 178.

35. Ibid., 182.

36. Irving Howe, *World of Our Fathers: The Journey of the East European Jews to America and the Life They Found and Made* (New York: Simon and Schuster, 1976), 558.

37. Mary Cass Canfield, "The Great American Art" *New Republic* 32 (November 22, 1922). Reprinted in Anthony Slide, ed., *Selected Vaudeville Criticism* (New York: Scarecrow Press, 1988), 225.

38. Deborah Dash Moore, *At Home in America: Second Generation New York Jews* (New York: Columbia University Press, 1981).

39. Eli Levi, "The Jew and Vaudeville," *B'nai Brith News* (May 1922), 9.

40. Joe Smith, "Dr. Kronkhite Revisited," in Myron Matlaw, *American Popular Entertainment Papers and Proceedings of the Conference on the History of American Popular Entertainment* (Westport, CT: Greenwood Press, 1979), 121–131.

41. Joe Smith, "Smith and Dale: Kaddish on the Road on the Orpheum Circuit, 1923–1924," *Western States Jewish History* 33, 3 (Spring 2001): 237–247.

42. Mark Slobin, *Tenement Songs: The Popular Music of the Jewish Immigrants* (Chicago: University of Illinois Press, 1982), 199.

43. Hasia Diner, *Lower East Side Memories: A Jewish Place in America* (Princeton, NJ: Princeton University Press, 2000), 51.

44. Unidentified clipping, Billy Rose Theatre Collection. Belle Baker Scrapbooks.

45. Barbara Grossman, *Funny Woman; The Life and Times of Fanny Brice* (Bloomington: Indiana University Press, 1991), 7.

46. Unidentified clipping, Billy Rose Theatre Collection.

47. In her autobiography, Sophie Tucker confirms that Brice did not speak Yiddish. She says that Brice learned the accent from Harry Delf, "a grand Jewish comedian who used to play the joints in Brooklyn and Coney Island." Sophie Tucker, *Some of These Days* (New York: Doubleday, 1945), 57.

48. Grossman, *Funny Woman*, 31. See also Andrew Erdman, "Blue Vaudeville: Sex, Morals and the Marketing of Amusement, 1895–1915" (Ph.D. diss., City University of New York Graduate Center, 2001).

49. Grossman, *Funny Woman*, 31.

50. "Why Belle Succeeds," *Detroit Journal* (October 24, 1919), Billy Rose Theatre Collection.

51. Undated clipping, *Detroit Journal*. Billy Rose Theatre Collection.

52. *New York Tribune* (September 15, 1912), 12. Billy Rose Theatre Collection; Undated clipping, *Cincinnati Commercial*. Billy Rose Theatre Collection.

53. Ethel E. Sanders, "Semitic Silhouettes—Ghetto Comedienne," *Opinion: A Journal of Jewish Life and Letters* (October 1932), 24.

54. Eddie Cantor with Jane Kesner Ardmore, *Take My Life* (New York: Doubleday, 1957), 15. In later life, Cantor proclaimed himself to be the "world's supreme delicatessen eater." Eddie Cantor, with David Freedman, *My Life Is in Your Hands* (New York: Harper and Brothers, 1928), 21

55. Cantor, *My Life,* 75. This joke expresses a nihilistic sentiment that one finds very seldom in Jewish humor, which characteristically expresses a kind of verbal shrug—a resigned attitude to the vicissitudes of life. Like the endless jokes of the period about Jews setting fires to collect insurance money, the material itself was clearly designed for a non-Jewish audience. George Jessel, *So Help Me* (New York: Random House, 1943), 124.

56. Seldes, *7 Lively Arts,* 180.

57. George Jessel, *This Way, Miss* (New York: Holt, 1955), 59–60. According to Jessel, Al Jolson found this routine particularly hilarious; Jolson's manager, Louis Epstein, would call Jessel wherever in the country he was playing, and ask Jessel to "sing a few bars of Harry Cooper." *This Way, Miss,* 60.

58. Nahma Sandrow, *Vagabond Stars* (New York: Harper & Row, 1977), 93.

59. "The Play: Ziegfeld Follies With Us Again," *New York Globe and Commercial Advertiser* (June 20, 1918), 17. Billy Rose Theatre Collection.

60. *New York Sun* (June 19, 1918), 22.

61. Cantor, *My Life,* 187–188.

62. Seldes, *7 Lively Arts,* 179.

63. See Sander Gilman, *The Jew's Body* (New York: Routledge, 1991).

64. Erdman, *Staging the Jew,* 37.

65. Cantor, *My Life,* 151. Jolson's performances were also, at least according to Herbert Goldman, tinged with homoeroticism. Goldman writes that Jolson, although married four times in his life, "occasionally kissed other men. Onstage, his work was filled with sly references to homosexuality, suggestive moistening of the lips, [and] risqué use of the behind and hips. . . . Audiences thought that it was daring humor; people in the business sometimes wondered." Herbert G. Goldman, *Jolson: The Legend Comes to Life* (New York: Oxford University Press, 1988), 66.

66. Herbert G. Goldman, *Banjo Eyes: Eddie Cantor and the Birth of Modern Stardom* (New York: Oxford University Press, 1997), 57–58.

67. Ibid.

68. Mark Slobin has reprinted the text of the song, which had two stanzas, the first in Yiddish and the second in English. In Yiddish the song is called "Levine mit zayn flaying mashin." The first two lines of the English stanza call Levine "the hero of your race" and "the greatest Hebrew ace." *Tenement Songs,* 200–201.

69. Eddie Cantor, *The Way I See It* (Englewood Cliffs, NJ: Prentice-Hall, 1959), 12.

70. Riv-Ellen Prell, *Fighting to Become Americans: Jews, Gender and the Anxiety of Assimilation* (Boston: Beacon Press, 1999), 29.

71. Transcribed from vocals by Fanny Brice, recorded August 11, 1921 (from Ziegfeld Follies of 1921). From "The Broadway Musical," vol. 1: 1918–1929, Chansons Actualites; CIN025. http://www.heptune.com/lyrics/secondha.html.

72. Alfred Kazin, *A Walker in the City* (New York: Harcourt, Brace and Company), 21–22.

73. Donald Weber, *Haunted in the New World: Jewish American Culture from Cahan to The Goldbergs* (Bloomington: Indiana University Press, 2005), 5.

74. Fran Stark, "My Mother, Fanny Brice," *Bazaar* (July 1968), 17. This was Brice's first child, Frances Brice Arnstein, who Brice described as looking, at her birth, "all wrinkled up and old, like a rabbi who just lost his synagogue." *Ladies' Home Journal* (December 1952), 60.

75. Another female vaudeville performer, Rhoda Bernard, also used a heavy Yiddish accent. She recorded a similar song to "Becky" called "Rosie Rosenblatt," about a

Jewish girl who also tries to dance professionally, although not in the ballet. Her boyfriend, Abie, tells her to "stop your turkey trot" and asks her, "ken you stay avay, from the cabaret?" George W. Meyer and Sam M. Lewis, "Rosie Rosenblatt" (New York: Pathé, 1916).

76. Howe, *World of Our Fathers,* 562.

77. Compare to the stereotypes set out by Prell in *Fighting,* 44–51; Seldes, *7 Lively Arts,* 191.

78. Prell, *Fighting,* 77.

79. June Sochen, "From Sophie Tucker to Barbara Streisand," in Joyce Antler, ed., *Talking Back: Images of Jewish Women in American Popular Culture* (Hanover, NH: Brandeis University Press, 1998), 71.

80. Ibid.

81. Prell, *Fighting.*

82. Grossman, *Funny Woman,* 172.

83. "Fannie Brice's Escape," *Variety* (October 10, 1914).

84. In 1930, a profile of Tucker in a Boston newspaper said that her son, Albert Edward, was then twenty-five years old, and "has of late years been on the stage, both with and without his mother. That kid is dearer to the 'Last of the Hot Mammas' than anything else in the world." Steve Clow, "How Sophie Tucker, 'Last of Red Hot Mammas,' Burned Her Way to Fame," *Boston Sunday Post* (March 16, 1930), 66.

85. Pamela Brown Lavitt, "'Coon Shouting' and the Jewish Ziegfeld Girl," *American Jewish History* (December 2000), 254 (emphasis in original); 261.

86. Quoted in John E. Dimeglio, *Vaudeville U.S.A.* (Bowling Green, OH: Bowling Green University Popular Press, 1973), 60.

87. Nora Ephron, "Sophie Tucker Looks Ahead," *New York Post* (September 6, 1964), 23.

88. Beverly Gray Bienstock, "The Changing Image of the American Jewish Mother," in Virginia Tufte and Barbara Myerhoff, eds., *Changing Images of the Family* (New Haven, CT: Yale University Press, 1979): 173–191.

89. Unidentified clipping, "Making a Revue for a Star" (October 14, 1925). Tucker Scrapbooks. Billy Rose Theatre Collection. Another clipping, from a later London appearance, called this song "the deeply impressive 'Yiddisher Mammy,' which Sophie has always dreaded trying to sing since her mother died." Unidentified, undated London clipping, probably from May 9, 1934. Tucker Scrapbooks. Billy Rose Theatre Collection.

90. J. T. Grein, "Criticisms in Cameo," *The Sketch* (October 1, 1930), 3. Tucker Scrapbooks. Billy Rose Theatre Collection.

91. Lewis Erenberg, *Steppin' Out: New York Nightlife and the Transformation of American Culture, 1890–1930* (Westport, CT: Greenwood Press, 1981), 201; ibid.

92. Tucker, *Some of These Days,* 260.

93. A. John Danhorn, "Our Friend the Drama," *The Musical Standard* (October 31, 1925). Tucker Scrapbooks. Billy Rose Theatre Collection. Paris audiences were divided on the song's merits; when Tucker tried to sing it there in 1928, she says that the Jews in the audience applauded the song while the Gentiles loudly booed it. Tucker gave up, and switched to her perennial favorite, "Happy Days Are Here Again." Tucker, *Some of These Days,* 258.

94. Slobin, *Tenement Songs,* 205.

95. Ibid.

96. Slobin translates the "kugel and tzimmes" line as "roast and dumplings," seemingly to avoid having to explain the Jewish foods. Slobin, *Tenement Songs,* 204; ibid.

97. Joyce Antler, *The Journey Home: Jewish Women and the American Century* (New York: The Free Press, 1997), 142; ibid.

98. Alex Berber, Jean Schwartz, and Eddie Cantor, "My Yiddisha Mammy," database of Performing Arts in America 1875–1923. New York Public Library Digitized Collections. http://digital.nypl.org/lpa/nypl/lpa_home4.html
99. Paula Hyman, "The Jewish Family: Looking for a Usable Past," in Susannah Heschel, ed., *On Being a Jewish Feminist* (New York: Schocken Books, 1983): 19–26.
100. Erika Duncan, "The Hungry Jewish Mother," in Heschel, *On Being a Jewish Feminist,* 28. However, Paula Hyman finds a very different picture of the Jewish mother in quoting the section of Michael Gold's autobiographical novel, *Jews Without Money* (1930), in which the communist writer praised his mother for her radical activities, including instigating a rent strike. He called her "that dark little woman with bright eyes, who hobbled about all day in bare feet, cursing in Elizabethan Yiddish, using the forbidden words 'ladies' do not use, smacking us, beating us, fighting with her neighbors, busy from morn to midnight in the tenement struggle for life." Quoted in Hyman, *Gender and Assimilation in Modern Jewish History: The Roles and Representations of Women* (Seattle: University of Washington Press, 1995), 128–129.
101. Snyder, *Voice of the City,* xvi. Snyder paraphrases Sophie Tucker that in New York and Chicago, the same people came every Monday to the matinee performance at particular theaters. Snyder, *Voice of the City,* 128.
102. Tucker, *Some of These Days,* 134.
103. Mordechai Kaplan, *Judaism as a Civilization: Towards a Reconstruction of American-Jewish Life* (New York: Thomas Yoseloff, 1957).
104. Quoted in Moore, *At Home in America,* 134.
105. Erenberg, *Steppin' Out,* 192.
106. Howe, *World of Our Fathers,* 566; ibid.
107. June Sochen, "Fanny Brice and Sophie Tucker: Blending the Particular with the Universal," in Sarah Blacher Cohen, ed., *From Hester Street to Hollywood: The Jewish-American Stage and Screen* (Bloomington: Indiana University Press, 1983), 44.
108. Sochen, "Fanny Brice," 44.

CHAPTER 2   JEWS ON BROADWAY

1. *New York Times* (January 9, 1927), 9.
2. The actors accepted a salary cut, which Nichols later restored retroactively. *New York Herald Tribune* (July 1, 1923), 23.
3. For example, the Chinese production was performed with an all-Chinese cast. But when the author was questioned in connection with her plagiarism lawsuit against the motion picture company that produced *The Cohens and the Kellys,* a film that capitalized on Jewish and Irish humor, she allegedly "professed ignorance of the fact that in Budapest and other European capitals the Jewish-Irish theme of her play is changed to fit racial conditions wherever it is produced." In "Real Life Abie Inspired Play, Author Reveals," unidentified newspaper (April 28, 1926), Billy Rose Theatre Collection.

    One critic, Alexander Woollcott, called it "unquestionably the most prosperous theatrical enterprise the world has ever known." *Philadelphia Inquirer* (May 17, 1925), 10. Perhaps the only precedent for such commercial success was the phenomenal popularity, in the nineteenth century, of the many stage versions of Harriet Beecher Stowe's novel, *Uncle Tom's Cabin.* A 1928 article by Benjamin de Casseres in *Theatre Magazine,* "A Non-Slush Probe into *Abie's Irish Rose,*" was subtitled, "From a Joke This Sociological Phenomenon Has Passed Into the Realm of 'Classic Instances' With 'Uncle Tom's Cabin'" (May 1928), 7.
4. "The Wonder of Our Stage Now Fairly Judged," *Boston Transcript* (May 15, 1924), 15.

5. Gilbert Seldes, "Jewish Plays and Jew-Plays in New York," *Menorah Journal* (April 1922): 236–240.

6. Gilbert Seldes, "Outline of a Preface," *New Republic* (May 25, 1927): 18–19.

7. Patterson James, *The Billboard* (June 10, 1922), 41.

8. Heywood Broun, *New York World* (May 28, 1922), 15; Broun, *New York Telegram* (August 2, 1931), 24.

9. Carolyn Joan Weiss, "The Jew as an Actor," *Baltimore Jewish Times* (July 7, 1922), 5; Elias Ginsburg, "A Plea for Jewish Drama," *Jewish Tribune* (January 5, 1923), 38.

10. Alison Smith, *New York Globe* (May 24, 1922). Billy Rose Theatre Collection.

11. "In Praise of Muni Wisenfrend," *New York Evening Post* (January 21, 1928), 30.

12. David Barzel, "Footlights and Stars on the Jewish Broadway," *Jewish Tribune* (December 4, 1925), 42.

13. Nahma Sandrow, *Vagabond Stars* (New York: Harper & Row, 1977), 260.

14. Telephone interview with Mike Burstyn, January 28, 2005.

15. Paul Muni, "English Theater Or Yiddish Theater?" *Der Tog* (November 5, 1926).

16. Leonard Prager, "Of Parents and Children: Jacob Gordin's *The Jewish King Lear*," *American Quarterly* 18, 3 (1966): 515.

17. Walter Ginsburg, "From Broadway to Second Avenue: The Yiddish Theatre in Greater New York Attracts the American Born Jew With Its Frankness and Realism," *The Day* (English Language Section of *Der Tog*), October 16, 1927.

18. A. Glantz, "The Great Conundrum From Broadway Called 'Abie's Irish Rose'," *Der Tog* (January 28, 1927), 3. The English words were transliterated into the Hebrew characters in which Yiddish is written, in much the same way that many English words that have entered Modern Hebrew are simply transliterated into Hebrew characters.

19. Addison Burkhardt, "My Yiddish Matinee Girl" (New York: Shapiro, Bernstein and Co., 1916).

20. David Carb, "A Major Impetus in the American Theatre: The Jew is Enacting Increasingly Important Role as Creator and Sponsor of our Native Drama," *American Hebrew* (November 22, 1929), 48.

21. Of Florenz Ziegfeld, another Jewish producer, Kibbitzer says that he is so lucky that if he "went down with the Titanic he'd come up with *Abie's Irish Rose*." J. P. McEvoy, *Show Girl* (New York: Simon and Schuster, 1928), 116.

22. Walter Prichard Eaton, "Jews in the American Theatre," *American Hebrew* (September 22, 1922), 464.

23. Eaton, "Jews in American Theatre," 464.

24. Thomas H. Dickinson, "The Jew in the Theater," *The Nation* (June 13, 1923), 689–90.

25. Jerry Eisenhour, *Joe Leblang's Cut-Rate Ticket Empire and the Broadway Theatre, 1894–1931* (Lewiston, NY: Edwin Mellen Press, 2003), 88–89.

26. Ludwig Satz, *New York Times* (September 26, 1926).

27. Dickinson, "The Jew in the Theatre," 690.

28. Harley Erdman, *Staging the Jew: The Performance of an American Ethnicity* (New Brunswick, NJ: Rutgers University Press, 1997), 114.

29. Harris Jay Griston, "The Merchant of Venice," *New York Times* (January 5, 1923), 16.

30. For opposing viewpoints, see J. Freed, "Is Shylock a Jew?" and Harris Jay Griston, "Revolutionizing the Shylock Label," *Jewish Forum* (February 1925), 9–15. See also A. Rosenthal, "Modern View of Shakespeare's Shylock," *B'nai Brith News* (March 1922), 11. These articles rely to some extent on the books by Maurice Packard, *Shylock Not a Jew* (Boston, 1919) and Gerald Friedlander, *Shakespeare and the Jew*. The debate continues to this day; for a modern treatment of the subject, see James Shapiro, *Shakespeare and the Jews*.

31. John Galsworthy, *Loyalties*, act 3, scene 1 in *Representative Plays by John Galsworthy* (New York: Charles Scribner's Sons, 1924), 447; Louis Harap, *Dramatic Encounters: The Jewish Presence in Twentieth-Century American Drama, Poetry, and Humor and the Black-Jewish Literary Relationship* (New York: Greenwood Press, 1987), 115. Among Harap's examples are Channing Pollock's *The Fool* (1920) and Owen Davis's *The Detour* (1921), both of which portray their Jewish character in relatively favorable terms.

32. Alan Dale, "Dialectic Decay Destroys Drama," *New York American* (May 28, 1922), 9. Billy Rose Theatre Collection.

33. Quoted by Mark Slobin, "Some Intersections of Jews, Music and Theater" in Sarah Blacher Cohen, ed., *From Hester Street to Hollywood: The Jewish-American Stage and Screen* (Bloomington, IN: Indiana University Press, 1983), 37.

34. Seldes, *7 Lively Arts,* 207; 215.

35. David Ewen, "The Jew as Cartoonist," *Jewish Forum* (August 1929), 355–356.

36. John Appel, "Abie the Agent, Gimpl the Matchmaker, Berl Schliemazel, et al." In Charles F. Hardy and Gail Stern, eds., *Ethnic Images in the Comics* (Philadelphia: Balch Institute for Ethnic Studies, 1986), 19.

37. Appel, "Abie the Agent," 18.

38. Harry Hershfield, "'Abie the Agent' Corrective for Jewish Caricatures," *American Hebrew* (June 24, 1921), 147; Appel, "Abie the Agent," 17; 17.

39. Seldes, *7 Lively Arts,* 201; 202.

40. Peter C. Marzio, Introduction to *Abie the Agent: A Complete Compilation: 1914–1915* (Westport, CT: Hyperion Press, 1977), vii–ix.

41. Thomas Craven, who reprinted Gross's version in his *Cartoon Cavalcade,* may have spoken for many non-Jews who said that the language is "extremely funny to those who can read it without effort." However, he said that to him it is "hard going, and by the time I have deciphered it, the humor is dead. Milt Gross is a true comedian, and no mistake, but I prefer his drawings to his dialect." Thomas Craven, *Cartoon Cavalcade* (New York: Simon and Schuster, 1943), 102.

42. Marzio, Introduction, xi.

43. Review of *Hello Broadway* from February 23, 1915, issue of the *New York Journal,* reprinted in Marzio, Introduction, ix.

44. Elias Lieberman, "He Makes a Nation Laugh—and Think," *American Hebrew* (October 7, 1921), 555.

45. Rick Marschall, *First Nemo Annual* (New York: Fantagraphics Books, 1985), 18.

46. John Appel, "Abie the Agent," http://www.balchinstitute.org/museum/comics/comics.html; ibid.

47. Robert Littell, "Abie's Irish Rose," *New Republic* (March 18, 1925), 98–99.

48. Difficulties encountered in using new technology was also part of the humor. As transcribed by Michael G. Corenthal, the classic routine begins: "Hullo! hullo! Are you dere? Hullo! Vot number do I vant? Vell, vot numbers have you got? Oh, excuse me, my mistook. I vant Central 248, please; yes, dot's right, 248. I say, Miss, am I supposed to keep on saying "Hullo!" and "Are you dere?" until you come back again? Vell, don't be long." *Cohen on the Telephone: A History of Jewish Recorded Humor and Popular Music, 1892–1942* (Milwaukee: Yesterday's Memories, 1984), 53.

49. Anne Nichols, *Abie's Irish Rose* (New York: Samuel French, 1924), act 1, p. 10.

50. Nichols, *Abie's Irish Rose,* act 1, p. 37; act. 1, p. 44.

51. Ibid., act. 2, p. 79.

52. In fact, the original title of the play was *Marriage in Triplicate. Encyclopedia of American Theatre,* 12.

53. A 1998 off-off-Broadway production, directed by Father Gary Seibert at the Theater at Holy Cross on West 42nd Street, also incorporated a Hanukkah menorah next to the Christmas tree, although none is called for in the stage directions.

54. Quoted in Henry L. Feingold, *A Time For Searching: Entering the Mainstream, 1920-1945* (Baltimore: Johns Hopkins University Press, 1992), p. 36.

55. Milton Herbert Gropper and Max Siegel, *We Americans* (New York: Samuel French, 1928), act 2, p. 60.

56. Ellen Schiff, ed., *Awake & Singing: 7 Classic Plays from the American Jewish Repertoire* (New York: Penguin Books, 1995), 4.

57. Carol Bird, "The Jew as a Human Being," *Theatre Magazine* (September 1921), 6 and reprinted in *B'nai Brith News* (June-July 1923), 14.

58. Ibid.

59. "Broad Comedy on Broadway," *Sioux Falls (South Dakota) Press* (May 14, 1922), 9. Billy Rose Theatre Collection. Newspapers throughout the United States frequently ran short articles on the latest Broadway offerings. Since "Hebrew" comics had toured the country for decades beginning in the late nineteenth century, it is perhaps understandable that the lead actors in *Partners Again* be described in such terms for a readership less knowledgable about Broadway than about vaudeville.

60. "Why Worry?" *Vogue* (October 1, 1918).

61. Erdman, *Staging the Jew*, 159.

62. See Albert Lee, *Henry Ford and the Jews* (New York: Stein and Day, 1980); Leonard Dinnerstein, *Antisemitism in America* (New York: Oxford University Press, 1994), 80–81.

63. Dinnerstein, *Antisemitism*, 81. Dinnerstein also points out that Ford's anti-Semitic articles garnered wide support from both educated and uneducated readers (and large numbers of Christian ministers), who wrote him to encourage his efforts to "expose" the Jewish "conspiracy." Dinnerstein, *Antisemitism*, 82.

64. David Halberstam, *The Reckoning* (New York: William Morrow & Co., 1986), 97.

65. A six-cylinder engine was significantly ahead of its time in 1922; Chevy did not start manufacturing cars with that engine until 1929; Ford waited until 1936 to follow suit. Halberstam, *The Reckoning*, 100.

66. Montague Glass, *Partners Again* (act 1, p. 20). Typescript. Billy Rose Theatre Collection.

67. St. John Ervine of the *New York Morning World* made fun of these aspirations in his review, writing, "What the people need is not liberty or equality or fraternity, but patent incinerators, frigidaire machines and nickel-in-the-slot telephones. When the poor man can burn his garbage in the heart of his home and keep his meat nicely frozen and call up all his friends, especially when he has nothing to say to them, then the millennium will be established in the Bronx, and heaven will be on earth on the lower east side." St. John Ervine, *New York Morning World*, (December 26, 1928), 19.

68. Bella and Samuel Spewack, *Poppa* (New York: Samuel French, 1929), act 2, p. 51.

69. *Poppa*, act 1, p. 29; act 2, p. 66.

70. Aben Kandel, "An American Dramatist Whose Humor is Universal," *American Hebrew* (January 17, 1930), 383; A. Glantz, "A Comedia Fun Yidishn Leben, Oyf Broadway," *Der Tog* (December 28, 1928).

71. Alexander Carr, "Perlmutter Speaks," *Theatre* (March 1, 1914), 38.

72. Arthur Hornblow, "The Theatre," *Theatre Magazine* (July 1922), 31.

73. Sulamith Ish-Kishor, "It Takes a Real Nordic to Make a Fine Cantor," *The Day* (November 14, 1925), 7.

74. Unidentified clipping, *Humoresque* file, Billy Rose Theater Collection.

75. B. Goldberg, "Fanny Hurst's 'Humoresque' at the Vanderbilt Theater," *Der Tog* (March 9, 1923), 3.

76. A. Glantz, "George Jessel Plays On Almost . . ." *Der Tog* (September 28, 1928).

77. "It's a Serious Business, Declare Abe and Mawruss," *Sunday News* (May 21, 1922), 19; *The Sun* (May 17, 1922), 22.

78. Undated clipping, Billy Rose Theatre Collection.
79. "The Theatre," *New York Tribune* (May 14, 1922), 16. Billy Rose Theatre Collection.
80. Nichols, *Abie's Irish Rose*, act 1, pp. 22–23.
81. *Brooklyn Jewish Chronicle* (February 29, 1924), 12.
82. *Theatre Magazine* (February, 1928), 97.
83. Anne Nichols, *Abie's Irish Rose*, typescript version (undated), Billy Rose Theatre Collection.
84. Nichols, *Abie's Irish Rose,* 1.
85. Moses Rischin has recorded that by 1916 only 23 percent of New York's Jews lived on the Lower East Side, compared to 50 percent in 1903 and 75 percent in 1892. *The Promised City: New York Jews 1870–1914* (Cambridge, MA: Harvard University Press, 1962), 93.
86. Newspaper photo of the diorama in an unidentified newspaper, Billy Rose Theatre Collection. The caption calls the diorama "probably the most original out-door bulletin ever used by a theatrical organization" and notes that it was erected "at a point where it is seen by thousands of motorists who daily pass that way." The sign was illuminated at night.
87. Deborah Dash Moore, *At Home in America: Second Generation New York Jews* (New York: Columbia University Press, 1981), 51; See Richard Plunz, *A History of Housing in New York* (New York: Columbia University Press, 1990). The photographer Carl Rosenstein still leads tours of the area, which he is trying to have landmarked as a historic district. See Christopher Gray, "Streetscapes/The Grand Concourse in the Bronx; Will it Be City's Thinnest, Longest Historic District?" *New York Times* (April 4, 1999), 7.
88. Jenna Weissman Joselit, "'A Set Table:' Jewish Domestic Culture in the New World, 1880–1950, in Susan L. Braunstein and Joselit, eds., *Getting Comfortable in New York: The American Jewish Home, 1880–1950* (New York: The Jewish Museum, 1990), 45–46.
89. Andrew R. Heinze, *Adapting to Abundance: Jewish Immigrants, Mass Consumption, and the Search for American Identity* (New York: Columbia University Press, 1990), 223.
90. John Corbin, "'Two Blocks Away' Liked," *New York Times* (August 31, 1921), 12. Billy Rose Theatre Collection.
91. Aaron Hoffman, *Two Blocks Away* (New York: Samuel French, 1925), act 2, p. 82.
92. Ibid.
93. Frank Rich (with Lisa Aronson), *The Theatre Art of Boris Aronson* (New York: Alfred A. Knopf, 1987), 36.
94. Osip Dymov, *Bronx Express*, in Nahma Sandrow, trans., *God, Man and Devil* (New York: Syracuse University Press, 1999), 294–295.
95. For the legacy of the metaphor of the melting pot in American culture, see Philip Gleason, "The Melting Pot: Symbol of Fusion or Confusion?" in *American Quarterly* 16 (1964): 20–46. Despite the comprehensiveness of his article, Gleason did not, however, seem to be familiar with *Bronx Express.*
    In Zangwill's play, it is not money but love (in the context of intermarriage with a Gentile) that will change the alien immigrant into a true American. See Werner Sollors, *Beyond Ethnicity* (New York: Oxford University Press, 1996).
96. Osip Dymov, Samuel R. Golding, and Owen Davis, *Bronx Express* (original English translation) act 2, p. 6, typescript, Billy Rose Theater Collection.
97. Ibid., act 2, p. 9; 9.
98. Ibid., act 2, p. 35.
99. Ibid., act 2, p. 26; act 3, p. 14.
100. Arthur Hornblow, "The Bronx Express," *Theatre Magazine* (July, 1922), 31.
101. V. E., "Osip Dymov's 'Bronx Express' on Broadway," *Der Tog* (May 12, 1922), 11.

102. Samuel O. Kuhn, "The Drama," *Jewish Forum* (May 1925), 109.

103. Unidentified Utica newspaper (May 27, 1924), 21. Billy Rose Theatre Collection; Julius Drachsler, "Intermarriage in New York City: A Statistical Study of the Amalgamation of European Peoples," *Studies in History, Economics and Public Law*, vol. 94, no. 2, whole number 213.

104. Riv-Ellen Prell, *Fighting to Become Americans: Jews, Gender and the Anxiety of Assimilation* (Boston: Beacon Press, 1999), 13.

105. Jenna Weissman Joselit, *The Wonders of America: Reinventing Jewish Culture, 1880–1950* (New York: Hill & Wang, 1994), 5.

106. Leon de Costa, *Kosher Kitty Kelly*, typescript, Library of Congress, act 1, p. 4.

107. Ibid., act 1, p. 14.

108. Ibid., act 2, p. 25.

109. Ibid., act 1, p. 8.

110. Ibid., act 2, p. 11.

111. Clipping, Billy Rose Theater Collection, *New York World*, June 16, 1925; Percy Hammond, "Another Pathetic Waif Left on Broadway's Friendly Doorstep," *New York Herald Tribune* (June 16, 1925).

112. Leon de Costa, *Kosher Kitty's Kids*, typescript, Billy Rose Theater Collection, Act II, p. 3–20; act. 1, p. 3–7.

113. Willard Mack and David Belasco, *Fanny*, typescript, Billy Rose Theater Collection, act 1, scene 1, p. 23.

114. Ibid, act 1, scene 2, p. 40.

115. Ibid., act. 2, scene I, p. 13

116. D. Solomon, "A Yiddish Maydel fun Der East Side Vos Fardint 2,600 Dollar a Voch af Broadway" (A Jewish Girl From the East Side Who Earns 2,600 Dollars a Week on Broadway), *Der Tog* (October 10, 1926).

117. Gilbert W. Gabriel, "The Cohens and the Cowboys," *New York Sun* (September 22, 1926), 29.

118. See Moses Rischin and John Livingston, eds., *Jews of the American West* (Detroit: Wayne State University Press, 1991) and Kenneth Libo, with Irving Howe, *We Lived There Too: In Their Own Words and Pictures, Pioneer Jews and the Westward Movement of America, 1630–1930* (New York: St. Martin's, 1984).

119. Harry Hershfield, "Fanny Brice Sent Abie 'Cuckoo' Laughing," *New York Journal* (September 28, 1926).

CHAPTER 3   JEWS IN SILENT FILM

1. "The Amateur Actor: A Short Story," (St. Paul-Minneapolis) *American Jewish World*, May 7, 1926, pp. 4, 18–19.

2. Quoted in Lester Friedman, *Hollywood's Image of the Jew* (New York: Frederick Ungar Publishing, 1982), 153.

3. Neil Gabler *An Empire of Their Own: How the Jews Invented Hollywood* (New York: Anchor Books, 1988), 56.

4. Julius Novick, "The Circle of Tradition is Broken," *Village Voice* (January 17, 1977).

5. Quoted in Gabler, *An Empire*, 277.

6. Quoted in George Harmon Knowles, *The Jazz Age Revisited: British Criticism of American Civilization During the 1920s* (Stanford: Stanford University Press, 1955), 121.

7. *Cinema* (February 21, 1924), reprinted in *Harrison's Reports* (April 5, 1924), 76.

8. Gabler, *An Empire*, 6.

9. Ibid., 34.

10. Ibid., 289.

11. "Adolph Zukor Campaign List," *Jewish Tribune* (October 23, 1925), 14.

12. Gabler, *An Empire,* 44.
13. Will H. Hays, "A Chronicle of Cinema Achievement," *American Hebrew* (November 22, 1929), 44. See also Franklin Gordon, "The Cinema at Its Peak," *American Hebrew* (March 7, 1930), 586.
14. "Joseph Levenson, Movie Censor," *American Hebrew* (July 29, 1921), 261.
15. Freda R. Bienstock, "A New York Jewess Invades the Field of the Showman," *Jewish Tribune* (September 25, 1925), 10, 17.
16. Gabler, *An Empire,* 140.
17. George Jessel, "Why I Alternate on Stage and Screen: A Player Who Frankly Avows That Only the Big Money Lured Him into Film Acting," *Theatre Magazine* (February 1928), 22.
18. Robert L. Carringer, ed., *The Jazz Singer* (Madison: University of Wisconsin Press, 1979), 145.
19. See Michael Rogin, *Blackface/White Noise.*
20. See Michael Alexander, *Jazz Age Jews.*
21. George F. Custen, *Twentieth Century's Fox: Darryl F. Zanuck and the Culture of Hollywood* (New York: BasicBooks, 1997), 102.
22. Michael Rogin, *Blackface/White Noise: Jewish Immigrants in the Hollywood Melting Pot* (Berkeley: University of California Press, 1996), 86; 100.
23. Custen, *Twentieth Century's Fox,* 102.
24. Custen, *Twentieth Century's Fox,* 104; 104. Custen also quotes a speech that Jack Warner planned to give at the film's expected fourth curtain call on opening night that announced, "The spirit of the play we feel is not the glorification of any one religion, creed, race, but has a universal theme. . . .'HONOR THY FATHER AND THY MOTHER." Custen, *Twentieth Century's Fox,* 105.
25. Gabler, *An Empire,* 143.
26. Gabler, *An Empire,* 144.
27. Walter Ginsburg, "Broadway's Favorite Comedian Began Life as a Cantor's Son," *The Day* (English-Language Section) (January 2, 1927).
28. Gabler, *An Empire,* 44.
29. Kevin Brownlow, *Behind the Mask of Innocence* (New York: Alfred A. Knopf, 1990), 390.
30. Review of "Humoresque," *Motion Picture News* (September 18, 1920), 4231.
31. Brownlow, *Behind the Mask,* 391.
32. Harry Alan Potamkin, *The Compound Cinema: The Film Writings of Harry Alan Potamkin. Selected, Arranged and Introduced by Lewis Jacobs* (New York: Teachers College Press, Columbia University, 1977), 368.
33. Unidentified newspaper, Chamberlin Scrapbooks, Academy of Motion Pictures Arts and Sciences. The same review mentions that at the end, the characters "buoy themselves with new dreams and ambition as they turn their faces towards a new land of promise—California." This seems to point to a different version of the film, with a different ending than the one we have.
34. R. Laurence Moore, *Religious Outsiders and the Making of Americans* (New York: Oxford University Press, 1986), xi.
35. Gilman M. Ostrander, "The Revolution in Morals," in John Braeman, Robert H. Brenner, and David Brody, eds., *Change and Continuity in Twentieth-Century America: The 1920's* (Bowling Green: Ohio State University Press, 1968), 343.
36. Ibid.
37. Patricia Erens, *The Jew in American Cinema* (Bloomington: Indiana University Press, 1984), 82.
38. In Leon de Costa's *Kosher Kitty's Kids,* Kitty asks Ginsburg if he has "ever seen the Irish-Jewish moving pictures" because "in them pictures the Irish always win."

Ginsburg retorts, "Sure! The Irish always win the fights and the Jewish people the money." *Kosher Kitty's Kids,* typescript, act 1, p. 5–6.

39. Kathryn Fuller, "Shadowland: American Audiences and the Movie-Going Experience in the Silent Film Era" (Ph.D. diss., Johns Hopkins University, 1993), 273.

40. Sean Dennis Cashman, *America in the Twenties and Thirties* (New York: New York University Press, 1989), 45. Cashman uses a figure of about 106 million for the entire United States population, plus about 12 million for America's overseas possessions, for a total population of 118 million.

41. Geoffrey Perrett, *America in the Twenties: A History* (New York: Simon and Schuster, 1982), 79.

42. Friedman, *Hollywood's Image,* 52.

43. Thomas Cripps, "The Movie Jew as an Image of Assimilation, 1903–1927," *Journal of Popular Film* 4 (1975): 197; Friedman is correct that these films were "[n]ot made as pseudodocumentaries to enlighten audiences about the beautiful ceremonies of Jewish religion or the more esoteric aspects of Jewish life." But in their focus on Jewish family life, and on the difficulties of being Jewish in a non-Jewish world, they obviously celebrate Jewish ethnicity. Friedman, *Hollywood's Image,* 53.

44. Friedman, *Hollywood's Image,* 53.

45. Andrew R. Heinze, *Adapting to Abundance: Jewish Immigrants, Mass Consumption, and the Search for American Identity* (New York: Columbia University Press, 1990).

46. Jenna Weissman Joselit, *The Wonders of America: Reinventing Jewish Culture, 1880–1950* (New York: Hill and Wang, 1994).

47. "The Cohens and the Kellys," *Exhibitors Herald* (September 25, 1926), 13.

48. Henry Jenkins, *What Made Pistachio Nuts? Early Sound Comedy and the Vaudeville Aesthetic* (New York: Columbia University Press, 1992), 179.

49. Jenkins, *What Made Pistachio Nuts?* 175.

50. Mark Winokur, *American Laughter: Immigrants, Ethnicity, and 1930s Film Comedy* (New York: St. Martin's Press, 1996), 153–154.

51. Oscar Handlin, *The Uprooted* (New York: Grosset & Dunlap, 1951).

52. Random House Reference, Words @ Random, Mavens' Word of the Day, March 4, 1999, http://www.randomhouse.com/wotd/index.pperl?date=19990304.

53. Although it might seem inappropriate to play up the stock market angle of the film, given that the stock market had just crashed the year before, the press sheet reported that, according to the Department of Commerce, only 4 percent of Americans were affected by the crash. And "even during the time of the smash the Broadway stage musical comedies inserted jokes about Wall Street and they got big laughs, many of them from the unfortunate victims." Thus, the studio concluded, "The Wall Street angle is good advertising." *Kibitzer* File, Billy Rose Theatre Collection.

54. Among the wacky celebrity definitions printed in the press sheet are those of Zeppo Marx ("A kibitzer is every one of my uncles"), Groucho Marx ("A kibitzer is a fellow who eats canned corn"), Fredric March ("A kibitzer is the helpful person who offers to hold your coat while you whip that truck driver who cut in ahead of you"), and Fay Wray ("A kibitzer is the man who dodges taking you to the night clubs because he says he doesn't dance"). Billy Rose Theatre Collection.

55. *Film Daily* (November 14, 1926), 11.

56. Donald Crafton, "The Jazz Singer's Reception in the Media and At the Box Office," in David Bordwell and Noel Carroll, eds., *Post-Theory: Reconstructing Film Studies* (Madison: University of Wisconsin Press, 1996), 468–478.

57. Janet Staiger, *Interpreting Films: Studies in the Historical Reception of American Film* (Princeton, NJ: Princeton University Press, 1992), 206–208.

58. *New York Times* (November 27, 1922), 18.

59. Lary May, *Screening Out the Past: The Birth of Mass Culture and the Motion Picture Industry* (New York: Oxford University Press, 1980), 147.

60. Quoted in Brownlow, *Behind the Mask,* 391.

61. Quoted in Brownlow, *Behind the Mask,* 411–412.

62. Unidentified review, *Hungry Hearts* File, Chamberlin Scrapbooks, Academy of Motion Pictures Arts and Sciences.

63. "Survivors of a Vanished Race in the Movie World," *New York Times,* January 18, 1920.

64. Harry Sabbath Bodin, "An Epic of the Immigrant: Screen Version of 'Hungry Hearts' on Broadway," *American Hebrew* (September 8, 1922), 387.

65. Undated Jewish newspaper review, quoted in Brownlow, *Behind the Mask,* 411–412.

66. *Harrison's Reports* (November 14, 1925), 182. Harrison was a former critic for *Motion Picture News* who left to form his own independent newspaper; he saw himself as championing the interests of the exhibitors against that of the studios, which, he felt, often took advantage of the movie house owners. He was also an early opponent of product placement in films.

67. A more recent, unpublished appraisal of *His People,* by the late film scholar William Everson, disputed the Jewishness of the theme. As Everson told his film classes at New York University:

    One is tempted to paraphrase the now-famous Levy's Bread ads and say that one doesn't have to be Jewish in order to appreciate *His People,* but that it most certainly helps. The Jewish ghetto is almost a character in its own right in the picture, or an object of worship. detail is there in order to make it a blockbuster for the Jewish trade, what emerges in really no more Jewish than a 10-meter set entirely on British cricket pitch would be essentially British. The British have never been really interested in playing cricket; the real game is in spectating, and murmuring "well-bowled" at appropriate intervals. So it is here; the cast is really playing a game which requires them to perform little rituals every so often, but the overall theme has far less traditional Jewish content than, for example, *The Jazz Singer.* Sweep all this extraneous detail away, and one is left with a staggeringly unsubtle sob-story of the "Stella Dallas" ilk.

    His People file. Museum of Modern Art Film Archive.

68. Judith Thisssen, "Jewish Immigrant Audiences in New York City, 1905–1914," in Melvyn Stokes and Richard Maltby, eds., *American Movie Audiences: From the Turn of the Century to the Early Sound Era* (London: British Film Institute, 1999), 15–28.

69. See Robert C. Allen, "Motion Picture Exhibition in Manhattan: Beyond the Nickelodeon," *Cinema Journal* 18, no. 2 (Spring 1979): 2–15; Ben Singer, "Manhattan Nickelodeons: New Data on Audience and Exhibitors," *Cinema Journal* 34, no. 3 (Spring 1995): 5–35; Robert C. Allen, "Manhattan Myopia; or, Oh! Iowa!," *Cinema Journal* 35, no. 3 (Spring 1996): 75; Sumiko Higashi, "Dialogue: Manhattan Nickelodeons," *Cinema Journal* 35, no. 3 (Spring 1996): 72–74.

    Leo Handel's pioneering study of Hollywood audiences focuses only on the 1940s, and even then has almost no discussion of the ethnic composition of the audience. Leo Handel, *Hollywood Looks at Its Audience: A Report of Film Audience Research* (Urbana: The University of Illinois Press, 1950).

70. Robert Allen, "Motion Picture Exhibition in Manhattan," 4.

71. By the time the film premiered, Yezierska had seemingly converted to Christianity. In "A Message of Faith" published in *Motion Picture Classics* in 1922, Yezierska sees the film medium as a bringer of Christian religious transformation, with the potential to reach millions of people who are "more hungry for beauty than they are for bread." And it is "because of the multitude that the screen is great. I love the masses and that is why I love the screen. When Christ preached He preached

to the multitude . . . [and] lifted them up." The Jewishness of the characters has been subsumed to the universality of the film's "message" of Christian redemption. Anzia Yezierska, "A Message of Faith," transcribed by Faith Service. *Motion Picture Classics* (November 1922), 41 and 86.

72. Miriam Hansen, *Babel and Babylon: Spectatorship in American Silent Film* (Cambridge, MA: Harvard University Press, 1991), 73. Hansen sees the producers pursuing a dual strategy of attempting to attract both the working-class nickelodeon clientele and the middle-class viewer. But Hansen stops her analysis of what she calls the "Ghetto" films before 1920. And those scholars who have focused on the middle-class audiences, like Lary May and Kathryn Fuller, do not analyze the middle-class reception of films about immigrants. See May, *Screening Out the Past* and Kathryn Helgesen Fuller, "Shadowland: American Audiences and the Movie-Going Experience in the Silent Film Era" (Ph.D. diss, Johns Hopkins University, 1992).

73. "Younger Generation (Dialog)," *Variety* (March 20, 1929), 9.

74. Hasia Diner, *Lower East Side Memories: A Jewish Place in America* (Princeton, NJ: Princeton University Press, 2000), 20.

75. Beth S. Wenger, "Memory as Identity: The Invention of the Lower East Side," *American Jewish History* 85 (March 1997): 4.

76. Lawrence W. Levine, "Progress and Nostalgia: The Self Image of the Nineteen Twenties," in Levine, *The Unpredictable Past: Explorations in American Cultural History* (New York: Oxford University Press, 1993), 191.

77. Hasia R. Diner, *Lower East Side Memories: A Jewish Place in America* (Princeton, NJ: Princeton University Press, 2000), 20.

78. Mario Maffi, *Gateway to the Promised Land: Ethnic Cultures on New York's Lower East Side* (New York: New York University Press, 1995), 285.

79. Of course, not all the people who viewed these films were Jewish. But the audience for them was clearly intended to be mostly Jewish, as evidenced by the films' focus on Jewish life and use of Yiddish expressions.

80. Jenna Weissman Joselit, "Telling Tales: Or, How a Slum Became a Shrine," *Jewish Social Studies* 2:2 (Winter 1996): 55–57.

81. Bodin, "An Epic of the Immigrant," 387.

82. An article in the *American Hebrew,* published just a few months before the premiere of Hungry Hearts, noted that Jews were beginning to move to the suburbs of Long Island and Westchester. Interestingly, the article speculates that "the first break in the solid city ranks of New York Jewry was made not by born-and-bred New Yorkers, but by men and women who came from the Middle West, the West and the South for business professional reasons to live in the metropolis." Their reason for leaving, the article suggested, was that they "could not accommodate themselves to the conditions of the New York apartments." "Suburbaniting It: The Trend of Home Life is Away from the City to the Country," *American Hebrew* (April 14, 1922), 606–608.

83. Freddie Schader, "The Younger Generation," *Motion Picture News* (March 23, 1929), 923.

84. May, *Screening Out the Past,* 158. Jews were also prominent in building movie theaters. See, for example, "Jack Shapiro: Builder of Cinema Palaces," *American Hebrew* (March 7, 1930), 612.

85. Eric Linklater, *Juan in America* (London: J. Cape and H. Smith, 1931) 392–393.

86. Douglas Gomery, "The Movie Palace Comes to America's Cities," in Richard Butsch, ed., *For Fun and Profit: The Transformation of Leisure into Consumption* (Philadelphia: Temple University Press, 1990), 139–140.

87. Richard Butsch, *The Making of American Audiences* (New York: Cambridge University Press, 2000), 161.

88. See, for example, Patricia Erens, "The Flapper: Hollywood's First Liberated Woman," in Laurence R. Broer and John D. Walther, eds., *Dancing Fools and Weary Blues: The Great Escape of the Twenties* (Bowling Green, OH: Bowling Green University Press, 1990), 130–139.

89. Sharon Pucker Rivo, "Projected Images: Portraits of Jewish Women in Early American Film," in Joyce Antler, ed., *Talking Back: Images of Jewish Women in American Culture* (Hanover, NH: University Press of New England, 1998), 34.

90. However, not all have agreed with this assessment over the years; for example, the film critic Harry Potamkin called *Humoresque* "the forerunner to the grimly funny lot born of *Abie's Irish Rose,* those fearful narrations of Irish-Jewish amities and enmities." Potamkin, *Compound Cinema,* 368.

91. Zelda F. Popkin, "Mother Love in Mean Streets," *The American Hebrew* (May 5, 1922), 700; ibid.

92. Neil Gabler, "Sound & Fury: The Making of the First Talkie, 'The Jazz Singer,' is a Story of Hollywood's Jewish Heritage." *Los Angeles Times Magazine* (July 31, 1988), 37.

93. Steve Whitfield, "Jazz Singers: A Hollywood Bomb—But, Inadvertently, An Accurate Portrayal of the American Jewish Condition," *Moment* (March-April, 1981), 24.

94. Ibid., 25.

CONCLUSION

1. Tad Friend, "Comedy First," *New Yorker* (April 19 and 26, 2004), 165.

2. Beth Wenger, *New York Jews and the Great Depression: Uncertain Promise* (Syracuse: Syracuse University Press, 1999), 4.

3. Clifford Odets, *Awake and Sing!* in Ellen Schiff, ed., *Awake and Singing: 7 Classic Plays from the American Jewish Repertoire* (New York: Signet, 1995), 260.

4. Steven Whitfield, *In Search of American Jewish Culture* (Hanover, NH: University Press of New England, 1999), 115.

5. Alfred Kazin, *Starting Out in the Thirties* (Boston: Little, Brown and Co., 1962), 80; 81.

6. Kazin, *Starting Out,* 82.

7. Henry Jenkins, *What Made Pistachio Nuts? Early Sound Comedy and the Vaudeville Aesthetic* (New York: Columbia University Press, 1992), 175.

8. Jenkins, *What Made Pistachio Nuts?,* 172.

9. John F. McClymer, "If the Irish Weren't Becoming White, What *Were* They Doing All Those Years?" http://www.assumption.edu/ahc/1920s/Historiography%20Discussion.html.

10. Samuel Heilman, *Portrait of American Jews: The Last Half of the Twentieth Century* (Seattle: University of Washington Press, 1995), 9.

11. Eli Lederhendler, *New York Jews and the Decline of Urban Ethnicity, 1950-1970* (Syracuse: Syracuse University Press, 2001), 205.

12. George Lipsitz, *Time Passages* (Minneapolis: University of Minnesota Press, 1990), 41.

13. George Robinson, "Kidding on the Square: Mickey Katz and the Barton Brothers Go Berserk," *New York Jewish Week* (September 29, 2000).

14. Joseph Foster, "Skunkcabbage By Any Other Name," *New Masses* (January 7, 1947).

15. Quoted in Patricia Erens, *The Jew in American Cinema* (Bloomington: Indiana University Press, 1984), 187.

16. Felicia Herman, "Jewish Leaders and the Motion Picture Industry." In Ava F. Kahn and Marc Dollinger, eds., *California Jews* (Lebanon, NH: Brandeis University Press, 2003), 108.

17. Nathan Guttman, "Jewish Bids to Amend 'Passion' Film Were Pointless," *Haaretz* (March 22, 2004). http://freerepublic.info/focus/f-news/1102761/posts.

18. Lester Friedman, *Hollywood's Image of the Jew* (New York: Frederick Ungar, 1982), 135.

19. Quoted in ibid., 128.

20. Jonathan Sarna, *American Judaism: A History* (New Haven, CT: Yale University Press, 2004), 222.

21. Myrna Katz Frommer and Harvey Frommer, *It Happened in the Catskills* (New York: Harcourt Brace Jovanovich, 1991), x; xi.

22. National Foundation for Jewish Culture, 330.

23. Norman Kleeblatt, curator, *Too Jewish?* (New York: Jewish Museum, 1996); *Too Jewish? Challenging Traditional Identities* (New Brunswick, NJ: Rutgers University Press, 1996). This exhibit of Jewish self-representation in contemporary art included sketches drawn by Art Spiegelman in the process of his work on the Holocaust-themed comic book, *Maus;* Dennis Kardon's set of plaster casts of Jewish noses; and Cary Liebowitz and Rhonda Lieberman's Hanukah menorah in the shape of lipsticks protruding from a Chanel pocketbook.

24. Michael Goldstein, "Reinventing Broadway," *New York Magazine* (May 29, 1995), 28.

25. Lane has actually made a career of playing Jewish shtick, such as in his roles as Nathan Detroit in the Broadway revival of *Guys and Dolls* and Pseudolus in Larry Gelbart's *A Funny Thing Happened on the Way to the Forum.* Casting non-Jewish actors in Jewish roles is nothing new; as I have pointed out, it happened even in the 1920s, in many of the plays that I have discussed. But there were still many prominent Jewish entertainers around, and they were a crucial part of the entertainment landscape. They are very few today and even those like Mandy Patinkin and Dudu Fisher who do sing Jewish music tend to be much more successful in mainstream Broadway musicals than in their "specialty" shows.

26. Kera Bolonik, "Oy Gay!: Will and Grace," *The Nation* (November 17, 2003).

BIBLIOGRAPHY

Alexander, Michael. *Jazz Age Jews*. Princeton, NJ: Princeton University Press, 2001.

Allen, Robert C. "Manhattan Myopia: or, Oh! Iowa!" *Cinema Journal* 35, 3 (Spring 1996): 75.

———. "Motion Picture Exhibition in Manhattan: Beyond the Nickelodeon." *Cinema Journal* 18, 2 (Spring 1979): 2–15.

Antler, Joyce. *The Journey Home: Jewish Women and the American Century*. New York: The Free Press, 1997.

———. *Talking Back: Images of Jewish Women in American Popular Culture*. Hanover, NH: Brandeis University Press, 1998.

Archdeacon, Thomas J. *Becoming American: An Ethnic History*. New York: The Free Press, 1983.

Bennett, David. *Party of Fear: From Nativist Movements to the New Right in American History*. Chapel Hill: University of North Carolina Press, 1988.

Berger, Arthur Asa. *Jewish Jesters: A Study in American Popular Comedy*. Cresskill, NJ: Hampton Press, 2001.

Berkson, Isaac. *Theories of Americanization*. New York: Columbia University Press, 1920.

Biale, David, Michael Galchinsky, and Susannah Heschel, eds. *Insider/Outsider: American Jews and Multiculturalism*. Berkeley: University of California Press, 1998.

Bienstock, Beverly Gray. "The Changing Image of the American Jewish Mother." In *Changing Images of the Family*, edited by Virginia Tufte and Barbara Myerhoff, 173–191. New Haven, CT: Yale University Press, 1979.

Boelhower, William. *Through a Glass Darkly: Ethnic Semiosis in American Literature*. Venezia, Italy: Edizioni Helvetica, 1984.

Brownlow, Kevin. *Behind the Mask of Innocence*. New York: Alfred A. Knopf, 1990.

Brucher, Richard. "Pernicious Nostalgia in Glengarry Glen Ross." In *David Mamet's Glengarry Glen Ross: Text and Performance,* ed. Leslie Kane, 211–225. New York: Garland Publishing, 1996.

Buhle, Paul. *From the Lower East Side to Hollywood: Jews in American Popular Culture*. New York: Verso Books, 2004.

Burgess, Robert E., and Ernest W. Park. *The City*. Chicago: University of Chicago Press, 1925.

Butler, Judith. *Bodies That Matter: On the Discursive Limits of 'Sex.'* New York: Routledge, 1993.

Butsch, Richard. *The Making of American Audiences*. New York: Cambridge University Press, 2000.

Byers, Albert. "Abie Eats." Franklin, OH: Eldridge Entertainment House, 1927.

Cahnman, Werner J. "Comments on the American Jewish Scene." Paper presented at the New York Conference on Acculturation, New York, 1965.

Canfield, Mary Cass. "The Great American Art." Reprinted in *Selected Vaudeville Criticism,* ed. Anthony Slide. New York: Scarecrow Press, 1988.

Cantor, Eddie. *My Life Is in Your Hands.* New York: Harper and Bros., 1928.

———. *The Way I See It.* Englewood Cliffs, NJ: Prentice-Hall, 1959.

Carringer, Robert, ed. *The Jazz Singer* [annotated screenplay]. Madison: University of Wisconsin Press, 1979.

Cashman, Sean Dennis. *America in the Twenties and Thirties.* New York: New York University Press, 1989.

Cesarani, David. "A Funny Thing Happened on the Way to the Suburbs: Social Change in Anglo-Jewry Between the Wars, 1914–1945." *Jewish Culture and History* 1, no. 1 (1998): 5–26.

Cimet, Adina. "Ambivalence Acknowledged: Jewish Identities and Language Strategies in Contemporary Mexico." In *The Collective and the Public in Latin America: Cultural Identities and Political Order,* ed. Luis Roniger and Tamar Herzog. Portland, OR: Sussex Academic Press, 2000.

Coleman, Edward D. *The Jew in English Drama.* New York: The New York Public Library and Ktav Publishing House, 1968.

Corenthal, Michael G. *Cohen on the Telephone: A History of Jewish Recorded Humor and Popular Music, 1892–1942.* Milwaukee: Yesterday's Memories, 1984.

Crafton, Donald. "The Jazz Singer's Reception in the Media and At the Box Office." In *Post-Theory: Reconstructing Film Studies,* ed. David Bordwell and Noel Carroll. Madison: University of Wisconsin Press, 1996.

Cripps, Thomas. "The Movie Jew as an Image of Assimilation, 1903–1927." *Journal of Popular Film* 4 (1975): 190–207.

Custen, George F. *Twentieth Century's Fox: Darryl F. Zanuck and the Culture of Hollywood.* New York: BasicBooks, 1997.

Dickinson, Thomas H. "The Jew in the Theater." *The Nation.* June 13, 1923: 689–691.

Dimeglio, John E. *Vaudeville U.S.A.* Bowling Green, OH: Bowling Green University Popular Press, 1973.

Diner, Hasia R. *Lower East Side Memories: A Jewish Place in America.* Princeton, NJ: Princeton University Press, 2000.

Dinnerstein, Leonard. *Antisemitism in America.* New York: Oxford University Press, 1994.

Distler, Paul Antonie. "The Rise and Fall of the Racial Comics in American Vaudeville." Ph.D. dissertation, Tulane University, 1963.

Dormon, James H. "American Popular Culture and the New Immigration Ethnics: The Vaudeville Stage and the Process of Ethnic Ascription." *Amerikastudien/American Studies* 36, no. 2 (1991): 179–193.

Douglas, Anne. *Terrible Honesty: Mongrel Manhattan in the 1920s.* New York: Farrar, Straus and Giroux, 1995.

Drachsler, Julius. "Intermarriage in New York City: A Statistical Study of the Amalgamation of European Peoples." Ph.D. dissertation, Columbia University, 1921.

Duncan, Erika. "The Hungry Jewish Mother." In *On Being a Jewish Feminist,* ed. Susannah Heschel. New York: Schocken Books, 1983.

Dymov, Osip. *Bronx Express.* In Nahma Sandrow, trans., *God, Man and Devil.* New York: Syracuse University Press, 1999.

Eisenhour, Jerry. *Joe Leblang's Cut-Rate Ticket Empire and the Broadway Theatre, 1894–1931.* Lewiston, NY: Edwin Mellen Press, 2003.

Erdman, Andrew. "Blue Vaudeville: Sex, Morals, and the Marketing of Amusement, 1895–1915." Ph.D. dissertation, City University of New York Graduate School, 2001.

Erdman, Harley. *Staging the Jew: The Performance of an American Ethnicity*. New Brunswick, NJ: Rutgers University Press, 1997.

Erenberg, Lewis. *Steppin' Out: New York Nightlife and the Transformation of American Culture, 1890–1930*. Westport, CT: Greenwood Press, 1981.

Erens, Patricia. "The Flapper: Hollywood's First Liberated Woman." In *Dancing Fools and Weary Blues: The Great Escape of the Twenties*, ed. Laurence R. Broer and John D. Walther. Bowling Green, OH: Bowling Green University Press, 1990.

———. *The Jew in American Cinema*. Bloomington: Indiana University Press, 1984.

Feingold, Henry L. *The Jewish People in America*. Vol. 4: *A Time for Searching: Entering the Mainstream, 1920–1945*. Baltimore: Johns Hopkins University Press, 1992.

Fields, Edmond, and L. Marc. *From the Bowery to Broadway: Lew Fields and the Roots of American Popular Theatre*. New York: Oxford University Press, 1993.

Friedlander, Gerald. *Shakespeare and the Jew*. New York: Dutton, 1921.

Friedman, Lester D. *Hollywood's Image of the Jew*. New York: Frederick Ungar, 1982.

Fuller, Kathryn. "Shadowland: American Movie Audiences and the Movie-Going Experience in the Silent Film Era." Ph.D. dissertation, Johns Hopkins University, 1993.

Gabler, Neil. *An Empire of Their Own: How the Jews Invented Hollywood*. New York: Anchor Books, 1988.

Galsworthy, John. *Representative Plays* by John Galsworthy. New York: Charles Scribner's Sons, 1924.

Gilbert, Douglas. *American Vaudeville: Its Life and Times*. New York: Dover Publications, 1940.

Gilman, Sander. *The Jew's Body*. New York: Routledge, 1991.

Gleason, Philip. "American Identity and Americanization." In *Harvard Encyclopedia of American Ethnic Groups*. Cambridge, MA: Harvard University Press, 1980.

———. "The Melting Pot: Symbol of Fusion or Confusion?" *American Quarterly* 16 (1964): 20–46.

Goffman, Erving. *The Presentation of Self in Everyday Life*. New York: Anchor Books, 1959.

Goldman, Herbert. *Banjo Eyes: Eddie Cantor and the Birth of Modern Stardom*. New York: Oxford University Press, 1997.

———. *Jolson: The Legend Comes to Life*. New York: Oxford University Press, 1988.

Gomery, Douglas. "The Movie Palace Comes to America's Cities." In *For Fun and Profit: The Transformation of Leisure into Consumption*, ed. Richard Butsch. Philadelphia: Temple University Press, 1990.

Gorelick, Sherry. *City College and the Jewish Poor*. New Brunswick, NJ: Rutgers University Press, 1981.

Grant, Madison. *The Passing of the White Race*. New York: Charles Scribner's Sons, 1921.

Green, Abel, and Joe Laurie, Jr. *Showbiz: From Vaude to Video*. New York: Henry Holt, 1951.

Gropper, Milton Herbert, and Max Siegel. *We Americans*. New York: Samuel French, 1928.

Grossman, Barbara. *Funny Woman: The Life and Times of Fanny Brice*. Bloomington: Indiana University Press, 1991.

Gurock, Jeffrey S. "Jewish Commitment and Continuity in Interwar Brooklyn." In *Jews of Brooklyn*, ed. Ilana Abramovitch and Sean Galvin. Hanover, NH: Brandeis University Press, 2002.

Halberstam, David. *The Reckoning*. New York: William Morrow, 1986.

Handel, Leo. *Hollywood Looks at Its Audience: A Report of Film Audience Research*. Urbana: University of Illinois Press, 1950.

Hansen, Miriam. *Babel and Babylon: Spectatorship in American Silent Film.* Cambridge, MA: Harvard University Press, 1991.

Hapgood, Hutchins. *The Spirit of the Ghetto.* New York: Schocken Books, 1966.

Harap, Louis. *Dramatic Encounters: The Jewish Presence in Twentieth-Century American Drama, Poetry, and Humor and the Black-Jewish Literary Relationship.* New York: Greenwood Press, 1987.

Heinze, Andrew R. *Adapting to Abundance: Jewish Immigrants, Mass Consumption, and the Search for American Identity.* New York: Columbia University Press, 1990.

Herberg, Will. *Protestant-Catholic-Jew: An Essay in American Religious Sociology.* Garden City, NY: Anchor Books, 1960.

Higashi, Sumiko. "Dialogue: Manhattan Nickelodeons." *Cinema Journal* 35, no. 3 (Spring 1996): 73–74.

Higham, John. *Strangers in the Land: Patterns of American Nativism, 1860–1925.* New York: Atheneum, 1971.

Hoberman, J. *Bridge of Light: Yiddish Film between Two Worlds.* Philadelphia: Temple University Press, 1995.

Hollinger, David. *Postethnic America: Beyond Multiculturalism.* New York: Basic Books, 1995.

Howe, Irving. *World of Our Fathers: The Journey of the East European Jews to America and the Life They Found and Made.* New York: Simon and Schuster, 1976.

Hyman, Paula. *Gender and Assimilation in Modern Jewish History: The Roles and Representation of Women.* Seattle: University of Washington Press, 1995.

———. "The Jewish Family: Looking for a Useable Past." In *On Being a Jewish Feminist,* ed. Susannah Heschel, 19–26. New York: Schocken Books, 1983.

Isman, Felix. *Weber and Fields.* New York: Boni and Liverright, 1924.

Jenkins, Henry. *What Made Pistachio Nuts? Early Sound Comedy and the Vaudeville Aesthetic.* New York: Columbia University Press, 1992.

Jessel, George. *So Help Me.* New York: Random House, 1943.

———. *This Way, Miss.* New York: Henry Holt, 1955.

Johnson, Carla. "Luckless in New York." *Journal of Popular Film and Television* 22, no. 3 (1994): 116–124.

Jolson, Harry as told to Alban Emley. *Mistah Jolson.* Hollywood, CA: House-Warven, 1951.

Joselit, Jenna Weissman. *Our Gang: Jewish Crime and the New York Jewish Community, 1900–1940.* Bloomington: Indiana University Press, 1983.

———. "A Set Table: Jewish Domestic Culture in the New World, 1880–1950." In *Getting Comfortable in New York: The American Jewish Home, 1880–1950,* ed. Susan L. Braunstein and Jenna Weissman Joselit. New York: The Jewish Museum, 1990.

———. "Telling Tales: Or, How a Slum Became a Shrine." *Jewish Social Studies* 2, no 2 (Winter 1996).

———. *The Wonders of America: Reinventing Jewish Culture, 1880–1950.* New York: Hill and Wang, 1994.

Kaiser, Arthur Leroy. *Hey! Teacher! A Humorous Entertainment (in Two Acts)* Chicago: Dramatic Publishing Company, 1928.

Kammen, Michael. *The Lively Arts: Gilbert Seldes and the Transformation of Cultural Criticism in the United States.* New York: Oxford University Press, 1996.

Kanfer, Stephan. *Groucho: The Life and Times of Julius Henry Marx.* New York: Alfred A. Knopf, 2000.

Kaplan, Mordechai. *Judaism as a Civilization.* New York: Thomas Yoseloff, 1957.

Kazin, Alfred. *A Walker in the City.* New York: Harcourt, Brace and Company, 1951.

Kessner, Thomas. *The Golden Door: Italian and Jewish Immigrant Mobility in New York City 1880–1915*. New York: Oxford University Press, 1977.

Kleeblat, Norman L., ed. *Too Jewish? Challenging Traditional Identities*. New York: The Jewish Museum, 1996.

Knowles, George Harmon. *The Jazz Age Revisited: British Criticism of American Civilization during the 1920s*. Stanford, CA: Stanford University Press, 1955.

Korelitz, Seth. "From Religion to Culture, From Race to Ethnicity." *American Jewish History* 85 (March 1997): 75–100.

Laurie, Joe Jr. *Vaudeville: From the Honky-Tonks to the Palace*. New York: Henry Holt, 1953.

Lavitt, Pamela Brown. "'Coon Shouting' and the Jewish Ziegfeld Girl." *American Jewish History* (December 2000).

Lederhendler, Eli. *New York Jews and the Decline of Urban Ethnicity, 1950–1970*. Syracuse, NY: Syracuse University Press, 2001.

Lee, Albert. *Henry Ford and the Jews*. New York: Stein and Day, 1980.

Levine, Lawrence. *The Unpredictable Past: Explorations in American Cultural History*. New York: Oxford University Press, 1993.

Levine, Peter. *From Ellis Island to Ebbets Field*. New York: Oxford University Press, 1992.

Levy, Clifton Harby. "How and Why New York Became the Greatest Jewish City in the World." *Jewish Forum* (1923).

Lewis, E. C. *Ish Ga Bibble (I Should Worry)*. Boston: Mutual Book Company, 1914.

Libo, Kenneth, with Irving Howe. *We Lived There Too: In Their Own Words and Pictures, Pioneer Jews and the Westward Movement of America, 1630–1930*. New York: St. Martin's Press, 1984.

Linklater, Eric. *Juan in America*. London: J. Cape and H. Smith, 1931.

Lipsitz, George. *Time Passages: Collective Memory and American Popular Culture*. Minneapolis: University of Minnesota Press, 1990.

Livingston, John, and Moses Rischin. *Jews of the American West*. Detroit: Wayne State University Press, 1991.

McClain, Ellen Jaffe. *Embracing the Stranger: Intermarriage and the Future of the American Jewish Community*. New York: BasicBooks, 1995.

Maffi, Mario. *Gateway to the Promised Land: Ethnic Cultures on New York's Lower East Side*. New York: New York University Press, 1995.

Mandel, Nora Lee. "Set Your VCR's: Jewish Women and Their Hair Appearing on TV This Season." *Lilith* (Fall 2001): 5.

Mantle, Burns. *Best Plays of 1921–22*. Boston: Small, Maynard and Co., 1922.

Marzio, Peter C. *Abie the Agent: A Complete Compilation, 1914–1915*. Westport, CT: Hyperion Press, 1977.

May, Lary. *Screening Out the Past: The Birth of Mass Culture and the Motion Picture Industry*. New York: Oxford University Press, 1980.

Mayo, Louise A. *The Ambivalent Image: Nineteenth Century America's Perception of the Jew*. Cranbury, NJ: Associated University Presses, 1988.

Merwin, Ted. "The Invention of Jewish Ethnicity in Anne Nichols' *Abie's Irish Rose*." *Journal of American Ethnic History* 20, no. 2 (Winter 2001): 3–37.

Montor, Henry. "Jewishness—and the Box Office: Why Broadway Stars are More Jewish Than Ever." *American Jewish World*, June 25, 1926.

Moore, Deborah Dash. *At Home in America: Second-Generation New York Jews*. New York: Columbia University Press, 1981.

Moore, R. Laurence. *Religious Outsiders and the Making of Americans*. New York: Oxford University Press, 1986.

Most, Andrea. *Making Americans: Jews and the Broadway Musical.* Cambridge, MA: Harvard University Press, 2004.

Mukdoni, A. "Trouble in the Yiddish Theater." *Jewish Digest* (November 1940): 63–65.

Mukerji, Chandra, and Michael Schudson, eds. *Rethinking Popular Culture.* Berkeley: University of California Press, 1991.

Nasaw, David. *Going Out: The Rise and Fall of Public Amusements.* New York: BasicBooks, 1993.

Nichols, Anne. *Abie's Irish Rose.* New York: Samuel French, 1924.

Ostrander, Gilman M. "The Revolution in Morals." In *Change and Continuity in Twentieth-Century America: The 1920s,* ed. Robert H. Brenner and David Brody. Columbus: Ohio State University Press, 1968.

Packard, Maurice. *Shakespeare Not a Jew.* Boston: Stratford Co., 1919.

———. *Shylock Not a Jew.* Boston, 1919.

Park, Robert E., and Ernest Burgess. *The City.* Chicago: University of Chicago Press, 1925.

Perlmutter, Ruth. "The Melting Pot and the Humoring of America: Hollywood and the Jew." *Film Reader* 5 (1982).

Perrett, Geoffrey. *America in the Twenties: A History.* New York: Simon and Schuster, 1982.

Plunz, Richard. *A History of Housing in New York.* New York: Columbia University Press, 1990.

Popkin, Henry. "The Vanishing Jew of Our Popular Culture." *Commentary,* July 1952.

Prell, Riv-Ellen. *Fighting to Become Americans: Jews, Gender, and the Anxiety of Assimilation.* Boston: Beacon Press, 1999.

Rich, Frank, with Lisa Aronson. *The Theatre Art of Boris Aronson.* New York: Alfred A. Knopf, 1987.

Rischin, Moses. *The Promised City: New York's Jews, 1870–1914.* Cambridge, MA: Harvard University Press, 1962.

Rivo, Sharon Pucker. "Projected Images: Portraits of Jewish Women in Early American Film." In *Talking Back: Images of Jewish Women in American Culture,* ed. Joyce Antler. Hanover, NH: University Press of New England, 1998.

Rogin, Michael. *Blackface/White Noise: Jewish Immigrants in the Hollywood Melting Pot.* Berkeley: University of California Press, 1996.

Romeyn, Esther. "My Other/My Self: Impersonation, Masquerade and the Theater of Identity in Turn-of-the-Century New York City," Ph.D. dissertation, University of Minnesota, 1998.

Sandrow, Nahma. *Vagabond Stars.* New York: Harper & Row, 1977.

Schiff, Ellen, ed. *Awake and Singing: 7 Classic Plays from the American Jewish Repertoire.* New York: Penguin Books, 1995.

———. *Awake and Singing: Six Great American Jewish Plays.* New York: Applause Books, 2004.

Seldes, Gilbert. "Jewish Plays and Jew-Plays in New York City." *Menorah Journal* (April 1922): 236–240.

———. *The 7 Lively Arts.* New York: Harper and Brothers, 1924.

Shapiro, James. *Shakespeare and the Jews.* New York: Columbia University Press, 1996.

Siegel, Milton, Herbert Gropper, and Max. *We Americans.* New York: Samuel French, 1928.

Singer, Ben. "Manhattan Nickelodeons: New Data on Audience and Exhibitors." *Cinema Journal* 34, no. 3 (Spring 1995): 5–35.

Sleszynski, Theodore. "The Second Generation of Immigrants in the Assimilative Process." In *The New Immigration,* ed. John J. Appel, 102–108. New York: Pitman Publishing, 1971.

Slide, Anthony. *The Encyclopedia of Vaudeville.* Westport, CT: Greenwood Press, 1994.

Slobin, Mark. *Tenement Songs: The Popular Music of the Jewish Immigrants.* Chicago: University of Illinois Press, 1982.

Smith, Joe. "Dr. Kronkhite Revisited." In *American Popular Entertainment Papers and Proceedings of the Conference on the History of American Popular Entertainment,* ed. Myron Matlaw. Westport, CT: Greenwood Press, 1979.

———. "Smith and Dale: Kaddish on the Road on the Orpheum Circuit, 1923–1924." *Western States Jewish History* 33 (Spring 2001): 237–247.

Snyder, Robert W. *Voice of the City: Vaudeville and Popular Culture in New York.* New York: Oxford University Press, 1989.

Sochen, June. "Fanny Brice and Sophie Tucker: Blending the Particular with the Universal." In *From Hester Street to Hollywood: The Jewish-American Stage and Screen,* ed. Sarah Blacher Cohen. Bloomington: Indiana University Press, 1983.

———. "From Sophie Tucker to Barbara Streisand." In *Talking Back: Images of Jewish Women in American Popular Culture,* ed. Joyce Antler. Hanover, NH: Brandeis University Press, 1998.

Sollors, Werner. *Beyond Ethnicity: Consent and Descent in American Culture.* New York: Oxford University Press, 1986.

———, ed. *The Invention of Ethnicity.* New York: Oxford University Press, 1984.

Solomon, Eric. "Jews and Baseball: A Cultural Love Story." In *Ethnicity and Sport in North American History and Culture,* ed. George Eisen and David K. Wiggins. Westport, CT: Greenwood Press, 1994.

Spewack, Bella, and Samuel Spewack. *Poppa.* New York: Samuel French, 1929.

Staiger, Janet. *Interpreting Films: Studies in the Historical Reception of American Film.* Princeton, NJ: Princeton University Press, 1996.

Stratton, Jon. *Coming Out Jewish: Constructing Ambivalent Identities.* London: Routledge, 2000.

Thissen, Judith. "Jewish Immigrant Audiences in New York City, 1905–1914." In *American Movie Audiences: From the Turn of the Century to the Early Sound Era,* ed. Melvyn Stokes and Richard Maltby. London: British Film Institute, 1999.

Tucker, Sophie. *Some of These Days.* New York: Doubleday, 1945.

Ultan, Lloyd, and Barbara Unger. *Bronx Accent: A Literary and Pictorial History of the Borough:* New Brunswick, NJ: Rutgers University Press, 2000.

Warshow, Robert. "Clifford Odets: Poet of the Jewish Middle Class." In *The Immediate Experience: Movies, Comics, Theatre and Other Aspects of Popular Culture.* Boston: Harvard University Press, 2002.

Wenger, Beth. "Introduction--Remembering the Lower East Side--A Conversation." In *Remembering the Lower East Side--American Jewish Reflections* , edited by Jeffrey Shandler, Beth Wenger, and Hasia R. Diner. Title? Bloomington: Indiana University Press, 2000.

———. "Memory as Identity: The Invention of the Lower East Side." *American Jewish History* 85 no. 4 (1997): 3–27.

Whitfield, Stephen J. *In Search of American Jewish Culture.* Hanover, NH: University Press of New England, 1999.

Wilson, Joan Hoff, ed. *The Twenties: The Critical Issues.* Boston: Little, Brown, 1972.

Winokur, Mark. *American Laughter: Immigrants, Ethnicity and 1930s Film Comedy.* New York: St. Martin's Press, 1996.

Yoffeh, Zalmen. "The Passing of the East Side." *Menorah Journal* (December 1929): 264–275.

INDEX

Page numbers in *italics* indicate illustrations.

About the Author

Ted Merwin is an assistant professor of religion and Judaic studies at Dickinson College, where he directs the Milton B. Asbell Center for Jewish Life. He also serves as chief theater critic for the New York *Jewish Week*, the largest-circulation Jewish newspaper in the United States. His reviews and articles are frequently reprinted in Jewish newspapers throughout the country.